BARCELONA PLAYS

A COLLECTION OF NEW PLAYS
BY CATALAN PLAYWRIGHTS

Vestibule of the Sala Beckett, Barcelona, where *Barcelona, mapa d'ombres* and *Plou a Barcelona* were first staged.
Photo: courtesy of the Sala Beckett

The Sala Petita of Barcelona's Teatre Nacional de Catalunya, site of the premiere productions of *Salamandra* and *Forasters*.
Photo: courtesy of the Teatre Nacional de Catalunya

BARCELONA PLAYS

A COLLECTION OF NEW PLAYS
BY CATALAN PLAYWRIGHTS

Translated by

Marion Peter Holt

and

Sharon G. Feldman

Martin E. Segal Theatre Center Publications
New York
© 2008

Library of Congress Cataloging-in-Publication Data

Barcelona plays : a collection of new plays by Catalan playwrights / translated by Marion Peter Holt and Sharon G. Feldman.
    p. cm.
ISBN 978-0-9790570-4-5
1. Catalan drama--Translations into English. 2. Catalan drama--21st century. 3. Barcelona (Spain)--Drama. I. Holt, Marion Peter. II. Feldman, Sharon G., 1962-

PC3975.E5B37 2008
849'.92608--dc22
                                2008042975

The translation of this work has been supported
with a grant from the Institut Ramon Llull.   LLLL Institut
                                                                     ramon llull

Copy-editing, typography, and design by Christopher Silsby
Cover design by Christopher Silsby and Marion Peter Holt

© 2008 Martin E. Segal Theatre Center
Daniel Gerould, Executive Director
Frank Hentschker, Director of Programs
Jan Stenzel, Director of Administration

TABLE OF CONTENTS

Barcelona's Teatre Nacional de Catalunya.

Photo: courtesy of the Teatre Nacional de Catalunya

The Sala Tallers of the Teatre Nacional de Catalunya.

Photo: courtesy of the Teatre Nacional de Catalunya

Preface

From the end of the Franco dictatorship in the mid-1970s to the first decade of the twenty-first century, Barcelona's theatre experienced a remarkable rebirth and transformation. Performance groups such as La Fura dels Baus, Els Joglars, Dagoll-Dagom, and La Cubana flourished with distinctive productions in which spectacle and movement usually overshadowed textual elements. In 1976, the Teatre Lliure (Free Theatre) was established by a talented group of actors, directors, and scenographers in their own flexible performance space. It quickly set new production standards with a repertory of international plays. Soon the Catalan language, suppressed for more than three decades, became the vehicle of expression for a new generation of playwrights waiting in the wings, challenging the spectacle and pantomime of the collectives with a "teatre de text" in which dialogue was the essence. In 1996 Catalonia would inaugurate its own National Theatre, housed in a modern, state-of-the art complex. Six years later, the pioneering Teatre Lliure expanded its facilities from its single stage in the Gràcia neighborhood to a reclaimed exhibition hall from the Barcelona International Exposition of 1929. Thus, a second modern theatre complex, with two distinctive performance spaces, was added to the city's growing production facilities. Barcelona has now become one of the most vibrant theatre centers in Europe, and works by Catalan playwrights are staged far beyond the city of their origin, in many languages.

Throughout the 1980s and 1990s, the image of the city itself had nearly disappeared from the Catalan stage. Leading playwrights were creating a type of Eurotheatre in which character names were eschewed in favor of generic names and specific locales were seldom essential to a play's theme or development. Toni Casares, artistic director of the Sala Beckett, a major alternative performance venue, chose to focus upon this absence in preparing the programming for the 2003-2004 season. In a series titled "The Action Takes Place in Barcelona," he took the initiative in encouraging both established and promising younger playwrights to create new dramatic works set in Barcelona and reflecting its diversity by dramatic evocation. The series, which included Lluïsa Cunillé's *Barcelona: Map of Shadows* and Pau Miró's *It's Raining in Barcelona*, earned Casares and the Beckett a prestigious Generalitat de Catalunya Prize. The same year, Sergi Belbel's *Strangers* had its premiere at the Teatre Nacional de Catalunya's Sala Petita. It is a play that does not name Barcelona explicitly, but we may assume this gripping story of a family over two generations and their interactions with two distinct waves of immigrants, does indeed relate directly to the cultural diversity of the Catalan capital. Josep M. Benet i Jornet's *Salamander*, which had its premiere in 2005, deals with the extinction of species, culture, and language, including the Catalan language. The early scenes are set in southern California where its reluctant protagonist sets off on a journey of discovery and revelation that leads him to a neighborhood in Barcelona where his grandfather had once lived. The interwoven subplot of the play deals with the Catalan diaspora brought on by the Spanish Civil War. All four plays offer contemporary perspectives of the city and at the same time transcend their locales in theme and theatrical viability. What these works have in common beyond their varied relationships to a specific city is a universality that enables their characters and dramatic conflicts to speak to audiences worldwide. These four plays also represent outstanding playwrights of three generations. Josep M. Benet i Jornet won his first literary award and achieved his first staging in 1963 when he was only twenty-three years old, but only after the demise of the Franco regime in 1975 could his talent flourish. He would become the leading exponent of thematically challenging and structurally innovative theatre in Catalan and an example for a rising generation of young dramatists. Sergi Belbel and Lluïsa Cunillé would arrive on the scene in the late 1980s and early 1990s as new and distinctive voices. Today yet another generation of young playwrights is continuing to demonstrate the impressive talent centered in Barcelona. The Teatre Nacional de Catalunya is helping their careers with its T-6 internships, appointments that assure the playwrights production opportunities at the TNC's Sala Tallers or at a cooperating alternative theatre in Barcelona. Pau Miró is one of the most promising of this new generation and one who has been selected by TNC for a T-6 internship.

Salamander

Josep M. Benet i Jornet

Josep M. Benet i Jornet

Photo: courtesy of the Teatre Nacional de Catalunya

Josep M. Benet i Jornet and *Salamander*

Since the premiere and brief run of his awarding-winning play, *Una vella, coneguda olor* (*An Old, Familiar Smell*) in 1964, Josep M. Benet i Jornet has been a major contributor to the revitalization of Catalan-language theatre. His plays have been staged not only in Barcelona but throughout Spain and Latin America; the critically acclaimed production of his *Fugaç* (*Fleeting*) in Paris (2005) and the recent publication of six of his plays in French translations attest to the growing recognition of his work in Europe. Despite the obstacles to staging Catalan theatre in the final decade of the Franco dictatorship, Benet remained active in Barcelona's evolving independent theatre movement. He experimented with varied dramatic forms in plays that confirmed him as the most promising member of a new generation of playwrights. If his early work had revealed the influence of Miller, Brecht, and the Spanish playwright Buero-Vallejo, his later plays invariably carried the stamp of his own distinctive theatrical voice.

Between 1965 and 1969, he wrote three quite different works set in the fictional land of Drudània, and in 1972 he experienced critical rejection of his most ambitious play up to that point, the inventive *Berenàveu a les fosques* (*You Were Lunching in the Dark*), in which he had combined techniques considered Brechtian (scenic projections and scene titles) and fluid temporal shifts with a fundamentally realistic dramatic mode. In 1971, he began writing *Revolta de bruixes* (*Witches' Revolt*), a play that a decade later would prove fundamental to his recognition throughout Spain. However, he suspended work on this play to write *La desaparició de Wendy* (*The Disappearance of Wendy*), a postmodernist experiment in which characters from existing children's literature were selectively integrated into a totally original play about the power of theatrical representation. *Revolta de bruixes* would finally have a critically acclaimed premiere in 1980 in a Spanish version at Spain's Centro Dramático Nacional. Long ignored by Barcelona's most important independent theatre company, the Teatre Lliure, he finally broke through that barrier in 1988 with the Lliure's successful staging of *El manuscrit de Ali Bei* (*The Manuscript of Ali Bei*).

In the 1990s, Benet demonstrated increasing daring in the use of structural innovations in thematically challenging plays, including *Desig* (*Desire*), 1991, *Fugaç* (*Fleeting*), 1994, *E.R.* (*Stages*), 1994, and *Testament* (*Legacy*), 1996; and in 2003 the Teatre Lliure produced one of his most memorable works, *L'habitació del nen* (*The Child's Room*), directed by Sergi Belbel. *Salamandra* (*Salamander*) opened at the Sala Petita of the Teatre Nacional de Catalunya in

October 2005 in a production directed by Toni Casares, with mixed reactions from both audiences and critics who were less than receptive to this complex and audience-challenging work. In 2006 Benet was commissioned by the Teatre Nacional to adapt Mercé Rodoreda's novel *La plaça del diamant* for a production to commemorate the revered novelist's centenary.

Salamander is Benet's most complex work and is unusual both in plot and scenic devices, incorporating cinematic elements with more conventional dramaturgy. Although it is hardly the reiterative play that some critics have maintained, it does present an exceptional variety of interrelated stories with recurring mythic and thematic intertext. In the first two deceptively casual scenes, Benet effectively introduced his principal characters: Emma, a biologist living alongside the desert of southern California; her adopted son Claud, a successful director of Hollywood films; Travis, Claud's boyhood friend who is filming a documentary on species extinction; Hilde, Travis's German assistant and lover; and The Man, Emma's loyal admirer. The actor who portrays The Man will, in the course of the play, assume the roles of several other diverse characters in various parts of the world. Claud is the obvious protagonist in the play; however, a shadow protagonist begins to assume identity in Scene 13, when Claud sifts through the shards of the past that he discovers in his father's isolated trailer. It is the unknown grandfather whose tragic fate will only gradually come to light. The playwright also provides a visual symbol of the underlying theme (threatened extinction) in the form of a wounded salamander that Travis has rescued and Emma has placed in a makeshift terrarium. A second visual symbol is a broken, discarded toy beast from Bavaria known as a *Wolpertinger*, which Claud's biological father had sent him.

Throughout the episodic play there are shifts from casual, naturalistic dialogue to reflective narrative monologues, which range from retellings of the past to a recalled dream filled with intertextual intimations. The twenty-eight scenes all take place at sunset in various parts of the world, and the extinction of day becomes a constant semiotic and scenic reminder of other extinctions. The frequent cuts from space to space or locale to locale suggest a cinematic intent, as do the accompanying projections of exterior scenes while an interior scene is in progress. This structuring is, of course, an intentional reflection of the medium in which both Claud and Travis work professionally. However, Benet's filmic form does not attempt to impose cinematic time on stage time but rather to alter the audience's perspective of the characters on stage, mediating the focus of attention as the camera does in film. When a character switches from conversation to monologue and a self-focusing dramatic mode, the effect is to some degree similar to the close-up in motion pictures.

As his story unfolds, Benet mingles Biblical and pagan archetypes with myths—the most central being the legend of the salamander's ability to regenerate itself after being consumed by fire. The broken antler of the German *Wolpertinger*, of quite different mythic origin, might well be interpreted as an obvious metaphor for the fracture in the protagonist's physical being (a life-changing wound to the groin). If its meaning is extended further to relate to the country of its origin, then it becomes a visual symbol of the destruction of German culture inflicted by the Nazis. The mother, Emma, acquires her own mythic character as a modern-day representation of the Roman earth-mother Maia, when she reveals how she and her late husband adopted Claud to avoid extinction of their own family and again when she becomes a de facto mother for Travis. As Claud and Travis resort to violence in reaction to their rivalry, they become obvious modern incarnations of Cain and Abel.

While a search for identity provides the dramatic momentum in *Salamander*, it is a search that thwarts audience expectation for this type of "journey" play. Claud only agrees to follow the leads he has discovered because the woman he loves, Hilde, goads him on continually from one country to another. Ultimately, he will abandon Hilde, unable to tell her about the fateful diagnosis he has received in Paris; in the penultimate scene, he rejects the identity he has discovered, crumpling and tossing away the eloquent farewell letter his grandfather had written before his death at Dachau. Benet has created a character who lacks most of the qualities we normally assign to a hero, yet his Claud remains strangely haunting at the end of the play, when all hope of continuing his Catalan bloodline is denied him.

MPH

David Selvas and Pep Cruz in *Salamandra* (2005), directed by Tony Casares.
Photo: courtesy of the Teatre Nacional de Catalunya

Cristina Genebat and Julio Manrique in *Salamandra* (2005), directed by Tony Casares.
Photo: courtesy of the Teatre Nacional de Catalunya

SALAMANDER

by

JOSEP M. BENET I JORNET

Translated by

Marion Peter Holt

I dedicate this story, in alphabetical order, to Sharon Feldman, Marion Peter Holt, Klaus Laabs, Irène Sadowska-Guillon and Wolfgang Schuch. In some cases they don't even know one another, but so it is. All of them, suddenly, one happy day, offered me their generous, openhearted friendship, their moving assistance, and, in fact, opened for me in that way areas I had never foreseen.

CHARACTERS

EMMA (age 60 to 65)

MAN (age 60 to 65)

CLAUD (age 35 to 40)

TRAVIS (age 35 to 40)

HILDE (age 30 to 35)

Bare stage. When appropriate, necessary physical elements are introduced. Upstage there is a screen. Places, but never people, are projected on it.

The action takes place over a spring at the beginning of the twenty-first century.

Light.

On the screen we see the exterior of an isolated house, with a welcoming look about it, situated in a semi-desert spot, near the Santa Rosa Mountains of southern California.

Sunset. The atmosphere is impregnated with a slight, almost imperceptible reddish tone. EMMA *and a* MAN.

EMMA: (*Relaxed.*) Have they got it under control?

MAN: (*Calmly.*) I don't know. It's all the same. The fire won't reach this far.

Pause.

EMMA: (*Changing the subject.*) So much for that. Well, you've seen that my son has a little crisis that's bothering him.

MAN: You think he ought to go up there?

EMMA: It's not all that important . . . (*Pause.*) If he does go, he'll get it out of his head once and for all.

Pause.

MAN: I'd like to live here.

EMMA: It wouldn't make things different. Come when you wish and, pardon my saying so, but your house is much better than this one.

MAN: (*Ironically.*) If you say so.

EMMA: Let it pass.

MAN: Don't worry.

EMMA: And who knows?

MAN: I'm the lucky one.

CLAUD *appears.*

CLAUD: Me, too. There's no phone coverage. I can't receive any calls on my cell phone.

EMMA: And the phone line is down, too.

CLAUD: So no one can bother me.

MAN: I've reported it and they'll fix it.

EMMA: I'd rather it stayed this way. I really mean it.

MAN: (*To CLAUD.*) Instead of resting, you're working.

CLAUD: No, just taking notes. I still don't know what I'm looking for. I have some ideas . . . imprecise ones. I really am getting some rest. Lying around . . . and mother is being a mother. (*He goes over to his mother and gives her a kiss.*) I love you.

MAN: You're not the only one.

EMMA: I see him . . . I see you on television . . . I can't avoid it . . . I love to see you. (*Teasing.*) When you were growing up we didn't foresee that possibility. (*Emphasizing the sentence with meaning.*) You're my son. You my son and I your mother. You understand?

CLAUD: And how. I don't know if you do.

EMMA: I do. And that doesn't exclude the other matter. You ought to make up your mind. And don't start telling me you already have. The letter only arrived today. You haven't had time to digest it.

CLAUD: The letter doesn't change a thing. It doesn't interest me.

MAN: Pardon me if I butt in. It's time for me to be on my way.

EMMA: What? Oh, no.

MAN: I have a forty-five minute drive.

CLAUD: Exactly. So if you leave now, you'll have spent more time in your car than here.

EMMA: Stay for dinner. And sleep over, if you want to.

MAN: It seems I have a lot of work waiting for me at home.

CLAUD: Nothing's waiting for you there. (*To* EMMA.) Is there any detail . . . some details you haven't explained to him.

EMMA: He's the only neighbor I have in God knows how many miles. Who else could I share things with?

CLAUD: Well, it seems perfect to me.

MAN: You two need to talk alone. It'll be better for you if I go.

CLAUD: A few weeks from now I'll be going to Europe.

MAN: Here, in the desert, the word Europe sounds almost exotic.

CLAUD: I'd like to work in Europe. Film part of the production, at least. I'm going to look for locations. I have a friend who knows Barcelona. Some sequences could be set there. So they've told me. I don't know for sure.

EMMA: And just what are you telling us now?

CLAUD: That a friend of mine will help me. (*To the* MAN.) And you know something? He's probably about your age. He looks a lot like you.

MAN: That's always happening to me, people who look like me.

CLAUD: Really. He's the kind of person who with two words already knows what you need. Stay for dinner.

MAN: No, no, I'm not staying. You and your mother eat alone. I'll think of you while I'm driving. Who's going to win, you or her?

EMMA: There's still light. The days are getting longer. You'll have an easy drive. Run on but come back soon. The moment you go I'll start missing you.

MAN: (*To* CLAUD, *referring to the mother.*) Did you know that I love her too?

CLAUD: For years.

MAN: That's why I always come back.

The MAN *disappears.*

CLAUD: Would you want him to sleep with you someday?

EMMA: You're a pain. I doubt it.

CLAUD: Shall we eat? I'll help you.

EMMA: I wouldn't want to take you from your work. (*Serious.*) Look, don't get upset. You have the box here.

Pause.

CLAUD: And the letter.

EMMA: It wasn't easy to find that damn box. It's falling apart.

CLAUD: Throw it out.

EMMA: Right. And everything that's in it.

CLAUD: It's nothing but junk.

EMMA: Throw it out? Not on your life. We'll open it and we'll rummage through the things. While we're talking. Even if it's for the last time. We haven't opened it in years.

CLAUD: You won't find anything that will convince me. I won't go. Seeing the place where that man lived doesn't interest me. A . . . a stranger. I won't go, Mother.

EMMA: We'll see. Open the box. Leave the letter for now, if you wish; and open the box. How hard is that?

Pause.

CLAUD: You win. All right.

CLAUD *goes to the rather large, dusty box. Sound of a car motor.*

CLAUD: Your boyfriend's leaving.

EMMA: But we never hear his car when he goes. It's not someone leaving, it's someone arriving.

CLAUD: Now? You weren't expecting anyone.

EMMA: Nobody. But no car comes here, in these mountains, by chance. Shit!

CLAUD: Mother . . .

EMMA: Oh, shit . . . who's coming to bother us? (SHE *goes upstage.* CLAUD *picks up an envelope that is on top of the box.* HE *hesitates. The car sound has stopped.* EMMA's *irritated expression changes.* SHE *is pleasantly surprised.*) It can't be! It's Travis! (CLAUD *drops the letter.*) And he's not alone.

* * *

On the screen we see another partial exterior view of the same house as before, EMMA's.

Sunset. CLAUD, TRAVIS, *and* HILDE. *The three of them are leaning over a small, improvised container that* TRAVIS *is holding.*

TRAVIS: What if it doesn't survive? What an awful loss!

HILDE: It's . . . it's pretty.

CLAUD: Since Mother can't hear me . . . is there any amphibian we can call "pretty?"

TRAVIS: (*To* CLAUD.) I wasn't expecting to find you here.

CLAUD: Then imagine if I could expect you to turn up suddenly at my mother's house. According to her, you haven't been here in four or five years. And just what are you doing poking through the rocks around here?

TRAVIS: I was coming down a ravine. I was coming down. I wanted to get to the bottom, where there's a stream, at the bottom of the gorge. In fact . . . if you can picture it, I was trying to see, if I could, creatures like this one. I'll tell you both all about it.

CLAUD: And the tiny creature was just crossing your path.

TRAVIS: Right under my nose. I didn't even notice. I'm a dope.

HILDE: You could mistake it for the vegetation.

TRAVIS: I stepped on it. I'd left it tailless. There's also a little wound. You see it? If we abandoned it, it would surely die. I don't know if it can survive.

EMMA *appears, carrying a container with water, a small bag of soil, some grass, and implements from the garden.*

EMMA: Not "can" it . . . I promise it will. (SHE *joins the group. While they talk, they improvise, under* EMMA's *direction, a terrarium in the container she has brought, and they transfer into it a small animal that perhaps we don't actually see.*) The desert salamander. Look what lovely eyes. It can't be dying.

HILDE: I read somewhere . . . they used to say that salamanders live on fire.

EMMA: Water! A lot of humidity, that's what they need. And worms. And larvae . . . Also plenty of grass. How am I going to find larvae for it?

CLAUD: Mother, you don't have to knock yourself out.

EMMA: A desert salamander, Claud! Don't you have any feelings?

TRAVIS: He does. Claud lives on feelings.

CLAUD: Travis, shut up.

EMMA: Travis, you could be fined. It's a protected species on the way to extinction. The fauna we have here . . .

CLAUD: As long as you don't mention it, no one will know a thing.

TRAVIS: Why, I was trying to find salamanders, in fact . . . We've obtained all the permissions in the world. They seemed delighted with my idea. Now we'll see what happens.

EMMA: Look at it. An incredible shade of green. And such a lovely face . . . That's that. I'll make a call. No, there's no line.

TRAVIS: I tried to reach you three or four times, Emma.

EMMA: The line's out. Travis, you'll have to take the car and head for the city. Give them the information, put up with the sermon you'll get and the instructions they have to give you. But you did well to come here. The poor creature wouldn't have lasted much longer without water. And here . . . I do know a thing or two.

TRAVIS: Seeing it in your hands makes me feel a lot better.

EMMA: Thanks. Did you hear him, son?

CLAUD: I heard him and I can hear you too. The idyll is beginning. Any moment you'll look for a quiet corner and you'll share secrets nonstop.

(*Pointedly.*) Maybe now you can let me have some peace, Mother.

They have finished with the terrarium.

EMMA: (*Who has understood him.*) I wouldn't think of it. (*To the other two.*) Now it's time for me to look after you.

HILDE: I don't want to be any bother.

EMMA: You've come with Travis, and you're very welcome. Hil . . . Hilde, you said?

HILDE: Yes, Hilde.

TRAVIS: German.

EMMA: Don't worry, there's plenty of room in this house. Well, provided you don't mind sharing the same bedroom. If not, relax; I'll see how . . .

TRAVIS: We'll be very happy to share the same bed. (*To* EMMA, *joking.*) Satisfied?

EMMA: Yes, indeed. Then that's settled.

TRAVIS: To finish the story, you don't know how difficult it was to get here.

HILDE: Through the fire.

TRAVIS: (*Satisfied.*) But we managed to get through it.

EMMA: Oh, you mean you wouldn't have come if it weren't for the salamander?

TRAVIS: Not come? I couldn't help coming. You were the one who never stopped talking about the desert salamander. Why do you think I was looking for one? If I finish this project, I'll have to put your name in the credits.

EMMA: (*To* HILDE.) Claud and Travis were inseparable when they were little.

TRAVIS: (*Changing the subject.*) Hilde is a wonderful researcher.

EMMA: Inseparable, the best friends in the world.

TRAVIS *and* CLAUD *look at each other and smile, skeptical.*

CLAUD: (*To* HILDE.) You'll feel at home in mother's house.

EMMA: I hope so. (*Back to her topic.*) Truly. Travis and Claud always went everywhere together.

TRAVIS: (*Cynically.*) Now not so much.

CLAUD: (*Apparently picking up on* TRAVIS*'s retort.*) The history of humanity is plagued with suppositions that must be amended later.

EMMA: What does that have to do with your friendship, silly?

CLAUD: I wasn't speaking of Travis and me. I was trying to explain to Hilde. Before, you were talking about the legend in which salamanders eat fire, and Mother cut you off.

EMMA: Child, I was providing scientific information.

CLAUD: That's what I meant. Science corrects itself constantly.

EMMA: Now you have to try to keep the salamander from burning to a crisp if you throw it in the fire.

CLAUD: We don't have the right to be sure about anything.

TRAVIS: (*Sardonic.*) Are you feeling all right, Claud?

EMMA: (*Quickly.*) He feels wonderful. And all of you have to help me fix supper. There's no escaping.

HILDE: (*To* CLAUD, *serious.*) Thank you.

TRAVIS: (*Suddenly.*) Hilde, it's obvious, tomorrow you have to go into the city. To explain the accident with the salamander and ask for instructions.

HILDE: It's a long way from here. You really think I should go there?

EMMA: We'll discuss it while we eat. Soup's on!

*   *   *

On the screen we see another partial, exterior view of the same house.

Sunset. EMMA *and* HILDE.

EMMA: Travis. The two of you arrived and I wasn't in the mood for visitors. But it's you and him. And I was so excited to see you. He and Claud, they were inseparable. Truly. I keep saying that, don't I? But the fact is . . . until . . . For years it looked like they had chosen the same career. And, in fact, they had, for sure. (*Pause.*) They still need each other. It seems to me. Raising a son . . . I'm a widow. Did Travis tell you that?

HILDE: Yes.

EMMA: For years now. My husband decided we'd have a son. I couldn't have children. When we adopted Claud, he was a six year old. My husband provided for us. He wanted a son because he knew he didn't have much time left. I mean, that meant a hasty adoption. We couldn't find a newborn anywhere. It had to be a six-year-old. Am I boring you?

HILDE: Not at all.

EMMA: I live alone. I like this place. It's wild, it's different. My husband liked it, and so do I. I was a professor of natural science. I'd jump in the car, and off I'd go. Or I'd stop and gape at something. That special fauna we have in these parts . . . Most days I see absolutely no one. It agrees with me. But then someone shows up and I can't stop talking . . . Claud's adopted. And now we have a small crisis at hand. Nothing important, really. Things are going well for Claud. Spectacularly well.

HILDE: He's good at his work.

EMMA: Especially now, since he premiered the last film. He's in demand. Then, without warning, he chucks it, says enough, and he's here with me. That happened two weeks ago. You can imagine how happy that makes me. (*Pause.*) And yesterday the letter came. His biological father has died. A drop out. An alcoholic without a steady job. He's dead and he's left his things to Claud. Nothing of any interest, according to what they tell us. For a long time we knew nothing about him. There's a letter from a neighbor that notifies us of his death, and also a letter from him addressed to Claud. Written a year ago. I've read it, Claud hasn't, he didn't want to. A distastful letter. He signs it with his first and last names. And it's handwritten . . . He doesn't ask for anything but it's written in a tone you'd use to apply for a job. That man remains so distant from my son . . . I calculated a bit. Claud was born when he . . . that man must have been, I don't know, twenty-seven at most. It was the time, how time passes, of the flower people and marijuana. Does it ring a bell that there was a time when the world was to change because of flower people and marijuana? The mother, the girl who was going with Claud's biological father . . . I say biological to point out the difference, I can't help myself. I can't help feeling disgust for him, and I also feel pity. The child was born and the mother disappeared four days later. She left a young man alone with an infant. Who knows what he thought of life, not then or later did he ever have a regular job, so it seems. You see, he lived in a trailer. One of those vehicles that stopped one day and was never moved again. After six years he puts the boy up for adoption. He gave him up, for certain. Claud doesn't remember any of it. I remember things that happened before I was six. He doesn't want to go up there. He doesn't want to know what his father has left him. He doesn't need anything from anybody. He's gone a lot further than his two fathers. But I say let him go. What does it cost him? The man died of cirrhosis. An alcoholic. But he never bothered us, never asked for anything. He knew where we were. He was sensible in his own way, and he came to know it. Why didn't he want to know about Claud? He had waited six years to give up a child who was in the way. (*She shows doubt.*) I suppose. But he never asked anything from us, rather he sent Claud little things, useless toys worth two, three, four dollars . . . Claud never knew where they came from but he played with them a while and then forgot about them. Or even worse. Toys that had belonged to the man's father when he was little . . . Grimy toys that maybe he'd repaired or cleaned up poorly before he sent them. Maybe they'd had some interest for him . . . I kept some of those strange objects. And finally it seemed that this man had forgotten us. He stopped sending things. He gave up. I don't know why, but he gave up. Do you think I'm making too many assumptions?

Pause.

HILDE: Yes.

EMMA: (*Surprised.*) Oh.

HILDE: Do you want to know what I think? Your son's biological father probably gave him up rather than ruin the life of a child he'd fathered blithely on drugs.

Long pause.

EMMA: Right. That's the box. There's the letter. The toys are inside. The ones I decided to save, I'm not sure just why. Yes, I do know. From superstition. (*Pause. A bit defiant.*) I'm going to tell Claud to go there, to go to the place where that poor man lived and decide if all he finds should really go in the garbage, or if, who can say . . . I'll tell him to go.

HILDE: I'm sorry, Emma.

EMMA: No. I'm glad you're here. That man . . . (*She is now beside the box and takes from it, little by little, objects with faded colors.*) One day he ran across Claud's name in a newspaper. Or he saw him on television. That's more likely. But he didn't say a thing . . . He had his dignity . . . that man who's so important is my son, I imagine he thought. (HILDE *is at* EMMA's *side.*) It doesn't matter if he was capable of understanding what his son was doing or if he only knew he'd become admired, sought after. He was just a poor nobody, a miserable soul. He would never have suggested to Claud that he come to see him while he was living. But now he's dead. If he doesn't go up there, it's no big deal, but if he does . . . Do you understand? The circle is complete. It's really over, and we'll forget him. (*Corrects herself.*) He'll forget him. Over once and for all. (*Pause.*) I'm certain he has memories from before he was six.

Suddenly something catches HILDE'*s attention,* SHE *puts her hand in the box and takes out a strange doll, covered with dust, limp, discolored, moth-eatern but with its original form recognizable. It is a kind of animal that could not really exist. Its body is that of a small mammal but the remnants of its feet are those of a bird; from its mouth, fangs like a vampire's still stick out; some bird wings still hang from its back; and it has, partially preserved, deer antlers.* HILDE'*s expression while she holds up the doll is a combination of surprise, eagerness, and repugnance.*

HILDE: What is this thing doing here?

EMMA: You see? It's one of that man's absurdities . . .

HILDE: (*Cutting her off.*) It has a broken antler. What is it doing here? A Wolpertinger.

*   *   *

On the screen we see another partial, exterior view of Emma's house.

Sunset. CLAUD *and* TRAVIS.

TRAVIS: Emma . . . When you see her suddenly drop everything, when all at once she scoots out with a plastic bag and says she's off to see what she can dig up . . . you think . . . She won't find a thing and the salamander . . . But then she returns, her hair a mess and looking like a cat that's caught the mouse, a look of mission accomplished . . . and with the bag half-full of little shapes that are slithering in wild mushrooms and . . . in what must be slime or . . . Only the salamander actually devours a bit of the things she gives it . . .

CLAUD: She knows what she's doing. In any case, you should go into the city.

TRAVIS: When I think about it, I don't want to force Hilde to travel to a strange place she's not familiar with.

CLAUD: Yes, of course, that's what I mean. You're the one who should go.

You're the one who's responsible for that little creature.

Pause.

TRAVIS: The salamander's surviving. At least for now.

CLAUD: Agreed. You're right. Letting the thing die is no catastrophe. It comes from a protected reserve, full of brothers and sisters and cousins who won't miss it . . . Even if it were the last of its species, it's all the same.

TRAVIS: (*Uncertain.*) No, it's not all the same, either. (*Brief pause.*) I was thinking that the desert salamander could be the species that would serve as an excuse to start my new documentary. That's why I've taped and photographed it, just in case.

CLAUD: What do you intend to do?

TRAVIS: It depends on the material I find. When you're working directly with reality, you can't be sure of what you'll find.

CLAUD: Reality. You'll give the public reality.

TRAVIS: I'll give it realities. It's about . . . Forget it.

CLAUD: What's it about? Your work matters to me. You can think what you like about me, but don't play-act. Don't get me pissed.

Pause.

TRAVIS: The idea is to speak again about extinction. Now in a more . . . ambiguous way. Beginning with the salamanders that are around here, in the Santa Rosa Mountains, explaining what it was for me to hear your mother talk. Did you notice that I was taping her while she was preparing the terrarium? If I hadn't had the accident with the creature, I still would have come to see her. How many years . . . ? (*Pause.*) Yes, I always felt better at your house, with your parents, than at mine, with my own parents.

CLAUD: Sure.

TRAVIS: Well, in a vague way, that's what I'm aiming for. Beginning with small amphibians, reptiles . . . Then other forms of life; humans even. When time comes to edit, I'll see.

CLAUD: Don't you find that . . . ? The degradation of the environment, its effects . . . Don't you find it less than exciting by now? That people talk about it, fine; that you're the one who talks about it . . .

TRAVIS: We'll see. I don't quite know what I'll do yet. (*Slight pause.*) Telling stories about love, don't you find that less than exciting by now?

Pause.

CLAUD: I saw your documentary. There were people who were upset over it. I know. You also make the news. I don't know what you'll do next, but that's a good documentary. (*Quickly.*) And I don't need to say more.

TRAVIS: I was lucky with Hilde. She didn't sleep while she was searching through archives. The crew is OK, but she . . . She's a ball of fire. (*Pause.*) I was struck the moment I saw her. And besides, I fell in love. I realized I didn't just desire her.

CLAUD: It's been a long long time since I've been in love.

TRAVIS: Hold it. It's not like before, in college, we'd bet on which of us would get the most inaccessible girl or which of us would make out the most in a semester. When I say I'm in love with Hilde I know exactly what I'm saying.

Pause.

CLAUD: Congratulations.

TRAVIS: I've also seen your fourth film, of course.

CLAUD: I have a public, we've been lucky.

TRAVIS: And you're doing what you want to do.

Pause.

CLAUD: Nobody could compete with us.

TRAVIS: You've started work on a new story.

CLAUD: Calmly. Yes, among other things. There won't be a romantic relationship, for sure. Here, with my mother, time slows down. There's no rush. Did you like my film or not?

TRAVIS: I saw it in Paris, at the Rex Cinema. It's exciting to discover the values you can find in a plot like that.

CLAUD: What does that mean?

TRAVIS: How many nominations do you foresee?

CLAUD: My films are honest.

TRAVIS: And you have a command of visual language like no one else. And you arrange things like God.

CLAUD: Did you like my film or not? Tell me!

Pause.

TRAVIS: It's infinitely better than the films that they normally show at the Rex. (*Takes a breath.*) It didn't interest me at all. You and I know each other. We know what we're thinking. What were you expecting? It didn't interest me. What difference does it make? What importance does it have? Huh?

* * *

On the screen we see another partial, exterior view of Emma's house.

Sunset. EMMA *is reading.* CLAUD *is taking notes on a pad. Silence.* EMMA *looks up.*

EMMA: Claud. (CLAUD *looks at her.*) That man's . . . letter . . .

CLAUD: I'm giving it thought, Mother, even if you don't believe it, I am.

EMMA *doesn't insist.* THEY *go back to what they were doing.* HILDE *appears.* SHE *is holding a piece of her clothing and a small travel case, with thread, needles, scissors . . . the indispensable items for sewing.* SHE *sees them, hesitates, and starts to leave.*

EMMA: Hilde. Why are you leaving?

HILDE: It'll be better if I . . . (SHE *corrects herself and speaks the truth.*) I don't want to disturb.

CLAUD *listens calmly to the brief exchange between the two women.*

EMMA: What do you mean disturb? Why, we aren't doing anything. And if you disturb us, so much the better.

HILDE: Oh, it doesn't matter. He's your son, you hardly ever see him. Now you're together, alone and at ease . . . I'm in the way.

SHE *starts to leave again.*

CLAUD: What were you going to do?

HILDE: Nothing, a button. Sew on a button.

EMMA: With those little scissors, and that . . . Why didn't you ask me . . . ? (SHE *gets up.*) I'll do it for you.

HILDE: (*Almost chillily.*) Thanks. No. I don't need any help.

EMMA: But, dear . . .

CLAUD: (*Interrupting, calmly.*) She doesn't need help. I think she's been doing things for herself for years. It's likely she has in her suitcase everything necessary to survive in any circumstances. (*To* HILDE.) Can't you sew on the button here, with us? (HE *gets up.*) Emma is reading, I'm jotting down notes that will probably never be of any use to me . . . you would be company.

EMMA: Stay, you're not in the way.

CLAUD: Not at all. (HE *goes over to her and, gently, leads her to a chair.*) Sit down. (HILDE *sits.*) That's that.

HILDE *remains a bit ill at ease.* EMMA *and* CLAUD *return to their places but wait there a beat, amused.*

HILDE: All right, then thank you.

Determined, SHE *starts to sew on the button.* EMMA *returns to her reading.* CLAUD *picks up his pad. But suddenly* HE *looks up and sits studying* HILDE. HILDE *doesn't notice yet, but* EMMA *does.* EMMA *doesn't say a word, but* CLAUD *does notice that his mother is aware he has been gazing at* HILDE. *Pause.*

CLAUD: I'm a film director. You can't help it. You don't just look, you frame . . . you try to understand how light works on a certain human image . . . (HILDE *has also looked up and realizes that* CLAUD *is talking about her.* HE *continues without emphasis.*) The outlines, the quality of the skin . . . , that instant of . . . grace.

Pause.

HILDE: (*Confused.*) What are you talking about?

EMMA: (*Matter of fact.*) Nothing. Just talk.

EMMA *goes back to her reading,* HILDE *returns to her button, and* CLAUD . . . CLAUD *keeps on looking at* HILDE: *simply looking at her.* HILDE *must be aware and does not return his look but neither is she self-conscious about it. Actually,* SHE *is relaxing.*

* * *

On the screen we see another partial, exterior view of Emma's house.

Sunset. CLAUD, *alone. The box is beside him.* HE *has the envelope in one hand and the letter it contained in the other.* HE *is reading.* HILDE *appears.* SHE *stands indecisive.* CLAUD *looks at her.*

CLAUD: You're not disturbing me now either. I was reading a letter. I've already finished.

HILDE: The letter from your biological father. Was it worth reading? Your mother told me something about it.

CLAUD: Are you curious to know what's in it?

HILDE: Burn it.

Pause.

CLAUD: That's an idea, a good idea.

CLAUD *takes matches from a pocket. Suddenly* HILDE *looks at the box.* CLAUD *strikes a match.*

HILDE: Wait!

CLAUD: I'm taking your advice. I'm burning it.

HILDE: Wait. (SHE *goes to* CLAUD's *side and blows out the match.*) Not yet. (*Hesitating.*) And what if I ask you to read it to me?

CLAUD: You want me to read it to you?

HILDE: Yes.

CLAUD: It's a terribly sad letter. Why does it interest you?

HILDE: I gave you the idea of burning it, right? I don't know if it interests me. Read it and then I'll ask you a question.

CLAUD: Has my mother told you that the man had no education, or if he did, he'd gone through a change.

HILDE: Yes. Will you read it to me?

CLAUD: Very well. (HE *reads.*) "Dear Mr. Claude," Claude with an "e" after the "d." He doesn't know how I spell it now. And "Dear Mr." but no last name. He can't put his own and neither can he put my father's. So he omits it. "I hope it won't bother you if I write you. I don't need anything from you and I'm well, thank you. It's hereby stated that they'll send you this letter after I'm gone. I only want to tell you I've seen your two pictures." I've directed four. I wonder which two pictures he's talking about? "I like the movies a lot. There are no movie theatres here but they showed one on TV, and a friend took me to Boise to see the other one. They're the best pictures I've ever seen." What kind of films do you suppose he saw? Boise's quite a distance from here, in Idaho, way up north. If you drove . . .

HILDE: Read the rest.

CLAUD: Sure. And wait, now comes the good part. "They're very intellectual pictures, but you never get bored, not for a minute." What do you think? Don't forget to tell Travis that this man found my films very intellectual.

HILDE: Travis says they're good, so there!

CLAUD: He doesn't think they're good.

HILDE: He can't say enough about them.

CLAUD: Yep. Like the dead man who writes to me. Why do you lie?

HILDE: I'm not lying. He gets enthusiastic about your setups, the way you move the dramatic action forward.

CLAUD: But he's never liked the films.

HILDE: Do you like his documentaries?

CLAUD: Yes. No. Yes, a lot. Look, a half-hour ago, only a half hour, I realized that my films don't interest him at all.

HILDE: He said that?

CLAUD: Yes.

HILDE: They don't interest him at all, maybe not. But he knows they're good. He talks about you often. About your cinematic style. And to recall when you were children, a couple of adolescents . . . Do you want me to tell you how you celebrated your eighteenth birthday? He talks a great deal about your films. He gets impatient but he respects them.

Pause.

CLAUD: My eighteenth birthday's of no importance. Yes it is, I'm sorry. He was also eighteen. That night we decided we'd always work . . . ; no, that we'd always create together. Create! For years we couldn't find any decent work. We managed best we could until we were twenty-four. And then . . . then he . . . , he let me down.

HILDE: What?

CLAUD: Yes, he let me down. Nothing important, yet it seemed so then. And, in any case, our relationship continued. Right up to this day, as you've seen. But our kind of prolonged adolescent relationship was over. Doesn't matter. It doesn't matter that what I'm doing doesn't interest him in the slightest.

HILDE: He speaks better of you than you do of him.

CLAUD: His documentaries are superb, fascinating, innovative. I'm sorry, I let myself get carried away. Because his opinion still matters to me. Yes, I admit it. Travis is my arbiter. And I'll never be able to escape from that. (*Pause.*) And now I'll burn the letter.

HILDE: Finish reading it first, will you?

CLAUD: You've already seen the style. It doesn't say anything else.

HILDE: Then, burn it. (*Looks at the box.*) No, really, why don't you finish reading it to me?

CLAUD: That person's opinion can't matter to me. Not his. So I don't understand your interest. I'll read it to you. (*But then* HE *looks at her perplexed.*) You're stubborn. And unexpectedly timid. Direct but reserved, reserved but insistent . . . You're . . . Can you explain to me who you are, Hilde?

HILDE: (*Smiles.*) You don't know what you're saying. Are you going to read?

CLAUD: Yes. "Intellectual pictures but not boring for a minute." OK. "If you'd stayed with me you wouldn't have had a chance to study, and you wouldn't be a great film director now. I'm not sorry you ended up in other hands." Thank you. "But I could have told you enough stories for a thousand pictures." He talks just like the stupidest of the admirers who ask for my autograph. "I've decided that when I die, my things will belong to you. Maybe they'll inspire you. I wasn't lucky. If there hadn't been a war, and my parents had stayed in Europe, who knows. (HILDE *is tense and goes to the box.* SHE *looks inside as* SHE *listens to the end of the letter.*) You'll find the letters my father wrote to my mother. Poor fellow, that was a drama for sure. A big one. Movies ought to have a happy ending, life has too much sadness. So, actually, I don't know if they'll be of any use to you. There're pictures too. I've very proud that you are my son. When I say so, nobody believes me. You don't bear my name, and I can't prove it. I won't take any more of your time." New paragraph. The first in the whole letter. "Forgive me." (*Slight pause.*) Another paragraph. "Respectfully . . ." And the signature. It's hard to make out. "Joe Bennett." That's it.

HILDE *takes from the box the same doll she discovered a moment before.*

HILDE: And now a question. Do you know what this is?

CLAUD: He sent it to me. Can I burn the letter?

HILDE: It's a Wolpertinger. I was born in Mittenwald. In Mittenwald there's a Wolpertinger museum. It's an imaginary animal. They invented it in my homeland. The only place you'll find one of them. A kind of goblin. An impertinent little monster. I was born surrounded with Wolpertingers.

CLAUD: The man who wrote this letter had nothing to do with Germany.

HILDE: In the letter, incidentally, he says if your grandparents had stayed in Europe . . .

CLAUD: I know nothing about that, about these grandparents. These grandparents don't interest me! Do you know what interests me? Do you know what I envy Travis most, at this moment? You.

Pause.

HILDE: Really? I interest you? Then you'll really be thrilled to know that I was born in Mittenwald, in Bavaria, near Munich. Munich's the capital. Mittenwald, apart from the Wolpertinger museum, is a town that has nothing special to offer. But not far from it there's a city that . . . You've probably never heard of Mittenwald, but you may have heard of that city. We're not so proud of it.

CLAUD: I hardly know Germany.

HILDE: Dachau. The city's called Dachau.

Pause.

CLAUD: The Nazis built an extermination camp there.

HILDE: A labor camp, not exactly an extermination camp. People think there's only one kind of hell. No, there's at least two. I was born in Mittenwald, not far from Dachau, and surrounded with Wolpertingers. Why would your father give you a Wolpertinger?

They remain silent.

* * *

On the screen we see another partial, exterior view of Emma's house.

Sunset. EMMA *and* TRAVIS.

TRAVIS: Hilde wasn't only an interesting, smart girl who captivates you in five minutes. She understood immediately what I was trying to do with the project about the Nazi camps, and she went directly to look for every document and every person anyone might need. As if her life depended on it. She urged me on. Imagine, me. It was hard for her to recognize that she had personal motives for . . .

EMMA: The Nazis and the second world war seem so remote . . . There've always been tragedies.

TRAVIS: My documentary was trying to be a bit different. The concentration camps were only a kind of excuse, a point of departure, as the salamander would be now. And Hilde . . .

EMMA: I'm glad a woman has finally caught you. Come here.

TRAVIS *goes closer.* EMMA *takes him in her arms.*

TRAVIS: My mother never did that to me.

EMMA: Claud doesn't like to be hugged.

TRAVIS: My parents . . .

EMMA: (SHE *releases* TRAVIS.) Enough of that. Your parents were normal parents, and I occupied a bigger place in your life. I hugged you because I'm happy. Would you say that I'm a happy woman?

TRAVIS: Maybe from time to time.

EMMA: Claud believes I'm happy. While my husband was living, I never stopped doing things, besides the classes. It was non-stop. You can't remember any of that. After he died, I stopped. Have you been listening to the radio?

TRAVIS: Yes.

EMMA: Have they talked about the fire?

TRAVIS: Yes. Nothing new.

EMMA: He left me, when you two were grown I moved here for good, and the hours pass. Look, now I have your salamander.

* * *

On the screen we see another partial, exterior view of Emma's house.

Sunset. CLAUD *and* TRAVIS. HILDE *enters immediately.*

CLAUD: The salamander will die.

TRAVIS: We'll see.

CLAUD: My new film . . .

TRAVIS: A sensational new film that will become . . .

CLAUD: (*Cutting him off, ironically.*) . . . another great success, yes. Well, in this film not only will there be a love story, but it will also be, quite straightforward, a melodrama. Maybe more than that but, for you, only a melodrama, and that's fine with me.

TRAVIS: Wonderful, I don't intend to argue the point. When we were kids and played cowboys and indians, we both wanted to be redskins, so leave it at that. I don't intend to get into an argument with you.

CLAUD: When we were kids, it was all in fun . . . (*To* HILDE, *who is already there.*) Until we were twenty-four, it was all in fun, as I told you.

TRAVIS: You told her what?

HILDE: (*Teasing.*) That at twenty-four you . . . let him down. Very hard?

TRAVIS: Please . . .

CLAUD: I didn't tell her anything else.

HILDE: Yes, that in fact it was not that important.

TRAVIS: Great. Why don't you explain it to me, Claud? That way I'll be able to judge whether it was important or not.

CLAUD: Fancy that! You don't even remember it.

TRAVIS: Refresh my memory.

Pause.

CLAUD: We were twenty-four. Finally, a minor producer was offering us a chance to direct our first feature film. A lousy formula picture. It was all the same. We revised the script. We spent whole nights planning it. And then the first meeting with the producer. I was shaking with emotion.

TRAVIS: Not me.

CLAUD: The first meeting with the producer. It was then. Suddenly, in front of those strangers, without consulting me, Travis began to present some ideas about direction that had nothing to do with the ones we had decided together. Nothing at all.

TRAVIS; I had just realized that the story didn't interest me and I tried to find a way out.

CLAUD: He was explaining it in front of those people and I didn't understand a thing. I tried to correct him and he cut me off and went on talking and dazzled that gang of morons that would pay for our work. I shut up, embarrassed, out of the game. Nobody even noticed me. They were all listening to him pour out ideas that suddenly were only his ideas.

HILDE: I was attracted to Travis because he doesn't tell lies. He gets excited about things and gets carried away but he doesn't lie.

TRAVIS: Let him say what he wants.

CLAUD: After the meeting I wanted to speak to him but, oh, he had work to do, some kind or other, and there was no time now. Next day, another meeting. And, once again, Travis's innovative ideas. It was the second day and, you know, I couldn't take any more of it. I jumped up. I spat out the indignation built up from twenty-four hours before. I shouted no, it wasn't that way, that it was my picture too, he was taking it away from me. Those people looked at me as if they were seeing a lunatic. Travis said nothing. He didn't open his mouth again. That's the way the meeting ended. But after a few hours, Travis, without telling me, went back to the producer and said he was leaving the project.

TRAVIS: I wasn't even interested in what I'd championed myself.

CLAUD: He said I was impossible to work with.

TRAVIS: You don't know what I said.

CLAUD: And that he was leaving it. They asked him to continue. They told him I was the one who should go . . . He said no. And disappeared. He behaved like a gentleman. The producers had to go along with my hysteria. I felt alone and paralysed. I didn't finish the film. Another person did. In any case, it was a failure. Low budget but a failure. Meanwhile, they offered Travis a proposal for a documentary. Or maybe they'd offered it to him before, and I didn't know it? It was offered . . . and until today. My career could have ended at twenty-four.

HILDE: It didn't.

CLAUD: What ended was the team of Travis and Claud.

TRAVIS: You came out the winner.

CLAUD: Yes. I'd be able to make a film about extinction without anyone seeing amphibians gliding through the water and grass.

TRAVIS: Obviously. I've told you I don't want to argue about it, Claud.

Long pause.

CLAUD: I like Hilde. I think she likes me, too.

HILDE *doesn't move. No one moves for a long moment. And suddenly* TRAVIS *leaps on top of* CLAUD. HE *catches him off guard.* HE *punches him in the stomach.* CLAUD *falls to his knees, the breath knocked out of him, gasping, his legs apart.*

HILDE: Travis, no! No!

TRAVIS, *unchanged, punches* CLAUD *once, twice, in the groin.* CLAUD *groans in pain.* HILDE *screams, runs up to* TRAVIS, *puts her arms around him from behind and pulls him off* CLAUD. TRAVIS *gets away from her and looks at her. Perhaps* SHE *is crying.* HILDE *looks at him, horrified. Suddenly, without saying a word,* TRAVIS, *leaves, disappears.* CLAUD *is writhing on the floor, with half-stiffled groans of pain.* HILDE *quickly kneels down beside him.*

HILDE: (*Crying out.*) Emma, Emma . . . !

*   *   *

On the screen we see another partial, exterior view of Emma's house.

Sunset. EMMA, CLAUD, *and* HILDE. CLAUD, *standing, is fastening his pants.* EMMA *has a small first aid kit and is standing beside him.* HILDE, *near the two of them.*

CLAUD: I'm much better.

EMMA: We'll call a doctor. Oh, no, the lines! We'll go to the emergency room.

CLAUD: Let's not exaggerate.

EMMA: These fights . . . How common and trashy! Who do you think you are?

HILDE: It was Travis.

EMMA: It was both of them, I'm sure. It still hurts, don't tell me it doesn't.

CLAUD: My balls, a little. But it's passing.

EMMA: You provoked him. Don't explain, it's all the same. There are many kinds of pain. Pain is not acceptable. Not your pain or the pain of the smallest animal. At least here, in my home. I don't want there to be any pain.

CLAUD: Where's Travis?

HILDE: He left.

EMMA: I didn't hear any car.

HILDE: Are you going to report him to the police?

EMMA: What do you mean?

CLAUD: Of course not.

EMMA: Naturally not. Try to relax. (SHE *has put away the first-aid items.*) I'll be right back.

CLAUD: Mother.

EMMA: What?

CLAUD: I'll go to Boise.

EMMA *looks at him and gives a sigh of relief.*

EMMA: You'll collect your father's things.

CLAUD: Are you calling him my father now?

EMMA: Don't confuse me. Will you do it?

CLAUD: I'll collect the stuff and I suppose I'll throw it in the trash. But I'll go. And in my car. It'll be relaxing to drive a few days. And it'll give me a chance to think about my next project . . .

EMMA: You won't change your mind?

CLAUD: No.

EMMA: Bless you, you idiot.

EMMA *leaves.* CLAUD *finishes arranging his clothes.*

CLAUD: What she doesn't know is that I'm going right away.

HILDE: You can't.

CLAUD: If it weren't for the problem with my balls, I assure you I . . .

HILDE; That's why you shouldn't go.

CLAUD: Of course.

HILDE: Travis is the one who should go. And me too.

CLAUD: My mother would prefer that you stayed. She wouldn't want to leave anything hanging. I have to go because you're staying. Poor mother. All alone against the Implacable Disorder of the Universe. Get it? It's a title for a grade-B movie. I'll take a look at the junk that man left me. Hilde . . . (*Pause.*) What I told you before is true.

HILDE: What did you tell me before?

Pause.

CLAUD· Goodbye.

*   *   *

On the screen we see another partial, exterior view of Emma's house.

Sunset. EMMA *and* HILDE. *Silence.* TRAVIS *appears, embarrassed. He looks at them and says nothing.*

HILDE: Idiot.

EMMA: (*To* HILDE.) Keep quiet. (*To* TRAVIS.) No sign of life from you for a whole day. And your car's in the garage. Where were you holed up?

TRAVIS: I've been walking.

EMMA: Amazing.

TRAVIS: Where's Claud?

HILDE: He's gone.

EMMA: He hasn't gone because of you, he hasn't gone to the end of the world. Just to do what he should do.

HILDE: You've been walking all night and all day?

TRAVIS: Yes.

EMMA: I'll fix you breakfast, dinner, and supper. And fast.

EMMA *disappears.*

TRAVIS: I'm sorry.

HILDE: The salamander is worse.

TRAVIS: It's getting worse?

HILDE: Well, I don't know what to do about it. I should have listened to you. I should have gone to the city, looked for information, and reported it.

TRAVIS: I'm the one who should have gone.

HILDE: No. (*Pause.*) If I hadn't been here, you wouldn't have had an excuse to get into a fight.

TRAVIS: We'd have found one.

HILDE: I'll take the car and go to San Diego.

TRAVIS: We'll both go.

HILDE: You haven't slept and you must be starving. I'll go alone.

TRAVIS: There's no reason for you to go. And they don't know we have the salamander.

HILDE: We'll feel better about it. You, too.

TRAVIS: I love you.

HILDE: Yes. It'll just be going and coming back, all right? Don't worry. I keep my eyes open.

TRAVIS: Not always. Hilde, the documentary must go forward.

HILDE: But there's no hurry. We can rest a bit.

TRAVIS: True. What's happened, Hilde?

HILDE: I don't know.

TRAVIS: Neither do I.

HILDE: I called you an idiot because I was furious with you. I'm not mad. I'm going.

TRAVIS: Wait. (HE *puts his arms around her and kisses her.* SHE *responds. Then* THEY *separate.*) Be sure to say goodbye to Emma.

HILDE: I will. Get some rest.

SHE *starts to leave.* SHE *changes her mind.* SHE *goes to the old box and takes out the doll, the Wolpertinger.*

TRAVIS: What are you doing?

HILDE: The little beast. It's missing one of its antlers and the other one . . . It'll keep me company during the drive.

TRAVIS: Watch out for the fire.

HILDE *disappears. Pause. Sound of a car leaving.* EMMA *appears with food and drink.*

TRAVIS *takes the drink and gulps down a few swallows.*

EMMA: What was that?

TRAVIS: What?

EMMA: A car just left.

TRAVIS: Didn't Hilde say goodbye to you?

EMMA: She's left?

TRAVIS: For the city. Didn't she tell you anything? She's worried about the salamander.

EMMA: What's wrong with the salamander?

TRAVIS: It seems it's gotten worse.

Pause.

EMMA: It's not worse.

Pause. Then TRAVIS *starts to eat quietly. Pause.*

TRAVIS: Sometimes Hilde's difficult and sometimes she isn't. She's had a complicated life.

EMMA: Eat and be quiet. Then off to bed. You'll sleep until your body tells you enough. What have you done?

TRAVIS: I'm sorry, Emma.

EMMA: You get some rest. Me, too. Afterwards we'll take care of the salamander. And we'll hope they'll come back. That Hilde will come back and that Claud will come back.

* * *

On the screen we see the exterior of an old trailer, almost a wreck.

Sunset. CLAUD *appears.* HE *looks all around, uneasily, and, perhaps, with a certain revulsion. Instinctively, without realizing it,* HE *places his hand on his groin. A grimace of discomfort. And instant later a* MAN *appears behind him.*

MAN: Is it as pretty as they say, California?

CLAUD: (*Removing his hand from where he had placed it, as if caught doing something improper.*) Huh? Oh, it depends.

MAN: (*Looking at the room.*) Now you've seen it.

CLAUD: Yes. I was expecting to find it dirty but not this bad.

MAN: (*As if* HE *were being blamed.*) He wasn't an orderly person. And he's been dead for weeks. Dust accumulates. In the letter I told you . . .

CLAUD: Leftovers.

MAN: You mean all the mess?

CLAUD: No, I mean the shit.

MAN: He was a good man.

CLAUD: Thanks for looking after him. Were you friends for a long time?

MAN: We went to Boise together to see one of your pictures.

CLAUD: Thanks for looking after him.

MAN: (*Affably but with dignity.*) You don't need to say that to me for a third time. (HE *goes up to some boxes.*) These are papers. Papers and photos. His clothes, too, but I don't think . . . Some of the papers had personal value for his father. Nobody's touched them.

CLAUD: Are they worth looking at?

MAN: Depends on who's looking, depends on why, the value of things changes.

CLAUD: Yes, I'm sorry. I don't mean to be disagreeable.

MAN: How was you trip? Would you like a cold beer? The bar's quite a distance. And the motel, forget it. You must have spent several days stuck in that car. Nice make. Are you very tired? I guess you won't be wanting to sleep here. If that's the case, I can look for somewhere you can stay.

CLAUD: I'm sure that won't be necessary. A couple of hours from now I'll be heading back.

Pause.

MAN: You're sure? You just got here and already you want to get behind a steering wheel again?

Pause.

CLAUD: Do you know? That man was not my father.

MAN: No. Joe didn't have a family. But, my friend, you want me to say it, right? An unlucky loser, that's what he was. You've been driving the interstate for days. Hope you didn't have any problem with the forest fires when you were getting close.

CLAUD: There's one in California, too, a fire.

MAN: You don't say. If you've got to spend even a couple of hours in a trailer full of dust, at least I can bring you a cold beer and a warm slice of pizza. Sound good? It's on me.

CLAUD: That would be nice, just what I need. I'll pay for the pizza and beer.

MAN: I said it's on me. Joe had his friends here. Where else? Right? He drank too much. No, he wasn't much good at keeping house. He only worked when he had no choice. When he livened up, he could be a funny guy. He never took up for long with any woman. Sometimes . . . You can imagine.

With one that was passing through, and that lasted a couple of weeks. I was the only one who believed him when you started showing up on TV, and he'd get excited and say that . . . that you were his son. I was the only one who believed him. Want to know why I believed him? Because Joe never told lies. I knew it. Sometimes he'd start to talk strange and he'd say he was speaking French and nobody took him seriously. But one day, that preacher from the Church of God heard him and said: that's French. A preacher who had his own church and wanted to save us from hell and brimstone because the end of the world was coming. So, when Joe, all kidding aside, opened his mouth you'd better listen to him. He wasn't a liar. He was a drunk and didn't give a shit about work. Funny guy. Only his hangovers made him cry. Then he'd say: where am I? Where did I want to be? That's it. He had no self-esteem. (*HE goes to the boxes and lightly kicks one of them, pushing it in CLAUD's direction. Pause.*) Know what I think? People without any self-respect, people without balls who've never tried to get out of their misery, they don't deserve any respect. Because we aren't really people. I'll tell you what we are. We're nobodies. On the other hand, people who've known what they wanted in life, and gone after it, those people aren't nobodies; those people, every one of them, are a bunch of sons of bitches. No . . . a bunch of . . . predators. (*Satisfied with himself.*) That word "predator," when somebody explained it to me, it stuck up here. Now I'll go get the beer and pizza.

HE *exits.* CLAUD *remains alone. Without approaching them yet,* HE *looks at the boxes. Mechanically, indecisive,* HE *puts his hand on his genitals again. Then* HE *takes a step toward the boxes.*

* * *

On the screen we see another partial, exterior view of Emma's house.

Sunset. EMMA *is handling the terrarium and* TRAVIS *is helping her.*

TRAVIS: In these canyons the predators can't do much harm to the salamanders, I think.

EMMA: There are many kinds of salamanders. If the salamanders disappear from the desert, it won't matter a lot. Anyhow, there're a few desert salamanders left. The situation's not so dramatic. You've picked the wrong creature for your documentary.

TRAVIS: No, it's right. (*Pause.*) I'll have to go, Emma.

EMMA: Right now it's a matter of saving this precious specimen we have at home. It's eaten some worms. I don't know. And you must wait until Hilde comes back.

TRAVIS: I'm getting tired of it. Where's she hiding out? Why isn't she here? What's she doing?

Pause.

EMMA: Try to relax.

TRAVIS: I don't know what's happened. And I need her, Emma.

EMMA: Maybe she got lost.

TRAVIS: No, not Hilde. I was thinking that . . .

EMMA: She's a very complicated girl. You said so yourself.

TRAVIS: She's had a complicated life. She feels comfortable with me, I'm sure of it. She needs me, too, and this is a respite for her. Because holding her in my arms . . . I dream of it. Holding her and not letting her escape. (HE *doubts.*) Troubled, contradictory . . . I don't care. But if need be, always ready to go into action. She's a person who's been wounded.

EMMA: (*Differing.*) Like the salamander, no. The salamander's not mentally troubled.

TRAVIS: When I met her, she was at loose ends. Not in her work. She's reliable in her work. But personally . . . she seemed as tense as a violin string. And with me, she began to relax. (*Pause.*) To San Diego. If she went to San Diego as she said, why not a word from her yet?

EMMA: After all, they probably didn't give it all that much importance. And with the phone out, this is the end of the world.

TRAVIS: It's been four days now. Maybe you're right, but I'm going anyhow. I'm of no use here.

EMMA: Well, thanks.

TRAVIS: I have to work. They're expecting me. There's this project and also other production ventures that I, well, I don't have to . . . but . . .

EMMA: You're stuck here without a car. I'll lend you mine.

TRAVIS: That's not necessary. I can . . .

EMMA: Stay a while longer. Tell me, what are you afraid of?

TRAVIS: Of looking ridiculous.

EMMA: That won't happen with me.

TRAVIS: It's already happened with you. I hit your son and instead of throwing me out, you want me to stay.

EMMA: What do you want? A scolding from me? Cain killed his brother Abel and God reprimanded him, but he didn't condemn the murderer. God's God and sees everything. I wasn't there when you and Claud had your fight. And nobody got killed, for one thing.

TRAVIS: And Claud and I aren't brothers.

EMMA: You know what'll happen if you go? She'll return immediately, it always turns out like that. And she won't find you here. Then what? What will she think if you abandon her over a slight delay?

TRAVIS: I'm nervous.

EMMA: Then pick up the salamander, help me. Careful. I want . . . Be useful. It'll take a moment. Are you listening to me?

TRAVIS: Yes, ma'am. (TRAVIS *sticks his hands into the terrarium.* HE *moves them around.*) It's not so easy. It's slippery. It gets away because . . .

EMMA: Grab it. You won't hurt it.

TRAVIS: (*Trapping something inside the terrarium.*) Got it!

EMMA: Great. Careful. If you can hold it, I can get a better look at the wound.

Suddenly TRAVIS *gives a start and lets what he was holding fall back into the terrarium..* HE *flaps his hand.*

TRAVIS: Oh, my God! Oh, ouch!

EMMA: What's wrong with you?

TRAVIS: My fingers . . . , my hand . . . ! It hurts . . . ! It hurts a lot . . . !

EMMA: (*Excited but not unpleasantly.*) Let's see. Hold it up! The rascal! It's defended itself! It's secreted poison!

TRAVIS: Poison?

EMMA: For self-defense, yes! Isn't it wonderful? It reacts!

TRAVIS: Poison . . . ? On my hands?

EMMA: Yes, a good sign! The instinct for self-defense! It has some life in it. Do you know what that means?

TRAVIS: Will they cut off my hands? Will I die?

EMMA: Not a chance! You'll give yourself a good scrubbing. Maybe with disinfectant . . . But especially soap. I guess I should keep an eye on you. Keep your hands away from your body. At least for a couple of days. (SHE *gives him a look.*) Now you'll have to stay.

TRAVIS: (*Calmer.*) Why do you want me to stay?

EMMA: I also have a right to feel anxious until your Hilde returns. Or . . . or until my Claud returns.

*   *   *

On the screen we see another views, now partial and exterior, of the old trailer.

Sunset. CLAUD, perplexed, seated among old papers, in front of the boxes. Near him a beer can and the remains of a pizza in a paper plate. HE puts down a piece of paper. HE looks at a photograph, puts it down, shows doubt. HE grabs the same piece of paper again. Suddenly HILDE appears, with the doll in her hand. CLAUD doesn't notice her. Pause. SHE makes some slight movement and causes a rustle. CLAUD turns around and sees the girl. HE sits dumbstruck. Pause.

HILDE: I brought the Wolpertinger.

CLAUD: What are you doing here?

HILDE shows him the Wolpertinger.

HILDE: Really, look, the Wolpertinger. It's missing an antler and part of the other one. It should have two of them.

CLAUD: Why have you come?

HILDE: Delighted to find you again. Are you happy to see me, too?

CLAUD: How did you get here? How . . . ?

HILDE: I'm good at research.

CLAUD: I can't believe it.

HILDE: I've come for the Wolpertinger's sake. Are all those your father's papers?

CLAUD: And Travis?

HILDE: With your mother. I suppose. As a matter of fact, you deserved the beating he gave you.

CLAUD: He caught me off-guard.

HILDE: (*With irony.*) I noticed.

CLAUD: Why have you come?

HILDE: Munich, Mittenwald, Dachau . . . Who was your father? Are all those his papers?

CLAUD: Yes.

HILDE: What do they say?

CLAUD: You haven't come to find out who my father was.

HILDE: Well, yes.

CLAUD: What does my father matter to you?

HILDE: I don't know whether he matters or not.

Pause.

CLAUD: Do you want me to have someone bring you a beer, a soda . . . ? How did you come? You must be exhausted.

HILDE: Have you read his papers?

CLAUD: My French isn't very good.

HILDE: Are they in French?

CLAUD: Most of them.

HILDE: And I read French fluently.

CLAUD: Why did you come? (*Pause.*) There are photographs too. Old ones. Very old, for the most part. Made in a city that's not American. Not in the north or south. Unless it could be Quebec. But I don't think so.

HILDE: Germany, maybe?

CLAUD: You can see stores with signs in French. I'd say they're photographs of Paris. Letters written in French and photos of Paris, for sure.

HILDE: (*As* SHE *looks for answers.*) Who are they photographs of?

CLAUD: Why did you come?

HILDE *picks up one of the photographs.*

HILDE: A girl. (*With tone of an expert.*) At the end of the 1930s.

CLAUD: Almost always the same girl, sometimes alone, sometimes with a boy. He's holding her by the waist, she's looking at him, she's always laughing. I'm sure he's the one who takes her picture. An ordinary young couple in love.

HILDE: How do you know that?

CLAUD: Here they're looking into the lens while they share a kiss. But the kiss isn't necessary to see that the boy desires the girl. And she feels the same way about him. Why did you come?

HILDE: Wait, are all the letters in French?

CLAUD: This one . . . (*Looking for it.*) This one's some kind of note. Kept in an envelope. On the envelope it says in English, in a different handwriting: "Copy of the letter I sent to the Greek," and inside, yes, there's a rough copy. But there's also a piece of paper with an address. The address is of a place named Milos. Who knows? (*Puts down the envelope, looks for another sheet of paper and shows it to her.*) Look, the other one . . . ; here I'm lost. It's not English, it's not French . . .

HILDE *takes it and looks at it.*

HILDE: Not German, not Italian . . . But it looks like a Romance language. (*Puts the sheet of paper down.*) Well, what do the letters explain?

CLAUD: A man is writing to a woman. She's here in America. She's pregnant, at the beginning. In some other letters she already has a son. A baby. He's in Europe. She's gone to America. The year is 1940. He misses her. I suppose she misses him, but there are no letters from her. What consoles him is that she's far away from the war.

HILDE: The Second World War began in 1939.

CLAUD: A couple who had to separate. He has stayed behind. He's writing from Paris. Why didn't he go with her? I've found one letter where all that is a lot clearer. How would he send that letter? France is in the hands of the Nazis. He is a member of a leftist party. He's not French but he has stayed in France to fight the invaders of France. And suddenly he's no longer writing from France. They've arrested him. See, this kind of blank postcard and with small handwriting. Do you know where he's sending them from?

HILDE: (*Passionately, almost triumphant, with complete certainty,* SHE *grabs the card that* HE *is showing her.*) From Dachau. From the work camp at Dachau. Who was this man?

CLAUD: My grandfather, I think. He's my grandfather and she's my grandmother. You read French better than me. They're the parents of the man who died in this trailer.

HILDE: He wrote you that he would have been able to tell you enough stories for a thousand films. Maybe it was true.

CLAUD: Yes, they've told me he never lied. He could have told the story of a man and a woman who desired each other. Are you happy now? Why did you come here?

HILDE: For all this.

CLAUD: You came because I was right.

HILDE: Right? Yes? In what way?

CLAUD: There are some things that just happen. You were capable of coming all the way here. Do you know why you came?

HILDE: (*On the defensive.*) I came for the Wolpertinger, for Dachau, for your father.

CLAUD: No.

HILDE: Yes. While . . . Travis . . .

CLAUD: Leave Travis out of it.

HILDE: He's finer than I can say. I've never loved him. Not Travis.

CLAUD *goes closer to* HILDE. HE *slowly puts his hands lightly over the girl's entire body.* SHE *trembles imperceptibly. Then perhaps* HE *takes her face between his hands. After that, perhaps* HE *lowers them and unfastens her clothes.* SHE *doesn't stop him.* HE *puts his hands and arms under her clothes and embraces her, holds her close and kisses her furiously.* HE *removes his mouth to catch his breath.*

CLAUD: Maybe you'll never love anyone, but if you want me half as much as I want you.

HILDE: Why did I come?

And now SHE *is the one who is embracing him.* THEY *kiss passionately. Their clothing is in the way.* THEY *begin to undress as* THEY *fall on their knees, wrapped in their embrace.*

*   *   *

On the screen we see another partial, exterior view of Emma's house.

Sunset. EMMA *and* TRAVIS *appear.* HE, *wet, is drying off with a towel. Both, relaxed.*

TRAVIS: I'm not five years old. I could have lathered myself without any help.

EMMA: Now you'll say you're embarrassed that you showed me your bare ass. Kids are hopeless, we have to keep an eye on them. (*Satisfied.*) You got clean and well disinfected. Does it still burn a bit?

TRAVIS: No.

EMMA: Just look at all the trouble you've caused, you poor salamander. And now cover yourself up a bit. Night's falling and so's the temperature. You men think it makes you feel more manly to pretend you aren't cold.

SHE *rubs him and* HE *lets her gladly. Perhaps* SHE *puts a light sweater on him.*

TRAVIS: Anything else?

EMMA: There now, handsome, that's it.

TRAVIS: All I need is my weekly allowance.

EMMA: What allowance?

TRAVIS: And for you to tell me I can come home as late as I please, but not to leave without . . .

EMMA: Without the keys.

TRAVIS: Without the rubbers.

EMMA: Oh, really! I'm not your mother. I'd never have said a thing like that.

TRAVIS: No, you said condoms. You said it a dozen times. You'd always say it to us. The weekends I had dinner with you. Claud and I were in a hurry to take the car and be off to live it up. But first we had to pass your inspection. As there's no father in this house, you'd say, I have to be father and mother. You looked happy. You used to check our clothes, you'd slip a few dollars in our jacket pockets, and you'd make sure we were carrying condoms.

EMMA: Never in my life.

THEY *look at each other, smiling. Suddenly* TRAVIS *embraces* EMMA *tenderly.* SHE *lets him. Pause.*

TRAVIS: It's as if night is always falling. Do you suppose the salamander will regrow it's tail? The wound is healing, it spits poison when it's angry . . . Have we saved it?

EMMA: Oh, let's hope so.

TRAVIS: And Hilde will come back, and we'll shoot more images of animals, of people, of towns, of species at risk.

EMMA: There's no species that isn't at risk.

TRAVIS: And Claud will come back full of ideas and he'll write the script of a melodrama that he'll turn, inarguably, into a movie classic. I'll have gone from here, and Claud will go . . . and you'll be living here all alone again.

Pause.

EMMA: A sensible woman must be certain that the boys in her home carry protection when they go out at night.

Pause. THEY *are still comfortably embracing.*

TRAVIS: And that reddish glow that's still in the sky?

*   *   *

On the screen we see another view, now partial and exterior, of the old trailer.

Sunset. A tattered and perhaps dirty blanket partly covers CLAUD'*s nude body.* HILDE, *also undressed, under some piece of clothing* SHE *has put over her, is reading intently some of the papers of* CLAUD'*s father. Suddenly* SHE *lets out a little cry of passionate recognition. And* CLAUD *awakens.* HE *sits up, looks at her.* SHE *doesn't notice until* HE *takes her arm, or touches her back with a certain concern.*

CLAUD: Hilde.

THEY *look at each other.* THEY *smile.*

HILDE: I woke you up.

CLAUD: Did you? I don't know. Come here.

HILDE *gives in to him, lets the piece of paper drop and lets him embrace her.* THEY *remain that way for a moment.*

HILDE: I've found the Wolpertinger.

CLAUD: You hadn't lost it.

HILDE: I've found the letters from your grandfather. He wrote very basic French.

CLAUD: Have you been reading for a long time?

HILDE: I let you sleep. (*Shyly.*) You've had a hard day.

CLAUD: We'll never stop holding each other, right, Hilde?

HILDE: (*With her mind already somewhere else.*) Never. (SHE *pulls away from him and picks up the piece of paper that she dropped.*) Listen. "I hope the doll I managed to get will reach you. They call them Wolpertingers, but the boy can name it whatever he likes. A kind of creature typical of these parts that, as far as I know, never existed. I love the two of you very much and I miss you, as always. Don't worry. I'm fine and someday I'll return. Then we'll be happy forever."

CLAUD: So what about it?

HILDE: Don't you understand?

CLAUD: A letter like all the others. I don't want to hear it. I want to make love again.

HILDE: Still more?

CLAUD: Still more.

HILDE: And that ache you felt . . . ?

CLAUD: It's nothing, it doesn't bother me anymore. And the bruise is fading.

HILDE: Wait. Relax. You ought to cover yourself.

CLAUD. No. And not you either.

HILDE: We're near Boise and it's getting cold. Men think it makes them feel more manly to pretend they aren't cold.

CLAUD *comes up to* HILDE *and puts the blanket over both their backs.*

CLAUD: Your body, my body and the blanket. We'll be warm.

HILDE: I've spent quite a while reading, yes. Your grandparents . . . she was French and I suppose he was Jewish, though I don't know from where. If he was Jewish, he didn't stay in France to face the Nazis. No way. Likely he had no choice but to stay. Yes, he was part of some resistance group. There are allusions but discreet ones, naturally. No, he wasn't French. There are gaps, who can say. (SHE *laughs.*) Keep your hands to yourself, you're making me nervous.

CLAUD: I won't.

HILDE: Listen. Your father's name was Joe Bennett. Your grandfather, Claude. Claude with the final "e" as in France. An "e" poorly written sometimes but which appears in all his signatures. You're named for your grandfather.

CLAUD: But I've always spelled my name without the final "e."

HILDE: Let me continue. There was the war. Everyone there took part. I've found her French passport. She was a Parisian. They got married. A young couple. She became pregnant. He was afraid he couldn't save himself and he decided that she and the unborn child would survive. She resisted but when the occasion came, he made her take a boat. Here, in the United States, they had no one, and when she arrived she suffered financial hardship. But her husband writes her and tells her to be brave, that at least bombs aren't falling and she's not in danger of being arrested. Your father was born at the end of spring, 1940. At least the child, here, would have the opportunities he'd need.

CLAUD: Well, fine.

HILDE: Your grandfather had a friend. Several, but one of them was Greek. In Paris, I mean. He was involved in politics, too. Your grandmother knew him well and your grandfather put his friend's regards at the end of some of the letters. A friend your grandfather was very close to. They ended up together at Dachau. On the postcards they allowed him to send from the camp he also put regards from his friend. Your grandfather died at Dachau, but his friend . . . who can say. The envelope with the copy and the note . . . you found the envelope. It's a copy of the letter your grandmother sent to the Greek island of Milos. After the war. Afterwards. She wanted to get in contact with that man. Or with his family. Who knows if she actually did. (*Pause.*) Claud, I want to know who your grandfather was.

CLAUD: You already know. Now let's leave it. Hilde, you and I, we . . .

HILDE: (*Impatient.*) Yes. Yes.

CLAUD: I let Travis beat me up because of you, and you have left Travis, with no explanation, because of me.

HILDE: Does your mother have mail delivery?

CLAUD: They deliver it once a week.

HILDE: I'll write Travis and you'll write your mother. We'll mail them from different cities. It's not necessary to hurt anyone.

CLAUD: Travis probably won't still be at my mother's house.

HILDE: I'll also send him an e-mail.

CLAUD: Maybe the telephone line's working again.

HILDE: Do you want to call her?

CLAUD: No.

HILDE: Do you want me to stay?

CLAUD: What do you think?

HILDE: At least for the moment I'm staying. I'll be able to help you with your work.

CLAUD: For sure!

HILDE: The script you're working on . . . Won't you have to look for locations in Europe?

CLAUD: It's what I wanted to do.

HILDE: I speak German, I speak French, I speak a little Spanish . . . I won't be a useless parasite.

CLAUD: Great, you'll be my interpreter.

Brief pause.

HILDE: Don't say no. Before going anywhere else, we'll go to Munich, then to Mittenwald, and we'll go to Dachau.

CLAUD: No.

HILDE: There are archives! We'll know when your grandfather died, maybe how he died . . .

CLAUD: What does that matter to us? And that work for me, you can do it by internet.

Pause.

HILDE: I was born in Mittenwald. When your grandfather was writing these postcards from Dachau, my family, not far away, in Mittenwald or Munich, were looking up at the sky to see if it was going to rain. As a child, I also had a Wolpertinger. Two years ago I found Travis. He was generous and had the kind of strength I needed.

CLAUD: (*Teasingly.*) You needed stength from someone else?

HILDE: But I refused to go near Mittenwald or Munich. We were preparing the documentary and I let Travis go to Dachau alone. There was no concrete reason for me to go, and I was afraid of returning. Now . . . I'll go to Mittenwald and I'll go to Dachau with you. Do you hear?

Pause. Suddenly CLAUD *bursts into laughter and embraces* HILDE.

CLAUD: Don't beg me, don't insist anymore! Fine, we'll go to Dachau. And afterwards, that'll be the end of it. Understood? The end of it.

HILDE: I'll make the reservations. Tourist or first class? First class. I was forgetting who you are.

* * *

On the screen we see another partial, exterior view of Emma's house.

Sunset. TRAVIS *is reading a letter.* EMMA *appears.* SHE *stands looking at him. Pause.*

EMMA: What does she have to say?

TRAVIS: How curious. You get a letter from Claud and I get one from Hilde. She explains that she's also sending me an e-mail, just in case . . . One for you, one for me. The same day.

EMMA: The mail only comes once a week. Where was Hilde's mailed from?

TRAVIS *looks at the envelope.*

TRAVIS: New York.

EMMA: Claud's is from Idaho, of course.

Pause.

TRAVIS: She's saying goodbye to me. Oh, and she didn't go to San Diego. (*Pause.* HE *looks directly at* EMMA.) What does Claud have to say?

EMMA: Just as he imagined, that man's home . . . A trailer. He was living in an old trailer without wheels. He hasn't found anything that's worth the bother, that when he could use his cell phone again he had a lot messages and it hasn't stopped ringing. He's accumulated a thousand commitments. He can't come back. He sends me kisses. (Pause.) In all honesty, I had him at home longer than I expected.

Pause.

TRAVIS: Hilde doesn't give me any explanation. Or even worse. She asks me to forgive her. In sad, agitated phrases. I won't see her again. It's over. (*Pause. When* HE *speaks, it is softly.*) Your son . . . I had him down. Shit! I should have finished the job.

EMMA: Don't say that! Don't start imagining things! I forbid it!

Pause.

TRAVIS: (*Without raising his voice.*) Well then . . . Damn my stupidity!

Pause.

EMMA: Leave the damning to someone else. Blaming yourself won't help. And you'll never hear it from me.

Pause.

TRAVIS: Whether you say it or I do. Claud and Hilde are together.

*   *   *

On the screen we see a general view of the town of Mittenwald, Germany.

Sunset. CLAUD *and* HILDE. CLAUD *is taking in the site of the town.*

CLAUD: Mittenwald. Photogenic. And peaceful. The streets are so clean . . . the people here take pride in these streets, for sure. And closeby, the mountain, magnificent. No one is talking about forest fires, they must be certain it's not their problem. And it's where you were born. From what you said about it, I was imagining it different, but I find it pretty. Do you really not want to see your family?

HILDE: (*As insisting adamantly on an idea already expressed.*) We've just come back from Dachau.

CLAUD: Let me have a breath of air. Don't you need to take a deep breath after Dachau?

HILDE: Not here.

CLAUD: Now we know that there's no Bennett in the records. No Bennett, no Fennett . . . Hilde, it's not certain that the man ended up here. Not at the Dachau camp, the one at Allach, or the one . . . what was it called?

HILDE: Dyckerhof.

CLAUD: Right. So, if you don't want to see your family, let's go back to Munich.

HILDE: That man was here. The postcards came from here.

CLAUD: It's late, the Wolpertinger museum must have already closed. Unless we stay over. Do you want to stay until tomorrow?

HILDE: No. Did you like the Dachau camp?

CLAUD: What are you talking about? What do you mean "like" the Dachau camp? Have you noticed me liking it, maybe? But my grandfather wasn't there. That's that.

HILDE: Did somebody invent them, the postcards?

CLAUD: Don't look at me that way. Have I done something wrong? We've visited the horror, we've confirmed what we wanted to . . . It's done. What option do we have? Maybe go to Paris, take care of several commitments there . . .

HILDE: (*Pleading.*) There is an option. Yes, there's one. The Greek friend. Milos is a Greek island.

CLAUD: Hilde, please. What are you saying now?

HILDE: The friend who was in the concentration camp with your grandfather. Milos is one of the Cyclades. Part of the Greek archipelago of the Cyclades. I've jotted down the airline and the ferry we have to take to go there.

Pause.

CLAUD: You're completely nuts.

HILDE: I'm asking you to. Please, please!

CLAUD: Hilde, what's going on? I'm serious about you, do you understand? One question. I already know it's all a lot of bullshit but . . . just what are you thinking? Forget Dachau for a minute. And you're serious about me, aren't you? I mean . . . I'm not talking about physical desire. Could you, perhaps, bring yourself to say that you love me?

HILDE: I don't know. (*With no change in tone.*) Do you know that seeing death, that seeing sights related to fear awakens the libido? Have you felt the urge to have sex? We haven't for two days. Let's look for an inn, not here, please, and make love. If you want to. And afterwards we'll talk about where we must go.

CLAUD: You can't say that you love me? Is it too soon to say it?

HILDE: I have said it.

CLAUD: I already know you desire me. I'm not asking if you desire me.

HILDE: It's not that it frightens me to think that I love someone.

Pause.

CLAUD: You've got me trapped.

HILDE: I had never . . . like with you, never. Never.

CLAUD: Sometimes I look at you and feel a kind of shiver . . . not like from the cold, but warm. Faster. You don't notice it.

Pause. HILDE *becomes more relaxed.*

HILDE: There are many different kinds of love. Of feelings. What did Travis tell you about me?

CLAUD: That you're . . . like some frightened creature. Troubled, he said. It doesn't matter to me.

HILDE: I can't help it, of course. (SHE *turns around, looking at the surroundings.*) I was born here, in Mittenwald. They organize interesting excursions from here. And in winter we have snow. You can ski.

CLAUD: I'm getting lost. Would you explain something to me?

HILDE: Yes. Won't it make a difference to you? Maybe it will interest you. I'm the daughter of a couple who quickly separated. Then I was just in the way. For both of them. No, it wasn't any big drama. My grandfather took me in. I went to live with him in Munich. I was very small and he was very old. His was a love story, the kind you like. He was a successful manufacturer, influential . . . until his wife died. Then he left the factories. He had lost his wife, years before she had saved his life, you see. He came to depend on me, came to terms with his own life by loving me. He would tell me stories, take me to the movies, console me if I had problems at school, scold me a little if I didn't behave . . . And, for example, he'd sit at my bedside if I had a fever. He'd sit beside me and from time to time he'd wipe my forehead with a handkerchief that smelled of his cologne. I must have loved him a lot too, because when I went off with my school to summer camp, I'd first, on the sly, fill a little bottle with his cologne, and that way, if I missed him . . . Once he bought me a Wolpertinger, the fabulous animal that for him represented the spirit of our land. When my grandfather spoke, sometimes he'd have a rhetorical tone in his voice. A little monster, that Wolpertinger.

CLAUD: A strange doll.

HILDE: In Munich . . . (*Becomes stronger.*) Here, too. In Munich sometimes there's a kind of silence. The least possible is said about things. At any rate, they told us about it in school. Tactfully. (SHE *smiles.*) With genuine tact. And they took us to visit it. The documentary Travis made . . . Actually . . .

CLAUD: I haven't seen it.

HILDE: No?

CLAUD: I haven't had a chance.

HILDE: You really should.

CLAUD: Naturally.

HILDE: You're a bastard.

CLAUD: I haven't had a chance! I'm always on the go! I didn't want him to think it didn't interest me, because it did. You can take me to a showing, if you want to.

HILDE: I will. In the documentary, the Nazi camps are a pretext. Travis wanted to speak of other matters. He compares the camps . . .

CLAUD: (*Cutting her off.*) Yes, I know that.

HILDE: For me it wasn't any pretext. I came home scared when they told me about it at school and took me to Dachau. Grandfather listened to me, I couldn't stop telling him what had happened at Dachau. And he finally had enough and interrupted me, uneasy, impatient, and he consoled me again, like the other times. He avoided the subject as much as he could, really bothered, resorting to caution. And suddenly he changed and said that if I had been a child in his times, the time when he was young, his wife, my grandmother would have seen to it that my life was easier than now. I didn't understand what he meant, but he threw off his caution and seemed to me sad and vulnerable. I didn't see him again with that face until he fell ill long afterwards, when I was nineteen. . I'd become an amusing and happy girl, and also bold, impulsive, a defender of marginal causes, concerned about the environment . . . you get the picture. Things like that. But now my grandfather was sick, with a fatal illness, and I loved him and I was taking care of him. No one else, just me. I stopped going to my classes at the university. If I was happy, it was because my grandfather had made it possible. I owed my happiness to my grandfather, and I'd be with him until the end. I filled the house with the scent of his cologne. Look, I was a naïve girl and a bit of a romantic, I'd be an idiot not to admit it . . . (*Pause.*) One day, while I was looking for papers about his medical history in his deak, I found other kinds of papers. Pornographic. (CLAUD *laughs, amused.*)   No. No. Not the kind of pornography you must be imagining. It wasn't that kind of pornography. It was newspaper clippings, some documents, and letters. When my grandfather had referred to the times when he'd have given me a better life, he was talking about the time of Hitler, of the Nazi era. He didn't involve himself in any special way. In reality, he couldn't, you know. But, for example, he refused to help the Jews. Him! Those letters from friends of his that he answered in a cold, icy manner . . . And you think you understand me when you don't. (*Pause to catch her breath.*) When the war ended, he didn't suffer any reprisals. None at all! And since it turned out that . . . a delicate subject. There was only his signature on some letters where he refused, in a cold, impersonal way, any help for his friends. Even . . . his own relatives. My grandfather, and his children, grew up, like me, in Munich and not in Mittenwald. I called my mother and told her what I'd found. It was so awful and it was . . . so beastly absurd! She listened to me without any surprise; I was simply talking about an inconvenient memory. I hung up in mid-sentence. Then, finally, I picked up the Wolpertinger, the spirit of the land, I went to my grandfather's bedside with the doll in one hand and the letters in the other and I asked him if he'd lived well near the extermination camp; pardon, the work camp. If he'd lived well, signing those letters . . . He looked at me, surprised and desolate. He replied, he had difficulty breathing, that at least we lived, that nothing could be done for those people, and that least we, thanks to Grandmother . . . (*Pause.*) But the problem is that we were Jews. He was a Jew.

CLAUD: What are you saying? Forgive me, but what are you saying?

HILDE: We were Jews!!

CLAUD: You're Jewish?

HILDE: It makes no difference to me what I am. But then it was different. And in spite of that . . . he was able to save himself. My grandfather wasn't the only case. Grandfather was Jewish but not his wife. No, she was Aryan. Pure Aryan blood . . . Grandmother came from an old prominent family, one of the mercantile families that had made the country rich centuries ago. But she married a Jew. In love. So much so that when the Nazis came to power she refused to divorce him, in spite of the fact that they demanded it at one point. On the contrary, she protected him tooth and nail, she saved him and she saved their children. But my grandfather and his father were very wary. Not one false step. Not even in secret did they risk giving aid to Jewish relatives, to Jewish friends . . . Nothing. Those desperate letters . . . their answers were brief and curt. Their letters were cold, as I've said, when they did respond. Well, of course, they didn't really hurt anyone . . . And that way nothing happened to him or to his family. He told me that to my face, lying in bed, as his filthy life was ending. He had spoken more than his condition permitted, so his breathing got worse. He stopped talking and was just looking at me. And I . . . I threw the Wolpertinger and papers on his bed, turned around, packed my bags, and left the house without ever entering his room again. He had saved his own skin but he had washed his hands of the blood of the others! Friends, relatives, uncles, cousins . . . ! Some of them died at Dachau. My father was Jewish like them. Do you understand? It's all the same, but I am really Jewish. Claud, it doesn't matter a shit to me, but I am a Jew! (*Catches her breath.*)   A week later they told me that my grandfather had only a few hours to live and that he kept asking for me, that the only thing that still interested him was to see me, his beloved granddaughter. Maybe he only wanted a caress, as repayment for all those he'd given me over the years. (*Pause.*)   I didn't go, of course I didn't go! I was an adolescent with principles. And he died. I didn't go to the funeral either. And then I fled from Dachau, Mittenwald, and Munich. I had never returned again. When Travis was here, you know, I didn't come with him. I never came back until today. A photogenic town. Now I realize it, you're right.

CLAUD: Hilde.

HILDE: All that . . . I have it in my head. It doesn't go away and it won't. Travis is the first man who has given me a little peace. And suddenly you appear and in a box you have a Wolpertinger and . . . I throw myself into your arms and . . . Maybe you think I came to look for you because I need to know who the man was that inherited a Wolpertinger. I do want to know, but it's not that. I have to believe it's not just that! I tremble too when I look at you!

CLAUD: Hilde, enough. Relax, relax . . . Look at me. Look at me! Make the reservations, Hilde; we're going to Milos. Then we'll see. Where did we leave the car? Let's get away from here. Let's go to Milos.

* * *

On the screen we see another partial, always exterior, view of Emma's house.

Sunset. EMMA *is holding the terrarium.* SHE *is not looking at it; her face shows her uneasiness.* TRAVIS *appears.*

TRAVIS: Nothing, I can't find it anywhere.

EMMA: It's not here; suddenly it's not here.

TRAVIS: But it hasn't died.

EMMA: It's not here. It couldn't get out of a terrarium, but it's not here.

TRAVIS: We've tried to find it, right? Is there anything left to do.

EMMA: It needs water. It won't find any. It won't survive.

TRAVIS: It'll use its wits.

EMMA: Don't talk just to be talking, it's not necessary. Why did it go?

TRAVIS: It was getting better. Thanks to you. It felt bold and . . .

EMMA: What will it do, alone? Its tail still has to grow back. Disoriented in a strange environment . . . (*Pause.*) You didn't mean to do it, but you've killed it.

TRAVIS· I wanted to save it! Why are you talking to me that way now? It's not like you, Emma! You should say that the salamander will find its way, that the sun won't kill it, that it will reach the water, that it will escape. That's the way you must talk!

EMMA *drops the terrarium. It shatters. Pause.*

EMMA: When are you leaving?

TRAVIS: Tomorrow. The rental car arrives tomorrow.

EMMA: You could have taken mine. At least until . . .

TRAVIS: I wouldn't think of it. (*Pause.*) The telephone line's repaired, I'm not leaving you cut off from the world.

Pause.

EMMA: Now I understand a dream I had.

TRAVIS: A dream?

EMMA: Last night I dreamed I was in Egypt, with my husband. Maybe at the Ramesseum, I don't remember what the Ramesseum looks like. I only saw an enormous wall that extended everywhere. Filled with carvings. Battles. The pharoah, in his chariot, expressionless . . . And they had cut the genitals from the conquered. A heap of amputated genitals, so that the conquered could be slaves but couldn't have offspring. A terribly realistic dreams. Except that the salamander was crawling along the wall, over the carvings. Green, beautiful, and with its long tail intact. (*Pause. Slowly.*) You know something? Claud's father didn't want to give up his child. But he wasn't sending him to school, he went around dressed any whatever way. I don't really know. I want to know the details. He couldn't support him. They took Claud away from him and gave him to us for adoption. (*Pause.*) I'll never tell Claud, that his father didn't want to give him up. You musn't either, if you see him again one day. (*Pause.*) I had to ask him to go to collect that man's things, don't you think?

Pause.

TRAVIS: Do you want me to stay a few more days?

EMMA: No, I want you to work.

TRAVIS: Yes. (*Pause.*) I'm sad too. Not angry anymore.

EMMA: Sad.

TRAVIS: Yes.

EMMA: But maybe . . .

TRAVIS: What?

EMMA: I don't know what I was going to say.

*   *   *

On the screen we see a sunset on the island of Milos, in the Aegean Sea.

Sunset. CLAUD, HILDE, *and the* MAN.

MAN: Milos is a relatively peaceful island. The sunset. What do you think of it? Like a fire, isn't it? Everyone says so, a fire. But no, the fact is the sun sinks into the water. On Milos they found the world's most famous statue of Venus. Beauty. They found her with her arms broken off. People who come already know that the statue's not kept here. If they come, it's to find this sunset. Better than the one on Sunion. No comparison. I haven't brought you to the top of the mountain. That's where the tourists are. Cultivated people, only a few of them . . . But in this kind of lookout, hidden by the church, you can see it just the same and we're alone. I don't know what it could be, the letter you're talking about. If your grandmother wrote it to my father, it must have been years ago . . . who can say. I can't tell you any more . . . For sure, for sure your grandfather was a friend of my father. Of all his group, my father was the only one to leave Dachau alive. He was very lucky. Someone has to be, right? He used to talk about it, about his companions. Not at first. As the years passed he started opening up. He spoke of the camp as if apologizing. He told about the horrors, casually, even modestly. It surprised me. Your grandfather was French, I imagine. My father wasn't a hero. He talked about the camp but there were things that weren't said. He wasn't Jewish. Your grandfather either, for sure. It's strange his name's not in the files. My father survived. He worked in the offices. So, it's obvious . . . there were more possibilities for getting out. You see? My father, before, was in another war. He was crazy, he had ideals. He'd gone to the war in Spain because he was crazy. Just before the World War there was a war in Spain. His side lost, he fled with another group, and crossed the border into France. The group he got involved with, the ones who sabotaged the Nazis, were mostly French. Also there was a Spaniard or two who'd come like him . . . But most of them French. For certain he was a friend of your grandfather and your grandfather was a terrific person, for sure. I don't remember any names. Wars are disgusting! That war dirtied everything. You'll have supper at my house and we won't talk anymore about it. The sunset, what do you think? I've seen enough, but . . . they say the first time you should watch it in silence. So I'll leave you. Only five minutes. You'll have time to tell me stories while we're eating. Maybe you two are in love. Reason enough to watch that fire alone, without anyone disturbing you. Five minutes. Then remember that you have to give me your address. You have e-mail, of course. An address to find you. You never know. If you don't mind.

HE disappears. CLAUD *and* HILDE *talk as they watch the sunset.*

HILDE: Do you think he really knows nothing about your grandfather?

CLAUD: Naturally he doesn't. He's a friendly person. He and his family. Well, he said it, it's possible that yes, my grandfather was at Dachau. That's something. Don't worry, we aren't sorry we came. (*Pause.*) I don't know what we're looking for, Hilde. There's nothing to find. And my father was not Jewish, that seems certain. You've done what you could, even got on my nerves. Forget it. Forget the ghosts and let it be.

HILDE: Do you want to turn back? Do you want to pick your locations in Barcelona?

CLAUD: One moment. So that you'll see that I want to exhaust every possibility . . . My grandmother. She was French. She lived in Paris. In any case, it's important to me to go to Paris. And we have . . .

HILDE: We have your grandmother's French passport. There's an address. I thought of that. But I didn't dare tell you.

CLAUD: We'll go to Paris. After all, I have things I have to attend to in Paris . . . meet some people . . . And we have the address, yes. Then you'll forget, agreed? Are you listening to me, Hilde?

HILDE: (*Happy, perhaps grateful.*) I heard you. Look at it. The sunset is really amazing.

* * *

On the screen we see another partial, exterior view of Emma's house.

Sunset. EMMA *and* TRAVIS.

TRAVIS: The car's ready, all my things are packed in the trunk. I'm off.

EMMA: You aren't forgetting anything?

TRAVIS: Nothing.

EMMA: I don't like for you to travel at night.

TRAVIS: It suits me. Spring is ending, I prefer not to drive under the California sun.

EMMA: Don't fall asleep.

TRAVIS: I won't.

EMMA: Well . . . I don't know if there's anything left for me to say.

Pause. THEY *look at each other. Pause.*

TRAVIS: Why didn't you adopt me?

EMMA: When will you stop repeating the same nonsense?

Pause.

TRAVIS: (*Natural.*) I would have wanted you to love me as much as you love Claud.

EMMA: That couldn't happen. But so what? (*Pause.*) Now listen. I do have something more to say to you. I wanted to say it yesterday. You'll make your film. And after this one there'll be another and another. Your documentaries will never be easy to watch, I predict. They'll never be enjoyable and never give comfort to anyone. Why should we care? A lot of people will be irritated with you and will ask you why you don't talk about the joy of living, even occasionally. But you won't give in. You won't, will you?

TRAVIS: I swear.

EMMA: No need. You don't have to swear for me. I'd like you to be different. But . . . in all truth . . . I also think that there has to be someone like you, someone who does what you do. Someone has to tell about the hell that's all around us. That somebody is you. That job has fallen to you.

TRAVIS: So it seems.

EMMA: And you'll never be a millionaire, but . . . you know what? On the other hand you'll find a lot of rewards in life. Maybe you'll end up with someone beside you, maybe not. Either way I want you to have children. You'll have children and your species won't die out.

TRAVIS: You're sure?

EMMA: Why do you ask? You're the one who has to be sure. You're the one.

TRAVIS: Agreed. How many children?

EMMA: Don't joke about it. It's a bargain.

TRAVIS: OK.

EMMA: What could I give you to seal the bargain? I should give that some thought. What could I . . . ?

TRAVIS: A kiss, how does that strike you? One kiss and that will be enough to certify that I'll have many offspring. As if you were marking me with a sign. As if you were . . . (HE *stops himself.*)

EMMA: As if I were.

TRAVIS *leans over a little and* EMMA *marks him with a warm kiss on his forehead.*

TRAVIS: Done. I'll never stop making unpleasant films and I'll have many children. No need for us to be so solemn all at once. Besides, I'll come back soon. Next time I won't wait so long, next time I'll come back soon.

EMMA: Liar. (*Pause.*) Do you have a lot of shots of our salamander?

TRAVIS: Indeed I do!

EMMA: Do you know what I'd like to suggest?

TRAVIS: What?

EMMA: With films, videos, whatever, there's a lot of footage, but afterwards most of the material is of no use to you and you throw it in the trash. I'd like for the salamander not to end up in the trash.

TRAVIS: It will open the film. Or it will be the ending. I've thought about it. I'll do it.

EMMA: Truly?

TRAVIS: You'll see.

EMMA *sighs.*

EMMA: I guess that's all. Hurry up, get started. It's a long trip.

TRAVIS: I'll drive fast. Everything goes fast.

EMMA: Be careful. Goodbye, and have a good trip. (*Pause.*) Son

*   *   *

On the screen we see the façade of an old luxury hotel in Paris.

Sunset. CLAUD *appears as he is finishing dressing. An instant later* HILDE *appears, still almost nude.* HE *smiles at her.*

HILDE: What are you doing?

CLAUD: You have to get dressed.

HILDE: We can have them send up dinner.

CLAUD: We have an appointment; if you'll go with me.

HILDE: (*Surprised and interested.*) Did you find out something?

CLAUD: Surprise. I found exactly the kind person we were looking for. A great nephew of my grandfather. He was a little unsure, but he said he'd meet me if I came there.

HILDE: (*Anxious.*) I'll throw my clothes on!

CLAUD: Wait. (HE *goes to her, takes her by the waist.*) What?

HILDE: (*Smiling.*) What?

CLAUD: You're relaxed, you're . . . well, you're beautiful.

HILDE: So are you. Listen . . . I find this hotel a little much. We didn't need a suite.

CLAUD: Don't be so modest. I can pay for it. They know who I am. I can't ask for something else.

HILDE: It'll be great to stroll through Paris with you. Spring has come. (*With ironic grandiloquence.*) The animals are mating . . .

CLAUD: Mating?

HILDE: And conceiving offspring. (*In a normal tone.*) It's the time for conceiving children.

CLAUD *gives her a kiss.*

CLAUD: Hurry up, get dressed.

HILDE: (*As* SHE *is leaving.*) That bruise. You've got to have it looked at. As a precaution. Really.

CLAUD: Get dressed. I want to be on time.

* * *

On the screen we see the façade of an old apartment house, humble and run down.

Sunset. CLAUD, HILDE, *and a* MAN.

MAN: What do you want to do here? I don't think there can be any of his papers or hers left anywhere. She was a cousin of my father. It's the kind of distant relative you lose touch with, don't you? She had lived here, needless to say. Next year you may not find me here. This ugly old building is an eye sore and will be coming down soon. As a boy, after the war, your grandparents sometimes came out to talk. Because you were coming, I've been searching to see if I could find . . . But no, only some mention in a kind of journal my uncle kept, years later. Members of the resistance. Everyone talked about the resistance. As if saying it lent some kind of self-justification. Resistance against the Nazi invaders of France. I'm a little skeptical, depending on who's doing all the talking. But he must have done something. I don't deny it. He probably came here as a refugee from another war. He was a foreigner, Spanish. From Barcelona, and . . .

HILDE: From Barcelona?

MAN: Yes. Certainly, but . . . but I don't remember anything else about him. It's true, yes, that she ended up in the United States and he went to a concentration camp. You think it was Dachau? I don't know that. But even if he did end up there, it's understandable that you didn't find him in the files, if you looked for him under Bennett, with two "n's" and two "t"s. According to my uncle's journal it was shorter. Or maybe he was wrong too. According to my uncle his name was Benet. I mean "B" "E" "N" "E" "T."

Pause.

CLAUD: But I've never called myself Bennett. Not Bennett or Benet. Never. In fact that man wasn't my grandfather and his wife wasn't my grandmother. In fact . . . Thank you very much. Thank you for receiving us. I shouldn't have troubled you. Now it's over and done. Don't you think so, Hilde? Done.

* * *

On the screen we see the open countryside, with Paris in the background.

Sunset. CLAUD *has placed a pile of papers on the ground and is burning them, adding others from time to time. Each time* HE *throws a sheet into the fire* HE *crumples it first in his fist with a mechanical and instinctive glance.*

CLAUD: I didn't want to burn them at the hotel. Or throw them into the trash. Maybe it would have been wrong, obscene, to throw the letters, the photos into the trash can . . . the things my . . . first father saved. And the fire won't be bigger than this little bonfire here. Hilde, are you listening to me?

HILDE: I don't want to sound ridiculous but you're burning your memory.

CLAUD: When you explained it to me . . . the story of your grandparents . . . I understood you, finally I understood you. And I said immediately: yes, we'll go to Milos. And we went. Now there's nothing more to do. There's no other place to look. Really, look for what? At any rate, we know more than we did at the beginning. But so what? There's nothing to save. Think about it: not even memory. Enough. I think you have the Wolpertinger at the hotel.

HILDE: Yes.

CLAUD: It's mine, actually. It won't matter to me if you keep it. But if it can awaken any feeling in you, it must be disgust. Because of the memories, throw it out. Get rid of it once and for all. (*Pause.*) Oh, tomorrow I have to . . . I have to see some people, those appointments. Not the reporters who called at the hotel but real obligations.

HILDE: Shall I go with you?

CLAUD: No, you'd be bored.

HILDE: I have to earn my keep. Now it's as if you were just keeping me.

CLAUD: No need tomorrow. I'll be running here and there all day. I need you at the hotel. If any call seems urgent to you, you can let me know on the cell phone. I may have it turned off for a while but . . . you can deal with it yourself. And check the e-mails I've received. If there're any that look interesting, you can print them for me to read later. You'll have earned your keep.

HILDE: Will we have dinner together.

CLAUD: I'm not sure. If I can, I'll let you know. By the way, Hilde, will you throw the Wolpertinger away?

HILDE: I don't know how to avoid it. Memories are a bit more than nothing. We say that a dead person, as long as someone remembers him, is not dead. And the people who've caused us some kind of pain . . . At least their names should be written down.

CLAUD: You're sick, Hilde. You let your grandfather die without you beside him. Fine. You cut off the little contact you had with your parents. Fine! And you've spent years trying to prove that you're different from them, that . . . ! Enough, Hilde! Haven't you heard that word? Haven't you understood it? Enough! Relax. You're not guilty of anything. Relax.

Pause.

HILDE: I love you, I want you to know that.

CLAUD: (*With a quiver.*) It's the first time you've told me that. If it's true . . . Wait, when people die, they're dead, however much they're remembered. They're dead. Period. When time passes, and when there's no one left who remembers them . . . It's not that then, finally, they die completely; it's that then, Hilde, the dead disappear. It's simply the same as if they'd never existed.

HILDE: No, there's what they've done, the things that have an effect on the ones who come after them.

CLAUD: There's nothing. (*To himself.*) What can there be? Are you sure you love me? You don't like love.

HILDE: I'm sure of it

CLAUD: Now you and I are living. It seems. Will you become my secretary tomorrow?

HILDE: Of course.

Suddenly CLAUD *has doubts about throwing a piece of paper, one of the last, into the fire.* HILDE *notices and* HE *is aware of it.*

CLAUD: It's the letter from my grandfather that I can't understand. Do you want me to keep it?

HILDE: (*Grateful.*) Yes, please.

CLAUD: Then I will. See? In my pocket.

CLAUD *smiles at Hilde.* SHE *smiles back. Pause.*

HILDE: Finished, then?

CLAUD: Wait. (HE *tosses a final piece of paper on the little bonfire.*) Now. Finished. Where do you want me to take you for dinner?

*   *   *

On the screen we see the façade of the old luxury hotel in Paris.

Sunset. HILDE, *alone, is clutching the battered Wolpertinger. A* MAN *enters with two hotel envelopes in his hand, one large and the other small.*

MAN: Pardon.

HILDE: Come in. (*Eager.*) Do you have the e-mail print-outs?

MAN: Yes. Here they are. (*Indicating the small envelope.*) Also, there's a message that came while you were out.

HILDE *has put down the Wolpertinger and takes the envelope.*

MAN: I hope you've had only pleasant news.

HILDE: On the computer screen I saw a message from Greece.

SHE *opens the big envelope impatiently.*

MAN: It's lovely, Greece. Can I take away the dinner service?

HILDE: Yes, thank you.

HILDE *is searching among the sheets in the envelope.*

MAN: (*As HE collects the dishes.*) We've had a splendid day. Spring is ending. It's a pleasure to go out on days like this.

HILDE *has found the specific sheet SHE was apparently looking for. SHE scans it. Brief, eager expression. SHE puts it aside and opens the small envelope.*

HILDE: (SHE *reads it, it must be short, and smiles.*) Yes, on days like this, going out . . . Today I was out only a while, I didn't feel like walking alone. (*Relaxes, upbeat.*) And now I see I'll have to go out again. Have you been to Greece?

MAN: No, miss, the world I've seen has been on television. But landscapes don't do much for me. But animals, that's another story . . . I like the documentaries about wild beasts. It's hard to believe. But they love one another, they fight . . .

HILDE: The big ones eat the little ones.

MAN: Only when they're hungry. Anything else?

HILDE: (SHE *looks at the MAN with a sudden suspicion.* SHE *points to the large envelope.*) Did you read those e-mails?

MAN: (*Surprised.*) No, miss. We never do that. And it's prohibited. Is there some problem?

HILDE: None at all, I'm sorry. (*More relaxed.*) One question. The Pont Neuf is the one that crosses the Seine at the end of the Ile de la Cité, isn't it?

MAN: Exactly. You know Paris.

HILDE: If I really knew it I wouldn't ask such an obvious question. Today I've felt a bit alone, you know. But the day will end well. I'll throw this piece of junk into the river. I'll look at old books . . . And I'll meet the man I love.

*   *   *

On the screen we see the Pont Neuf and the secondhand book stalls set up along the Seine in Paris.

Sunset. HILDE *appears strolling with a calm look.* SHE *is carrying a bag over her shoulder.* SHE *walks up to a bookstand.* SHE *casually browses through the books.*

MAN: Are you looking for something specific, miss?

HILDE: No, thanks. I'm killing time, I have a date.

MAN: Springtime, the Pont Neuf and a pretty girl who has a date.

HILDE: (*Amused.*) A date with my lover.

MAN: I'm happy for him. You're a foreigner.

HILDE: So's he.

MAN: Will you be in Paris long?

HILDE: I don't think so. We have to go to Barcelona.

MAN: What a pity. But you'll remember it. How about a gift for your lover? A book's a good keepsake.

HILDE: I wouldn't know which book to buy. I'm sorry.

MAN: I know which book you should buy. (HE *picks up a small volume.*) Look, read the title.

HILDE: (*Reading, even more amused.*) "Last Letters of Two Barcelona Lovers." Fancy that! Well, well!

MAN: Isn't it exactly the book you need?

HILDE: Well . . . I don't recognize . . . the authors. Do you recommend it?

MAN: To you, yes. To you, today, yes. It's short, you can read it quickly. Written at the beginning of the nineteenth century. Written by second-rate French writers but . . . The story's about two foreign lovers in Barcelona. Letters they exchange.

HILDE: Letters?

MAN: We follow the whole story through their letters.

HILDE: Letters. Really? Does it end well?

MAN: Like all melodramas. They have to get the reader's eyes wet.

HILDE: You've convinced me. Is this the price?

MAN: You noticed? Hardly expensive. (*As* HILDE *pays.*) I was closing the stall. I'm leaving late. It seemed I was waiting for you. My last customer of the day. Here, and thank you. (HE *closes up the tiny stall.*) There you see it, now you don't, no more books. Let them sleep, and until tomorrow. Is your lover late?

HILDE: No. I came early. He asked me to meet him here. And now I see him. He's coming. He's crossing the bridge. On time.

MAN: I won't disturb you. Have a good evening. And when you come back to Paris you know where to find me.

HILDE: I'll remember.

The MAN *leaves.* HILDE *is alone for a moment, the book in her hand.* SHE *is excited.* CLAUD *appears.* SHE *runs to him and embraces him.* HE *tries to restrain himself but* HE *can't and* HE *responds.*

CLAUD: Hilde . . .

HILDE: Things go well?

CLAUD: What?

HILDE: Did everything go well?

CLAUD: Which things?

HILDE: (*Laughing.*) How should I know? If I don't know what you've been doing!

CLAUD: I've dealt with some matters that . . . were worrying me.

HILDE: (*Impatient, her mind elsewhere.*) And now they aren't worrying you.

CLAUD: They can't worry me anymore.

HILDE: (*Without giving it any importance.*) Very enigmatic. But what I'm bringing you . . . ! (*Anxiously.*) It's not all finished, Claud! Now maybe it is. Look! (SHE *opens her bag and takes out the paper on which the e-mail is printed.*) Our friend from Milos. He's sent you a message! A message, do you understand?

CLAUD: What does he want now?

HILDE: To explain something, to tell you what he didn't tell you when we were at his house.

CLAUD: (*Tired, without much interest.*) And if he didn't tell us when we were there, why now?

HILDE: He couldn't bring himself to. From modesty, from . . . from shame!

CLAUD: What's this all about?

HILDE: He knows how your grandfather died! Or . . . or why he died! He doesn't remember anything about any letter his wife sent, he didn't deceive us about that, but as a boy he heard more than once about why your grandfather died. Do you understand?

CLAUD: Yes.

HILDE: It's a story of . . . petty betrayal, dirty miserable betrayal . . . while . . .

CLAUD: While what?

HILDE: In his message he must have softened the truth, or so I imagine. Let's see. Your grandfather and his Greek friend. Both of them fought in the Spanish Civil War, together. He knows your grandfather was Spanish, while with us he mentioned only French companions. Instinctively, to avoid the truth. Now he's telling you and apologizing. And they ended up in Dachau. The Greek friend went to work in the camp offices but not your grandfather. We know that too. But . . . (*Impatient.*) I'll read. "Since he was working in the office, my father had better chances of surviving. The work was a lot easier and sometimes there was an extra food ration. From the office he could even, in some measure, help his other friends, some of his less fortunate friends, as most were. Only some of them, those who, for one reason or another, it seemed important for them to keep on the list. He had to decide with a cool head. It was necessary to understand who was really indispensable. The time came when your grandfather felt that he was getting weak and asked for help. Asked his friend. They had fought together so many times . . . But my father didn't help him. He couldn't. There was a consultation, and the hard, sad decision was that his friend was not a necessary person. They let him die, there was no way out. But he always felt remorse for abandoning him. He remembered your grandfather's sunken, hopeless eyes. As I am witness, he never stopped remembering him. At least, at great risk, he gave him a way to write a letter to his wife. Not the usual neutral postcard, a real letter. His last letter. I don't remember what kind of connections he could have had, but the letter was written and the letter left the camp. A few weeks later your grandfather was dead." (*Pause.* HILDE *looks at* CLAUD.)   My obsession for searching . . . Going to Milos did serve some purpose! At least for finally knowing!

CLAUD: (*A bit unfocussed.*) Your mania: the utility of knowing. You still haven't gotten rid of the Wolpertinger?

HILDE: I'll throw it in the river. I'm sorry . . . I've gotten rid of a great burden by knowing. And yes, it's enough. We won't talk about it again if you don't want to. But you have this message. You have it. We've tied up the loose ends. Are you all right?

CLAUD: Why?

HILDE: (*Uncomfortable.*) You're not reacting. It was a pathetic betrayal, Claud! Why aren't you reacting? (*And* SHE *is the one who reacts, excitedly.*) Agreed, it's done and over. I don't want you to . . . We'll talk about it later. Let's see if at least this will make you laugh. I've just bought a book. A nineteenth-century novelette that's very sad. Here. "Last Letters of Two Barcelona Lovers."

While HILDE *is handing him the book,* CLAUD *makes no move to take it. Pause.*

CLAUD: (*Softly.*) Hilde, there won't be two Barcelona lovers.

HILDE: Aren't we going there? Have you changed your mind?

CLAUD: I don't want . . . I wouldn't want you to suffer. (*Pause.*) It's over, you and I have to go our own ways.

Pause.

HILDE: We have to part? Separate? Do I understand what I've just heard?

Pause.

CLAUD: Yes.

HILDE: Why? Who did you see today?

CLAUD: You're the most . . . you're a marvel and . . . (*Pause.*) There's no other way to . . .

HILDE: Just explain what's happened.

CLAUD: There's nothing to explain.

Pause.

HILDE: You're leaving me? Because I told you I loved you? I'd never said that to anyone. Even to Travis. Did you suspect I'd like to have children with you?

CLAUD: Hilde.

Pause.

HILDE: What is it? What? You desire me. You can't deny you desire me.

CLAUD: No, I can't.

HILDE: You want me passionately, you bastard!

CLAUD: Yes.

HILDE: Then . . . (*Pause. Frenetic.*) No, Claud. Please no. Explain it to me, Claud!

CLAUD: (*Tense and distant at the same time.*) It's just that I don't want to prolong it. Uh . . . I'm thinking more of you than myself. Remember that, in reality, I didn't interest you. You were looking for a . . . you were looking for other things in me.

HILDE: Now what are you saying?

CLAUD: I don't know.

HILDE: (*Furious.*) I'm not a good co-worker. I'm a fool, right? I'm insufferable and I can't be taught. I live in a fantasy world. I'll always be sick. Just an . . . unbalanced, troubled person. I can't help it. And you can't put up with it. I haven't stopped spoiling your life. Yes, it's obvious. Yes, indeed! And now what? It's not your question but . . . now what? (*Desperate.*) Now what about me? What do I do?

CLAUD: (*Neutral.*) You'll find a job. You're a good co-worker. I'll see that you get a good job. I myself . . .

HILDE *slaps him.*

HILDE: I'm not talking about a job! Don't you dare make it sound like I'm talking about a job!

CLAUD: I'm sorry.

Pause.

HILDE: (*Crushed.*) I was getting used to the fact you could no longer . . .

CLAUD: It's not that.

HILDE: What have you done to me? You're also one of those people who bite their tongue while they're asking for forgiveness, aren't you?

CLAUD: (*With effort. HE is suffering. HE is trying unsuccessfully to find adequate words.*) I want you to go on with your life. A few weeks from now . . . you know how to manage alone. You do. You must try . . . you must not think about me, OK? You probably won't.

HILDE: Just shut up! (*Pause. Very softly.*) What have you done to me?

CLAUD: Stay at the hotel as long as you wish. I'll have my things picked up.

HILDE: Oh, you don't even intend to set foot there again.

CLAUD: (*Utterly tense.*) But before . . . Before I'd like to . . . You don't know how much I'd like to . . .

HILDE: Tell me it's only a joke.

CLAUD: (*Hiding his total despair.*) I'd like you to know . . . I'd like . . .

HILDE: Do you know how I feel? You hadn't loved before. Really, no one.

CLAUD: (*Helpless.*) I'd like . . .

Pause.

HILDE: If you have to go, then go. (HE *stays, quiet, looking at her.*) Why are you looking at me? Don't look at me! (*Pause.*) I don't want you to see me cry. (*Pause.*) I can't move. Don't you see it? You go. Don't look at me. Go away!

CLAUD *reacts.*

CLAUD: Yes. (*Takes a deep breath.*) Yes, Hilde.

HE *turns his back and leaves.* HILDE *remains alone. Pause.* SHE *lets out a single sob. Then, with fury,* SHE *throws away the book she has bought, perhaps into the river. Pause.* SHE *is unsteady.* SHE *doesn't know what to seize onto. Perhaps* SHE *puts away the e-mail printout.* SHE *finds the Wolpertinger,* SHE *seizes it furiously and starts to throw it away too. But then* SHE *stops and studies it.*

HILDE: No. You're missing an antler and a half. You're horrible. And come what may, you're staying with me. Wherever I go, if I live or die . . . you stay with me.

SHE *pulls herself together, arranges her clothing with an instinctive and unnecessary motion, looks at the river, looks at the sky, and then leaves.*

*   *   *

On the screen we see again a partial, exterior view of Emma's house.

Sunset. EMMA, *alone. A phone rings.* SHE *picks it up.*

EMMA: Yes, hello. (*Very brief pause.*) Claud! Where are you? Paris, how I envy you, I'll never go back there again. What? I can't hear you very well. Oh, and why from a taxi? Why aren't you calling me from the hotel or, if I may ask, from the Place des Vosges? On the way to the airport? I like Orly better, maybe because . . . Yes, I'm fine. Alone. Fine. And where are you going now, Claud? I can't hear you well. Claud, has something happened to you? What can I say, it seemed so to me. You have to tell me what? It's curious, yesterday I spoke with Travis. Him yesterday and you today. Him? Alone, too. I can't hear you, son. Yes, Travis. Look, I'm the one who called him. Now that the line's working again . . . He wouldn't have called me. You can't stop being friends, Claud. He said he was calm and relaxed, but I'm not so sure. I'm never sure with you two. Oh, me! Nothing, I sighed. I said it was just a sigh! And now explain why you're calling me. Why are you calling me, Claud? You said you had to tell me something or other. You only wanted to hear my voice? That's not true. You can spend months without hearing my voice. I'm glad you called me but . . . In fact, I don't like it because . . . if you don't call me it means everything is going well. But if you do . . . Wait, I can't hear you. Claud? Claud? Claud, yes, now I do, go on. I'm listening. You're alone too, Travis? Oh, I mean Claud. What with my head and this phone and the lousy coverage! Sorry. Are you alone? You've called me to tell me who knows what, and you aren't telling me, and I get the feeling you're not telling me because I had a conversation with Travis and now you no longer . . . Yes, and besides the battery in your cell phone is getting worse, and on top of all that you sound strange, and shut up and don't tell me I'm wrong. (*Pause.*) Forget the salamander. It disappeared. Then I do have something to say. You're on edge, you're ill, maybe you think you shouldn't have called me. Yes, you should have called me. Do you know why? At least because I say so . . . Claud! Claud, can you hear me? Claud, yes, to tell you that, look, I don't want to know anything you don't feel like telling me. And to remind you . . . Claud? To remind you that I'm your mother and to send you a kiss. Do you hear me? Hear what I'm saying to you? Can you hear me? Did you hear me, Travis? (*Corrects herself, annoyed with herself.*) Claud, shit! I asked if you could hear me, Claud. Answer! Claud! The connection's not broken! Claud! If you hear me, say so. Say something so that I can hear you. (*Pause. Softer.*) Claud. (*Encouraged again, and for an instant.*) Claud! Now! What are you saying? I can't hear you well, you said goodbye? Claud!

Pause. SHE *gives up and puts down the phone.* SHE *remains in a daze.*

* * *

On the screen we see a small plaza situated at the edge of the old part of Barcelona.

Sunset. CLAUD *and a* MAN.

MAN: Did you have a good trip, from Paris to Barcelona? Did you see the fire from the plane? You don't look so well.

CLAUD: I'm fine. Happy to meet up with you.

MAN: Excited about getting to work?

CLAUD: I'll try to generate some excitement.

MAN: I've picked out a few places. You weren't too precise about the locations you wanted.

CLAUD: I have a better idea now.

MAN: We can consider this plaza as the entrance into a kind of environment . . . the ambience you asked for. Behind you a church from the beginning of the twentieth century, in front a medieval one . . . The feminine image on top of the fountain is a saint who protected the city . . . But the people who lived here, the ones who made all this, have disappeared, have become extinct, or nearly. Maybe I'm exaggerating. They left for other neighborhoods of the same city or disappeared. It's a neighborhood that was always inhabited by families with little buying power. Now, too. But now the change is brutal . . . Almost all are recent immigrants, African, Asian, Latin American immigrants . . . You get the picture? They've made the neighborhood theirs but they don't know what these churches are or what this fountain means. (*Pause.*) How is it? What you want?

CLAUD: It may serve the purpose.

MAN: (*Sighs.*) Claud, either you explan to me better what kind of film you have in mind, or I won't be able to help you. A melodrama, a love story, a certain kind of ambience . . . there's nothing specific there. Nothing to work with.

CLAUD: You're right. Forgive me. (*Up to this point we have seen him distracted; suddenly* HE *tries to focus.*) I'll try. The story I want to tell . . . At least in part . . . Let's see. I'll go as far as I can. Actually, it's a rather conventional subject. I'll begin.

MAN: I'm listening.

CLAUD: Imagine . . . On one hand, there are two friends, or two brothers, I'm not sure about it. In any case, they've known each other from childhood. They have a love-hate relationship, they're in the same profession but have oposing ways of understanding it. Perhaps, in reality, each of them thinks the other is right. Fine. Now we see them, and afterwards we have the girl.

MAN: They both fall in love with the same girl.

CLAUD: Predictable, inevitable. They fall in love with the same girl and come to blows over her.

MAN: Literally.

CLAUD: Literally. A brief and brutal fight. Perhaps without realizing what he's doing, one of them kicks the other one in the testicles. Once, or twice . . .

MAN: Stop.

CLAUD: Twice would have been enough. (*As* HE *is talking,* HE *becomes involved in what* HE *is telling.*) And so, the girl, also inevitably, chooses, from the two, the one who received the kick. Then . . . try to imagine it. Ever since he was kicked, the guy's testicles haven't stopped causing him pain. But what does it matter when you really desire a woman? Days of sex, days of unflagging passion . . . perhaps days of love if the thing we call love really exists . . . Etcetera. But . . . there's a but, don't forget. The pain in his testicles still hasn't gone away. And he notices, besides, that the place he received the blow has a dark bruise. Not exactly a hematoma. And as the days pass, it grows larger. He tries to forget about it. He loves the girl. Suppose it's true, suppose it's more than desire, suppose it's love. In short, something right out of a movie. A savage love he'd never felt before. And she . . . she, simply, says that, really, she'd never loved any man before.

MAN: Does she only say it, or is it true?

CLAUD: It's true. For sure. It's true. But he begins to have difficulty making love. She doesn't notice. He tries to hide it and she's not aware, or at least she pretends she isn't. Perhaps . . . I don't know. They don't talk about it, only some allusion, and in any case they want to be together. They travel. Other things happen that aren't relevant. They arrive in a great European city. Not this one. Much larger. And then, one day, he disappears. For almost an entire day he leaves the girl alone. He doesn't tell her where he's going or who he'll be seeing. (*Pause.*) Actually, he has set aside this day because he's having a medical examination. He has friends, money, influence . . . He's gone to the best hospital, the best specialist . . . He's scared. A long, exhaustive medical examination. He is more and more afraid, but he hides it. And the faces around him don't look exactly happy. His fear increases. With good reason. When he leaves the hospital he knows the diagnosis. Without the shadow of a doubt. He has two choices, either he lets them operate or he dies. But . . . if they operate he won't have sex again. If they operate, they'll have to . . . Do you get it? It won't be only that he can't have children. It will be . . . nothing. They'll have to castrate him, that's how things stand.

MAN: Hard!

CLAUD: (HE *smiles.*) Yes.

MAN: And what does he decide?

CLAUD: I think he probably doesn't know. What interests him is another decision. The other one. He makes another decision. We've agreed he loves the girl. He thinks he could live with her always. It doesn't matter that she can be irritating, that she forces him to uncover old, disagreeable histories . . .

MAN: Wait, you're losing me.

CLAUD: I'll explain that part another time. He loves the girl, he could have married her, he could have had children, in fact she wants to have children . . . And that will never happen. No children, or, soon . . . Well, he decides he has to break up with her. And that he won't tell her the reason, he won't tell her why.

MAN: Won't he let her choose?

CLAUD: She's in love. She'd say that she would stay with him. He breaks with her abruptly, just as I've told you, without giving her any explanation. He sees her collapse in front of him and he can't bear it, and he's desperate, and has to hide it. Act strong, cold, play the son of a bitch. She doesn't hide her feelings. Why should she pretend she doesn't understand a thing, that she loves hm and doesn't want to be left alone? But he, on the other hand, has to stand fast. He, come what may, is lost. She, too? If she fights back, no. He hopes she'll fight back. He hopes for it, wants it. If you knew how insistently he was praying to any God who'd listen that she would fight back and walk away . . . She's such a fragile girl . . . and . . . and . . . , and he has to leave her there, in the middle of the city, seeing the pain on her face, without being able to express his own, his despair. I can imagine quite well how wrenching it is for him when, unable to say a word, a single word of comfort, he must turn his back on the girl, and walk away, leave her forever, however long that forever lasts.

MAN: What else?

CLAUD: (*Tired.*) Haven't you had enough for today?

MAN: It's a melodrama. You'll have to develop it. But how does Barcelona figure in?

CLAUD: (*Breathes deeply. Recovers his calm.*) You'll understand it in time. And a neighborhood like this could be right, really. But enough for now. Now take me to eat. Let's talk about other things, all right?

MAN: All right.

CLAUD: Oh . . . wait. I also wanted to ask you . . . I don't know if you 'll have an answer. It's simply a matter of curiosity. While I was flying here, I was reading a guide book about Barcelona. Thumbing through it. In the guidebook there was a reference to a language. I don't know, maybe a dialect . . . (*Emphatic.*) Do they speak something here that isn't Spanish?

MAN: What was that? I was thinking over your story.

CLAUD: You don't like it.

MAN: I'll wait until you have the screenplay clearer. What were you saying? Here, something that's not Spanish. Yes, Catalan.

CLAUD: And there are people who really speak it? Or is it like Welsh, for example.

MAN: They speak it, really.

CLAUD: Oh I have an old document, a letter . . . It's another story. It could be . . . surely not, but . . . the person who wrote the letter was born here. Could he have written the letter in . . . in Catalan?

MAN: He could have. Still could now.

CLAUD: You mean that . . . ? Do you know someone who'd be able to tell me if the letter is written in that language?

MAN: Me. I have many talents, didn't you know that?

CLAUD: You.

MAN: Whenever you wish.

CLAUD: (*Expectant and cautious.*) I have it here, the letter.

The MAN, *with naturalness, holds out his hand. Only then does* CLAUD *make up his mind and searches in his pockets to find the letter.* HE *hands it to the* MAN.

MAN: Yes, it's Catalan. Yes. (HE *looks up and sees the expression on* CLAUD's *face.*) Do you want me to try?

CLAUD: What?

MAN: To read it. Translate it.

CLAUD: You can do that, too?

MAN: More or less.

Pause.

CLAUD: Please.

The MAN *examines the text, calmly, indifferent, trying to figure it out. Then, slowly,* HE *begins to translate.*

MAN: For example, in this part the writing is clearer. In fact it's very clear, as if it were written with someone in mind he doesn't know very well . . . Let's say he was thinking of someone like me. (*The* MAN *reads, bit by bit, impassively and with few hesitations.*) "Life is hard here. I know you're waiting for me. Be prepared for anything that may happen. At least, maybe someone will make sure that this letter, so different from the cards I write you from time to time, will reach you. They've promised me. Forgive me for writing you in Catalan. You don't understand it very well but you'll make an effort; my French isn't very expressive and I don't want to speak to you in any other way. It would make me so happy to see you again, and see my son at least once in my life . . . When I'm cold, I think of your body. I've always fought for lost causes, forgive me for that. If I die, I want you to live and not despair, and if you do, I want you to keep going in any case. For our son's ske. You must enable him to . . ." There's a phrase here I don't understand. "I never stop thinking of my son's future and the future of my son's children. Try to see that they are happy. We won't be, but they can. The world where I live, the music in the names of the things in my world, will disappear. Their world . . . I don't know what it will be, but they'll have one, whatever it's like, and it musn't disappear. Don't let that happen. Don't let their world disappear. Sometime, if you'd like to, tell my son about the place I'm from. So that he'll know that other universes existed and so that he'll defend his own. And you . . . Look, if you're too sad, remember when we walked arm in arm along the Boulevard Poissonnière, when instead of having a meal, we decided to buy a Croque-Monsieur and went to see the marvelous American films at the Rex Cinema. Those days existed. Happiness existed. I love you. Goodbye." And it's signed "Claudi." (*Pause.*) A depressing letter. Where was it written?

CLAUD: At Dachau.

MAN: Oh. (*Pause.*) The Rex Cinema. They showed your last film there . . .

CLAUD: (*Interrupting him.*) Yes. (*Pause.*) Then what is Catalan?

MAN: (*With his mind still on the letter.*) Huh? (HE *recovers rapidly.* HE *looks for a way to answer.*) Oh, nothing. I don't know . . . , like this neighborhood. A phenomenon on the way to extinction.

CLAUD: On the way to extinction? (CLAUD *laughs, suddenly amused, bitterly amused.*) The protagonist of my film . . . I'd say that he's in the same boat. (*Slight pause.*) You know, maybe I'll stay in Barcelona for a few days. (*The* MAN *starts to return the letter to him.*) I don't need it, you can throw it away. Throw it away. Really. (*Slight pause. Then energetically, almost disagreeably.*) Throw it away.

* * *

On the screen we see a partial, exterior view of Emma's house.

Apparently it is sunset. EMMA *and the* MAN, *seated tranquilly, holding drinks.*

MAN: Have you had any news from your son?

EMMA: No.

MAN: And from Travis?

EMMA: Not from him either.

MAN: You're certain?

EMMA: It's just that I don't feel like talking about it.

Pause.

MAN: It's the last day of spring.

EMMA: Thanks for coming.

MAN: Thanks for having me.

EMMA: Don't talk nonsense.

The image on the screen begins to dissolve until it disappears. Upstage, half in shadow, separate and equidistant, the figures of CLAUD, TRAVIS, and HILDE begin to appear. THEY are walking. THEY are walking silently without moving from the spot. The atmosphere has a reddish tinge that quickly increases.

EMMA: Almost no one likes salamanders. That one was especially beautiful.

MAN: The ancients believed that salamanders, in the fire . . .

EMMA: (*Patiently.*) That they ate fire.

MAN: They must have had some reason to say it.

EMMA: Ignorance.

MAN: Something else.

Pause.

EMMA: It looks like sun doesn't want to set and that night will never come.

MAN: The sun has already gone down. It's the fire, Emma.

EMMA: Oh, the fire.

MAN: It won't reach this far.

EMMA: (*Unsure.*) It won't, will it? Not here.

The MAN *looks at* EMMA. *Without moving from where he is sitting,* HE *holds out his hand. Pause.* EMMA *extends hers and they meet halfway. Silence. Upstage, the three figures,* CLAUD, TRAVIS, *and* HILDE, *continue walking, separate and tireless. Then, little by little, the figure of a beautiful salamander appears. And suddenly, both the figures of the three young people and those of the two older ones freeze their rapid or slow movements. The reddish tinge increases a bit more, while the figure of the salamander presides over it all. And suddenly there is total BLACKOUT.*

ACKNOWLEDGEMENTS

Although in the writing of my plays I would often use information and help that different individuals had offered me, I'd never had the courtesy to attribute the debt of gratitude I had contracted. On this occasion the debts are very evident, numerous, fundamental, and at least for once I must recognize them in explicit form. With even more reason because some of the assistance came from close and patient friends, and in other cases it came to me from persons with whom I'd never spoken in my life. In short, this work would not exist, in any form, without a group of collaborations that I hardly dare call providential. So then . . .

My thanks to Sharon Feldman and Marion Peter Holt for their research and their concerned and enthusiastic thoughts about some proper names, about the California desert, and about the appropriateness of other locations in the United States.

My thanks also to Klaus Laabs for some proper names and for his information relating to Dachau . . . and because he readily understood what kind of small detail I was looking for.

By way of Klaus, my thanks to Florian Borchmeyer because, Déu meu, out of the blue he offered me the crucial existence of the *Wolpertinger*.

My thanks to Jaume Terradas because he heard me out, not as a scientist listening to an illiterate, but as writer to writer, and thus revealed to me the existence of the lovely salamanders that survive in the California desert.

And, finally, my thanks to Esteve Miralles, who guided me, patient and unfazed, through the etymologies of several proper names, the names I needed.

Strangers

Sergi Belbel

Sergi Belbel

Photo: courtesy of the playwright

Sergi Belbel and *Strangers*

Sergi Belbel (Terrassa, 1963) is at the forefront of Spain's post-Franco theatrical landscape. An accomplished playwright, director, and translator, Belbel has authored more than twenty plays and received a succession of awards for his achievements as a dramatist and director. He has played a leading role in reinvigorating, in democratic times, the tradition of text-based drama in Catalan and has served as Artistic Director of the Teatre Nacional de Catalunya since 2006. At the same time, he is currently one of the most coveted playwrights in Europe, and his presence on the international theatre scene is unrivaled by that of any other living dramatist from Spain. In addition to *Strangers* (*Forasters*, 2003), five of Belbel's plays have appeared in print in English.

Strangers premiered at the Teatre Nacional de Catalunya under Belbel's direction during the fall of 2004. The play was commissioned in conjunction with the controversial "Fòrum Universal de les Cultures Barcelona-2004" and, as such, touches upon an array of timely issues around which the Fòrum was conceived: cultural and ethnic diversity, displacement and migration, racism and ethnocentricity, assimilation and integration. Belbel's two-part "family melodrama" portrays the saga of a European family whose pain and trauma, both physical and existential, emerge as part of a foreboding cycle of repetition. Through a curious play of temporal and spatial interactions, parallelisms, and collisions, *Strangers* appears to manifest an awareness on the part of Belbel that theatrical performance, in essence, hinges upon a tenuous rapport between the living and the dead, a process of substitution through which we resuscitate or reincarnate past lives. Belbel's play hence proposes a relationship between collective memory and the theatre spectacle that is grounded in strategies of substitution; that is, through the employment of an array of characters who appear before the audience as specters from the past.[1]

The scenic space is, ostensibly, a large urban apartment occupied by several generations of the same bourgeois European family over the course of two centuries (the present-day twenty-first century and the 1960s). In typical Belbelian fashion, the text proposes an intriguing casting strategy that produces a kind of temporal vacillation, entailing effects of doubling, repetition, and even simultaneity, as the two strands of time appear to intermingle and intersect. According to the proposed scheme, the actor who portrays the grandfather during the twentieth century is also the father in the twenty-first, the mother during the twentieth century is the daughter during the twenty-first, and so on. Belbel's casting strategy yields potentially unanticipated visual effects, whereby many of the characters in the play appear to evolve in adulthood into duplicate images of their parents. With this effect of theatrical ghosting, the faces of the characters are blurred and confused in a crisis of distinctions that visually accentuates the notions of repetition and memory. Time progresses yet it also appears to stand still.

Although Belbel is accustomed to playing on a global stage, curiously, this is the first play that he has written that, at least on one level, appears to address the specific cultural and historical realities of his own city. Although he does not name Barcelona explicitly in the text (or in any of his texts, for that matter), there are several aspects of the context that are distinctly reminiscent of the multicultural and multiethnic conditions that have shaped the evolution of this city, as well as Catalunya, throughout the two centuries. Whereas, during the post-civil war years, Catalunya, with its ever-increasing industrialization and economic prosperity, became a prominent focal point for large waves of migration from economically underdeveloped areas of Spain, during the post-Franco years (especially the 1990s and the present decade), Catalunya became once again a popular destination for thousands of immigrants, from various points of the globe, especially Africa and Latin America. Thus, to be a "stranger" in Barcelona during the decades depicted here is a state of being that carries with it multiple connotations. Belbel takes full advantage of the ambiguous, polysemous value of his title, transferring metonymically all those meanings that the term "stranger" connotes to the spatial geography of the apartment building in which the action takes place.

In the most literal sense, Belbel's employment of the term refers to the family living upstairs, in the invisible space of the apartment situated directly above that which is depicted on stage. The twentieth-century inhabitants of the upstairs apartment are characterized as immigrants from another culture. Seemingly underprivileged and unassimilated, their presence poses a series of cultural, ethnic, and/or racial points of contrast with the members of the bourgeois European family living downstairs. In the twenty-first century, the cultural gap between these different worlds is even more pronounced, for the upstairs neighbors are described as *émigrés,* not only from another culture, but also another continent. The upstairs apartment is never revealed to the spectator yet the space is evoked in acoustic terms and referenced through several cultural clichés often associated with immigrant populations. Despite the clichés and, perhaps, in a conscious move to unravel, critique, or deconstruct them, Belbel's plot creates an upstairs/downstairs dialectic in which the two worlds collide and then intermingle and overlap within the same urban apartment building.

This unraveling occurs in the sense that Belbel does not confine the meaning of the title to the foregoing literal interpretations. He manipulates the notion of a "stranger" or "foreigner" in an existential—even Camusian—sense, creating a degree of uncertainty as to whether it is the immigrant family living upstairs or the assimilated family downstairs who are indeed the "strangers." The boundaries distinguishing the two apartments/two worlds, upstairs/downstairs, invisible/visible, become increasingly porous as the action begins to undermine the traditional, staid, culturally homogeneous bourgeois space of melodrama and gives way to signs of cultural hybridization or even *mestisatge*. The lack of difference culminates with the revelation that a neighbor from upstairs has purchased the downstairs apartment. Having once belonged to the invisible upstairs realm, his appropriation of the downstairs space sets in motion a series of ethno-national connotations with regard to the migratory space that is Barcelona, Catalunya, Spain, or Europe. What was once a space of invisibility will now become visible.

Given the ties and parallels that Belbel tends to establish between plot and structure, it is possible to read an analogous replication of these cross-cultural relationships and ethno-racial ambiguities in the temporal ambiguity of the play. It is in this lack of distinctions that the expressive power of the play emerges, for just as two worlds collide, so do two temporal planes. There is an aura of inevitability that pervades *Strangers* as though there were a secret and elusive pattern at work, somehow fatalistically condemning the characters to relive the lives of their predecessors. Barriers among human beings are shattered, spatial boundaries are ruptured, and layers of time are traversed. In *Strangers*, memory consequently is established not only in an individual sense, but also in a collective sense: the historical memory of an entire people. Belbel's play compels us to contemplate the present and the future in relation to the past and to reflect in a collective, self-conscious sense upon where we have been and where we are going.

SGF

NOTE

1. Cf. Joseph Roach, *Cities of the Dead: Circum-Atlantic Performance* (New York: Columbia University Press, 1996) and "History, Memory, Necrophilia," in *The Ends of Performance*, ed. Peggy Phelan and Jill Lane (New York: New York University Press, 1997), 23-30.

Forasters (2004) at the Teatre Nacional de Catalunya, directed by Sergi Belbel.
Photo: courtesy of the Teatre Nacional de Catalunya

Anna Lizaran holding Marcel Montanyès in the Teatre Nacional de Catalunya production of *Forasters* (2004).

Photo: courtesy of the Teatre Nacional de Catalunya

STRANGERS

(A Family Melodrama in Two Periods)

by

SERGI BELBEL

Translated by

Sharon G. Feldman

TIME

Twentieth century, mid 1960s.

Early twenty-first century. Almost forty years later.

SPACE

A large apartment in a city center. Living-dining room and bedroom, separated by a door. In the living room there are two more doors, one that opens onto a hallway and the other onto a hallway that leads to the remaining bedrooms. The ceiling should be visible. There could be some detail in the décor that varies from one period to the other. The same goes for the costumes and characterizations. The changes should be instantaneous; although it is the lighting, weak and yellowish during the 1960s, white and more potent during the twentieth century, that best distinguishes the two moments in time.

CHARACTERS

TWENTIETH CENTURY (1960s)

GRANDFATHER

FATHER

MOTHER

SON

DAUGHTER

FEMALE NEIGHBOR

BOY

MALE NEIGHBOR

HUSBAND

CHARACTERS

TWENTY-FIRST CENTURY

FATHER: actor who plays the GRANDFATHER in the twentieth century

DAUGHTER: actress who plays the MOTHER in the twentieth century

SON: actor who plays the FATHER in the twentieth century

GRANDSON: actor who plays the SON in the twentieth century

GRANDDAUGHTER: actress who plays the DAUGHTER in the twentieth century

MAID: actress who plays the FEMALE NEIGHBOR in the twentieth century*

ORPHAN: actor who plays the BOY in the twentieth century*

YOUNG MAN: actor who plays the MALE NEIGHBOR in the twentieth century*

MAN: actor who plays the HUSBAND in the twentieth century.

The actors who play the MAID, ORPHAN, *and* YOUNG MAN *in the twenty-first century and, correspondingly, the* FEMALE NEIGHBOR, BOY, *and* MALE NEIGHBOR *in the twentieth century should offer well-differentiated interpretations and characterizations. The* FEMALE NEIGHBOR, MAID, BOY, *and* ORPHAN *could even be played by different actors.*

For the remaining doublings, a certain degree of confusion is desirable and even encouraged. The NEIGHBORS *from the twentieth century belong to a different culture. Those from the twenty-first century are, in addition, from a different continent.*

PROLOGUE

Home. Early twenty-first century.

The SON, *fifty-five years old, speaks with a well groomed, forty-eight-year-old* MAN.

MAN: Does anyone live here anymore?

SON: No. The furniture is here because, until a few days ago, my father was living here with . . . the woman who takes care of him. They won't take it away. He's gone to live in a much smaller place and doesn't have room for it.

MAN: An old folk's home.

SON: No. (*Pause.*) Not exactly. A retirement community, or whatever they call it. (*Pause.*) If you want, you can come back to the apartment another day and take a closer look around.

MAN: No. Thanks.

SON: Well. (*Pause.*) Think about it and give us a call. OK?

MAN: No. That won't be necessary. I'll take it.

SON: (*Pause.*) Excuse me?

MAN: I assume I need to work out the details with you, or . . . ? (*Pause.*) Conditions of the contract, down payment, closing . . . ?

SON: Yes. I'm the owner.

MAN: Oh, all right. Do you mind if we discuss it now?

SON: No. (*Pause.*) Excuse me. Have we met before?

MAN: (*Pause.*) No. You must have me confused with someone else. (*Pause.*) Why do you ask?

SON: Because . . . I thought . . . (*Pause.*) Never mind, it doesn't matter.

MAN: No. What's important now is . . . (*Pause.*) . . . that this apartment will be mine.

SON: (*Pause.*) What did you say?

MAN: I mean . . . it's perfectly natural for you to confuse me with someone you know and care about. I suppose it must be hard to sell the place you've lived in your entire life to . . . a stranger. You want to believe you know me, so you don't feel like you're handing over your entire box of memories to a . . . to someone you don't know.

SON: Maybe that's it. (*Pause.*) But don't worry, it's not like I have so many good memories here, either. For the past few years only my father has lived here. (*Pause.*) What makes you think I care about the . . . the person you remind me of?

MAN: (*Pause.*): Is it all right if I write you a check for twenty percent today and then the rest the day of the closing? (*Pause.*) By the way . . . that "For Sale" sign on the balcony . . . you won't be needing it anymore, will you? (*Pause.*) So you might as well take it down now.

Darkness.

PART ONE

SCENE 1

Twentieth century. The 1960s. Home. The door that connects the living room with the bedroom is open.

In the bedroom, the MOTHER, forty-four years old, in bed, gravely ill. At her side, the DAUGHTER, seventeen years old.

In the living room, the FATHER, forty-five years old, and the SON, twenty, sitting at the table. THEY are having breakfast. The SON reads a book and consults his class notes.

MOTHER: (*To the* DAUGHTER.) Close the door.

DAUGHTER: Are you cold?

MOTHER: No. Close the door.

The DAUGHTER *gets up and goes toward the door.*

FATHER: (*To the* SON.) Why aren't you eating?

SON: I'm not hungry.

FATHER: (*To the* DAUGHTER, *who is closing the door.*) Why are you closing the door?

DAUGHTER: Mom asked me to.

FATHER: Is she cold?

DAUGHTER: No.

The DAUGHTER *closes the door. The* FATHER *gets up.*

FATHER: (*To the* SON.) Eat up.

SON: I'm not hungry.

FATHER: You have to eat. You can't go off to campus without having breakfast.

SON: Why not?

FATHER: Because you can't, and stop looking at me like that. Eat up.

SON: I don't feel like it. I'll throw up.

DAUGHTER: (*To the* MOTHER.) Why did you want me to close the door?

MOTHER: So your father doesn't hear what I have to say to you.

DAUGHTER: You shouldn't talk; the doctor doesn't want you to exert yourself.

MOTHER: The doctor can go to hell.

DAUGHTER: If Dad hears you . . .

MOTHER: That's why I made you close the door. Understand? So he doesn't hear me.

DAUGHTER: What did you want to tell me?

MOTHER: Help me sit up a bit.

The DAUGHTER *helps the* MOTHER *sit up in bed.*

FATHER: (*To the* SON.) Would you stop reading and finish your breakfast already?

SON: I'm studying. I have an exam.

FATHER: This is no time to study. You've had plenty of days to do it. (*Pause.*) I'm going to shave. When I come out of the bathroom, I want to see that whole plate cleaned, do you hear me? You're wasting away and you need to eat.

SON: You make a lousy mother.

FATHER: What?

SON: Nothing.

The FATHER *exits through the door to the hallway. The* SON *grunts with anger, looks at the food, and makes a face. The* GRANDFATHER *enters from the same door. Seventy-five years old. He wears pajamas.* HE *stands behind the* SON, *who does not see him.*

GRANDFATHER: Good morning!

SON: Oh, you scared me . . . You don't look so good.

GRANDFATHER: I was up all night. My god. What nightmares . . . I dreamt your grandmother rose up from the grave. She was scolding me with a vengeance. What screams . . . She hit me and everything. She was furious with me, because she said that lately I've been eating too much and it's not good for my health. Of course, she, you see, used to eat like a chicken and look where she is now, sprouting geraniums. What a night, god, what a night . . .

SON: Yeah, yeah. Come on, grandpa, don't talk so much and open your mouth.

The GRANDFATHER *opens his mouth and the* SON *crams down all his untouched food. The* GRANDFATHER *chews with extraordinary gluttony and, while he eats, continues to mutter a series of incomprehensible words. Meanwhile, in the bedroom:*

DAUGHTER: Are you all right like that? (*Pause.*) Go ahead, talk to me.

MOTHER: Well all right. I'll talk. This what I wanted to tell you. That from now on I plan to talk. I won't leave here with anything bottled up, I'm telling you that right now. Now that you're here, I'll begin with you. I don't want to leave this world without having told you a few things . . .

DAUGHTER: Now is not the time . . .

MOTHER: When, if not now? You think I don't know what's going on? It won't be long before I lose my head completely. And once I'm unconscious, I'm not coming back, dear.

DAUGHTER: Mom, please . . .

MOTHER: Don't tell me "please" or give me any of that crap. First I want you to tell me something. (*Pause.*) Have you been with a man yet?

DAUGHTER: What?

MOTHER: If you've gone to bed yet with that stupid friend of your brother's . . .

DAUGHTER: Whaaat?

MOTHER: Don't give me that face and answer me.

DAUGHTER: Mom . . .

MOTHER: Answer me.

DAUGHTER: Hmm . . . No . . . Well . . .

MOTHER: Well?

DAUGHTER: No, but . . . I mean yes, uh, I mean no . . .

MOTHER: What's it going to be? Yes or no?

DAUGHTER: It's just that I don't know why you want me to tell you.

MOTHER: Oh, dear, you just seem so dull, and you think you're so outgoing! Don't look at me like that. Come on. Woman to woman: have you ever done it, yes or no?

DAUGHTER: All the way . . . no.

MOTHER: I see. Making out and maybe a bit more?

DAUGHTER: Not even that.

MOTHER: That's fine. And do you like it?

DAUGHTER: What?

MOTHER: Well "that," when he touches you, when you make out . . .

DAUGHTER: Mom!

MOTHER: Will you stop pretending to be a saint? I'm talking to you about serious things, about important things in life. And before I kick off, I'd like to . . . (SHE *makes a grimace of pain.*) You see? It gets worse every time.

DAUGHTER: You want your medicine?

MOTHER: These pills don't do anything for me anymore. I'll tell your father to call the doctor and have him prescribe some injections again. It's the only thing that calms the pain.

DAUGHTER: What injections?

MOTHER: Morphine, dear. When you're at the end of the line like me, there's nothing better. It costs a fortune and it's hard to get, but I still have some savings and good contacts with some very important doctors thanks to one of *my* relatives, of course, the son of one of your grandmother's cousins, who's very well connected. (*Pause.*) So what's it going to be?

DAUGHTER: What?

MOTHER: Your brother's friend. Do you think he's "the one"?

DAUGHTER: I don't want to talk about it now.

MOTHER: It's not him.

DAUGHTER: Please . . .

MOTHER: It's not him. You're not in love with him. And he isn't either.

DAUGHTER: What do you know?

MOTHER: You've known each other for years. If you really liked each other, you would have discovered what a man is a long time ago.

DAUGHTER: I know what a man is.

MOTHER: Until you've had one inside you, you can't possibly know.

DAUGHTER: But what are you saying? What's got into you? Are you . . . crazy? You've never talked to me like this before!

MOTHER: I've never been on the verge of death.

DAUGHTER: You're not on the verge of death.

The MOTHER *smacks the daughter.*

MOTHER: I am on the verge of death. Don't ever contradict me again. Damn it! I've had enough lies in this life.

DAUGHTER: You hurt me.

MOTHER: I'm sorry.

DAUGHTER: I've had enough of the way you all treat each other in this house!

MOTHER: Come on, come on, don't exaggerate.

The DAUGHTER *holds back her tears.* SHE *gives the* MOTHER *a look of rage. The* MOTHER *looks at her, unperturbed.*

Meanwhile, in the living room, the SON *has finished feeding his entire breakfast to the* GRANDFATHER. *The* FATHER *enters, wiping off some remaining shaving cream from his chin with a towel. The* SON *quickly closes his book.*

FATHER: *(To the* GRANDFATHER.*)* Hi, Dad. (HE *looks at his* SON'*s empty plate.*) Did you finish it all? That's what I like to see. *(To the* GRANDFATHER.*)* He didn't want to eat his breakfast.

GRANDFATHER: You can tell they haven't lived through a war, these kids . . .

FATHER: Have you had breakfast, Dad?

GRANDFATHER: No.

The SON *looks at him and smiles. Suddenly, upstairs, on the floor above, noises are heard, banging, footsteps, dragging of furniture, etc.*

SON: What is that?

MOTHER: What is that?

FATHER: The new neighbors.

DAUGHTER: I don't know. It's coming from upstairs.

FATHER: They're moving in today.

SON: Who are they?

FATHER: I don't know. Nice people I hope.

MOTHER: I don't think I can take that noise.

SON: I'm leaving, I'm late.

MOTHER: How god-awful! With the headache I have!

FATHER: You could've given your grandfather something for breakfast, you know?

MOTHER: Tell them to stop it right now.

DAUGHTER: Mom, please. Now? It's nine in the morning, and they have a right to make as much noise as they want.

MOTHER: Even if they live above a woman who's practically at death's door?

FATHER: It's like the ceiling is going to cave in on top of us.

Above, massive laughter is heard, screams and applause. The PEOPLE BELOW *quietly look at the ceiling.*

MOTHER: They're laughing.

Pause. Suddenly, the noises stop. Silence. The PEOPLE BELOW, *immobile, looking at the ceiling.*

GRANDFATHER: (*To the* FATHER.) Son, breakfast, I'm starving.

Darkness.

SCENE 2

Twenty-first century.

The FATHER, *in the bedroom, lying in bed. Eighty-three years old. A "foreign"* MAID, *probably Latin American, approximately fifty years old, changes the bed linens while the* FATHER *remains on top.* SHE *speaks with an accent.*

MAID: It would be a lot easier if you would get up.

FATHER: I said I want my little pill.

MAID: Not today. I'm tired.

FATHER: Tired of what? If you give it to me, I'll get up afterwards and you can make up the bed in peace.

MAID: What a guy, my god.

FATHER: Tired of what?

MAID: Of you.

FATHER: I'm more tired of your ridiculous habits and I'm not complaining.

MAID: You don't complain? And what ridiculous habits do I have, let's see.

FATHER: This obsession with cleaning that drives me crazy. You can't remain still for single moment in the entire day. In a house where nothing has gone on since God knows when. And you're always tiki tiki tiki tiki cleaning like you're possessed, every corner, every piece of furniture, the legs of the chairs, the china plate by plate, the glassware and the silverware that no one ever uses.

MAID: It's all covered in dust.

FATHER: That's not true.

MAID: If I didn't take care of it, I'd get bored.

FATHER: You do it so you don't have to be with me. That way you have the perfect excuse to say you're tired and don't want to do what I want.

MAID: It's not normal what you want at your age.

FATHER: Well, you certainly like it enough, don't you?

MAID: Now what should I say?

FATHER: Yes. With all the appropriate screams.

MAID: That's not true.

The FATHER *takes advantage of the fact that the* MAID *is very close to him and touches her rear with both hands.*

FATHER: Oh, what a nice little ass, my god, it's so nice, damn.

MAID: Keep your hands still.

FATHER: And if I try it without the pill?

MAID: I said not today.

FATHER: And I say yes! This is my house, and here, what I say goes, damn it!

MAID: I have to go to the store.

FATHER: You can go tomorrow.

MAID: Tomorrow is my day off, and I have to visit my family.

FATHER: I'm your family.

MAID: No.

FATHER: I'll fire you. I'll talk to my son, who's been dying to get rid of you ever since you came here to . . . work, and he'll put you out on the street. And just what family do you have to go and visit, pray tell?

MAID: My cousins.

FATHER: Your cousins? What cousins? You don't have anyone here; your whole family stayed in your country, dying of hunger, and if it weren't for the money I give you, you'd be there too, and you'd have already died of malnutrition or some horrible disease.

MAID: Shut up!

FATHER: I don't feel like it. It'll kill me, it'll kill me and you'll have to live the rest of your life with my death on your conscience, you unappreciative, nasty, selfish, mean, unsophisticated, woman, whale, cow, mule!

MAID: Oh . . . you really are like a little child . . .

FATHER: Me? (*The* MAID *nods yes.*) Come on!

MAID: So you want to fire me, do you? Well as long as you don't call a lawyer, if you know what I mean.

FATHER: It was . . . it was just a figure of speech, woman . . . Don't take it that way . . . Will you forgive me? I've been bad, haven't I? Well, you know what they do to little boys who behave badly? A spanking. Come on, come on, go ahead. I deserve it, don't I?

MAID: I said no!

The doorbell rings.

MAID: Someone's at the door.

FATHER: What did you say, woman? It's been years since anyone's called at this door. Find yourself a better excuse to get away from me.

MAID: I said someone's at the door. But since you're deafer than a doornail . . .

FATHER: I have a very fine sense of hearing.

MAID: Oh yes, of course.

The doorbell rings again.

FATHER: Someone's at the door. (*The* MAID *laughs and goes to open it.*) You
see what a fine sense of hearing I have?

The MAID *goes to open the door. The* DAUGHTER *appears, fifty-five years old,
accompanied by a* BOY *of nineteen, the* GRANDSON. THEY *are carrying suitcases
and bags. In the bedroom, the* FATHER *gets up, grabs a walking stick, and, with some
effort, makes his way to a dresser.* HE *opens it and looks for a container of pills.* HE *finds
it and takes one of them. Then, after giving it some thought,* HE *takes two more.*

MAID: May I help you?

DAUGHTER: Who are you?

MAID: And you?

DAUGHTER: Where's my brother?

MAID: Excuse me?

DAUGHTER: We were supposed to see each other today at this time. (SHE
looks her up and down.) You must be the famous cleaning woman, huh?

MAID: Famous?

DAUGHTER: This is my son. Say hello to the woman, dear.

GRANDSON: Hello.

MAID: You . . . are . . . my boss's daughter?

DAUGHTER: Yes.

GRANDSON: Such ugly furniture.

DAUGHTER: It's not ugly, stupid, it's old.

GRANDSON: Oh.

Tension. The MAID *looks the* DAUGHTER *over and says something under her breath in her native language, a kind of lament or prayer for the difficult days that* SHE *believes are about to come. The* GRANDSON *sits down in a chair, takes out his personal data organizer and begins playing Pac-Man.*

DAUGHTER: What did you say?

MAID: No . . . it can't be . . . I thought that . . . excuse me, but nobody told me . . . I'm sorry, but I don't think your father is expecting you. He has a delicate heart, and since it's been so many years since . . .

DAUGHTER: Where is he?

FATHER: (*From the bedroom.*) What's taking you so long?! I'm waiting for you!! This stuff takes effect immediately!! Your little boy has been veeeeeery bad and needs to be punished with a good spaaaaaanking!

Silence in the living room. The MAID, *the* DAUGHTER, *and the* GRANDSON *look at each other. Suddenly, very loud music is heard, definitely not Western in style, coming from the apartment upstairs.*

FATHER: Oh, no, no no!!! Not now, for the love of god! (*Pause.*) Turn off that goddamn music, fucking foreigners, and stop bothering the hell out of me right now!!!

Darkness.

SCENE 3

Twentieth century.

In the bedroom, the MOTHER, *in a nightgown, is standing.* SHE *is beating off the dust and airing out the mattress and pillows. Next to her, clean linens and pillowcases, folded. The* SON *enters through the living room door, crosses the room, and opens the door to the bedroom. The* MOTHER *doesn't see him and continues beating the mattress.* SHE *does so with nervous gesturers, in an awkward manner. Her hands and arms no longer respond as before, and* SHE *is frustrated and angry with herself. The* SON *watches her.* SHE *grabs a clean, folded sheet, tries to unfold it and inadvertently drops it on the floor.* SHE *then becomes conscious of her* SON*'s presence and looks at him.* SHE *does not like him to see her this way at all.*

MOTHER: What are you doing?

SON: Let me help you.

MOTHER: No. That won't be necessary. I said no! I want to do it myself. Come on, stay with me for a while in the living room, I'll make the bed up later.

The MOTHER *leans on him.* THEY *walk toward the living room. Some noises are heard upstairs.* SHE *looks at the ceiling: running, screams, incomprehensible words. The* SON *sits the* MOTHER *down in an armchair.* HE *makes her comfortable with cushions and covers her legs with a blanket as* THEY *chat.*

MOTHER: Have you all spoken with those lowlifes?

SON: Yes.

MOTHER: Have you told them that I would like to die in peace?

SON: Mom, you're not dying, don't be such a pain.

MOTHER: Here, the only pains are your father, your sister and you, who don't stop with all your foolishness. I'm already dead. Inside I'm completely dead. Decayed. It's just a matter of the decay extending everywhere. It's horrible to see your body fail you this way when your mind still functions . . . (*Noises above.*) Who are they?

SON: They're not from here. They come from somewhere to the south.

MOTHER: I can tell, but where, exactly? What are they? A family?

SON: Yes, and from what I can tell, a very large one.

MOTHER: How did they end up in a city and a neighborhood like ours?

SON: I don't know. But from the looks of them, they don't seem to have much money. They have horrible taste in clothing. The mother goes around all made up, even to go out to the market. Yesterday I ran into her on the stairs and she held me up with her blabbing . . . I couldn't understand a word she was saying, she mutters away and yells and laughs like a hysterical nutcase.

MOTHER: You didn't ask her anything?

SON: No. I could barely get a word in edgewise.

MOTHER: And what did she say?

SON: Uh! That she was so happy to be here, that they've lived here for years, in a smaller apartment on the outskirts, that they came here because her husband was suffering from I don't know what kind of grave disease, and that they recommended treatment in a hospital here, and first just the two of them came, I don't know how many years ago, and they liked it so much here that they decided to sell what they had down there and move here permanently with the rest of the family. And all that in an incredible mishmash of languages, and when you talk to her, either she doesn't understand anything, or she doesn't listen to you, and she just says yes yes to everything you say.

MOTHER: What does her husband do?

SON: I didn't ask.

MOTHER: Are you really that stupid or are you just pretending?

SON: Why do you want to know?

MOTHER: The last thing I'll hear before I kick off will be the screams, the laughter and the cries of those people. I'd at least like to be informed about who they are. I don't want to go to the other neighborhood filled with questions left unanswered. You know me, don't you? Come on. Go upstairs and invite that woman and one of her kids to have tea or coffee with me.

SON: Whaaaat?

MOTHER: You heard me. Go ahead, get upstairs.

SON: No.

MOTHER: Don't you want to give your mother, who's about to kick off, just a small measure of happiness? Imagine the next time you see me will be in front of a grey tombstone next to a ditch in the ground with a little tear rolling down your face. Even now that I already have one foot on the other side, you're still incapable of doing anything for me? Imbecile.

SON: I don't like it when you insult me. And I've never stopped doing things for you all my life.

MOTHER: Yes, helping me fold sheets, cooking, ironing, setting the table, and washing the dishes. Everything that never occurred to your sister to do.

SON: And that seems like very little to you?

MOTHER. I think it's awful. Sometimes, when you're in the kitchen, I look at you and it seems like you're enjoying it and everything! That's not the kind of help I expect from you, idiot.

SON: Don't insult me!

MOTHER: I'm not insulting you. I'm just telling you what you've been, what you are, and what you will be your entire life. An idiot. A shameless jerk, even more spineless than your father, which is already saying a lot!

SON: All this because I don't want to go upstairs and invite that scum?

MOTHER: Even if you don't do it, you'll continue to be that way. (SHE *doubles over from the pain. The* SON *moves closer to her.* SHE *lets out a very loud belch in her* SON'*s face.*) Ruaaaaa!

SON: (HE *steps back, as a reflex, and takes a hand to his nose.*) Oh!

MOTHER: It smells bad, doesn't it?

SON: It's disgusting.

MOTHER: Am I decaying or am I not decaying inside? (SHE *places a hand on her head.*) But here, I'm still pretty much intact. Unfortunately.

Suddenly, the MOTHER *begins to cry. The* SON *looks away, pretending not to see, so that the* MOTHER *thinks that* HE *does not know that* SHE *is crying.*

MOTHER: Oh . . . I've got something in my eye . . .

The GRANDFATHER *enters through the hallway door, accompanied by a ten-year-old* BOY *who is very shy.*

GRANDFATHER: I found this kid crying hysterically in the stairwell.

MOTHER: Who is it?

SON: I think he's the youngest son of the people upstairs.

MOTHER: What's your name, little boy?

GRANDFATHER: Would you like a cookie?

SON: What were you doing in the stairwell? You couldn't get into your house?

GRANDFATHER: A cookie?

SON: You want me to let your mom know you're here? (*Pause.*) Is something wrong? (*Pause.*) Do you understand what I'm saying?

BOY: Yes.

GRANDFATHER: A cookie, yes or no?

MOTHER: Is your mother upstairs? (*Pause. To the* SON.) Go and tell them he's here.

GRANDFATHER: But, don't you like cookies? I've never met a boy who doesn't like cookies. You're the first. (HE *leaves, grumbling.*)

MOTHER: You couldn't get into your house? (*The* BOY *shakes his head no.*) Why? Did they punish you? (*The* BOY *doesn't say anything.*) Don't you want to tell me your name?

The GRANDFATHER *returns with a tin of cookies.* HE *has opened it and is eating one of them with enthusiasm.*

GRANDFATHER: You never tasted better cookies in your life. Do you want one or not? If you don't take it, I'll eat it, OK?

SON: Leave him alone, grandpa.

GRANDFATHER: Well then I'll eat it. Mmm . . . delicious . . . (HE *offers him another cookie.*) What? (*Pause.*) It's your loss.

The BOY *looks at the* GRANDFATHER *and smiles. The* MOTHER *observes the* BOY *and is moved without knowing exactly why.*

MOTHER: (*To the* SON.) Go and look for his mother.

BOY: No!

The BOY *moves closer to the* GRANDFATHER *and takes a cookie from him.*

GRANDFATHER: Oh, my, my . . . We really have to be insistent with you, don't we?

BOY: Thank you. (*Pause.*) You . . . are . . . all . . . really . . . (*Pause.*) nice . . .

GRANDFATHER: And you're very stubborn.

MOTHER: (*To the* BOY.) Don't pay attention to him. He's my father-in-law. He's a nasty, disagreeable old man, but he's not a bad person.

GRANDFATHER: She's the mean one. (HE *goes toward a piece of furniture and grabs a wooden box. Pause.*) Do you like it?

BOY: Yes . . . It's . . . really . . . nice.

GRANDFATHER: Well I won't give you anything from this, you're too little. Come on, now, you already have a cookie, right? What more do you want? Go on. Get out!

The BOY *smiles at the* MOTHER, *gives her a kiss on the cheek, and goes running out. The* MOTHER *is surprised by the kiss but contains her emotion. Silence. The* GRANDFATHER *opens the box and takes out a cigar.* HE *lights it up.*

GRANDFATHER: In the end, he took it. What a stupid little boy, for the love of god. I was about to give him a little smack to see if he would react, because it was so clear that he wanted a cookie . . . And since those people only understand things if you hit them over the head with them . . . Did you see how skinny he was? I'd say they must be dying of hunger. Where have you ever seen a mother and father who don't feed their children? (*Pause.*) Miserable people. And on top of that, they act so proud. Because he didn't take it because of pride. He was dying of hunger. And then they say we're not generous! Next time I won't insist so much. Let him die!

SON: Grandpa, you shouldn't smoke in front of Mom! And especially that disgusting thing.

GRANDFATHER: Disgusting? Come on, shut up, shut up, what do you know, you boiled trout? This is one of the best things in life, kiddo. I'm leaving. (*Pause.*) Lowlifes, we're beginning to be surrounded on all sides by lowlifes and we going to have to pay for it, listen to what I'm telling you, and remember . . . (HE *exits.*)

SON: (*Referring to the* BOY.) Did you see how he was dressed?

MOTHER: I didn't notice. (SHE *makes a grimace of pain.*)

SON: What's the matter?

MOTHER: Go away. I want to be alone.

The SON *leaves. Once alone, the* MOTHER *begins to cry.*

SCENE 4

Twenty-first century.

In the living room, the DAUGHTER, *the* GRANDSON *with the electronic game, the* MAID *and the* FATHER, *who has left the bedroom and is leaning on his walking stick. The music of the* NEIGHBORS *above, at high volume. Voices are heard.*

FATHER: Why have you come?

DAUGHTER: (*To the* GRANDSON.) This is your grandfather. (*Pause.*) Give him a kiss. (*To the* FATHER.) He's the youngest. The other three . . . weren't able to make it.

The GRANDSON *gets up reluctantly and goes toward the* FATHER. HE *extends his hand to him.*

FATHER: Hi. (HE *doesn't correspond.*) No. That's not necessary. (*Pause.*) When I was little I too thought it was repulsive to kiss old people. The stench would remain in my nose for the rest of the day, and the contact with their flabby, sweaty skin made me nauseous. The same thing happens to you, doesn't it? I understand, believe me. (*Pause.*) Go ahead, go ahead, sit down.

GRANDSON: All right. It's up to you. (*Pause.*) My brothers and sisters send their regards.

FATHER: How can they send their regards if they don't even know me. (*Pause.*) And not a word from your father?

GRANDSON: (*Pause.*) I haven't seen him in years.

FATHER: Oh. (*Silence. The* MAID *moves closer to the* FATHER.) I'm all right.

DAUGHTER: Can we talk . . . alone?

FATHER: Are you referring to her? She lives here. There's nothing that she can't hear.

MAID: I have to go to the store.

FATHER: Not now. (*Pause.*) Why have you come?

DAUGHTER: (*Pause.*) I'm dying.

FATHER: (*Tense pause.*) Me too.

The FATHER *goes to his bedroom. The music from above suddenly stops. Only footsteps are heard. The* FATHER *in the bedroom and the* DAUGHTER *in the living room cry in silence. Darkness.*

SCENE 5

Twentieth century.

In the living room, the MOTHER, *the* FEMALE NEIGHBOR, *and the* SON. *They are having tea and cookies. The* FEMALE NEIGHBOR *speaks the language with difficulty. In the bedroom, the* GRANDFATHER *continually rummages through all the drawers and closets.*

MOTHER: And as you can surely understand, I would like to spend my few remaining days in peace and tranquility.

FEMALE NEIGHBOR: Yes, yes.

MOTHER: You understand, right?

FEMALE NEIGHBOR: Yes, yes.

MOTHER: You'll try not to make so much noise, right?

FEMALE NEIGHBOR: Yes, yes.

MOTHER: Would you like some more tea?

FEMALE NEIGHBOR: Yes, yes. (*The* MOTHER *looks at the* SON. HE *grabs the teapot.* HE *is about to pour.*) No, no.

The SON *leaves the teapot and looks at the* MOTHER.

MOTHER: How many are you, at home?

FEMALE NEIGHBOR: Huh?

MOTHER: How many sons do you have?

FEMALE NEIGHBOR: Sons? Oh. Yes, yes. And daughters.

MOTHER: How many?

FEMALE NEIGHBOR: Three daughters. And two sons.

MOTHER: The boy is yours?

FEMALE NEIGHBOR: Yes, yes. The little one. He's a very good boy.

MOTHER: Yes.

FEMALE NEIGHBOR· Very good boy. *(Pause.)* The little one.

MOTHER: Yes, yes. (SHE *looks at the* SON, *who can't help but laugh.*)

FEMALE NEIGHBOR: On the other hand, the big one . . . the big one . . .
      uy uy uy . . .

MOTHER: Uy uy uy?

FEMALE NEIGHBOR: Uy uy uy . . .

MOTHER: Uy uy uy, what?

FEMALE NEIGHBOR: Uy uy uy. Yes, yes. (*SHE laughs.*) Tee hee hee.

MOTHER: *(To the* SON.) Uy uy uy?

SON: Go figure.

MOTHER: (*To the* FEMALE NEIGHBOR.) Why do you say uy uy uy?

FEMALE NEIGHBOR: (*With tone of complicity.*) Because he's twenty years old . . .

MOTHER: Is he the oldest?

FEMALE NEIGHBOR: He's the oldest. Yes, yes. Twenty. You know? The age of . . . Uy uy uy. You know what I mean, right?

MOTHER: Yes, of course, of course. (SHE *looks at the* SON.)

SON: She must mean he's a stud.

FEMALE NEIGHBOR: A stud, yes, yes. Tee hee hee. He's a stud. The little one no, the little one is a very good boy.

MOTHER: And the three girls?

FEMALE NEIGHBOR: Uy uy uy . . . The three.

MOTHER: Well now. How old are they?

FEMALE NEIGHBOR: Three handfuls, the three of them. Tee hee hee. They're very difficult, very difficult. They don't help me with the chores, at home. Even though I insist. There's no way.

MOTHER: Does your husband work?

FEMALE NEIGHBOR: Yes, yes.

MOTHER: What does he do for a living?

FEMALE NEIGHBOR: Thank you for the tea. I'm must be going. (SHE *gets up.*)

MOTHER: Don't leave me hanging, please . . .

FEMALE NEIGHBOR: My husband . . . is on his way home right now. I haven't made . . . dinner.

MOTHER: (*To the* SON.) Go with her. (*To the* FEMALE NEIGHBOR.) You'll remember the favor I asked, right?

FEMALE NEIGHBOR: Yes, yes.

MOTHER: What favor did I ask of you?

FEMALE NEIGHBOR: Thank you for everything.

MOTHER: What favor did I ask for?

FEMALE NEIGHBOR: My husband . . . is coming home now.

MOTHER: God.

FEMALE NEIGHBOR: What?

MOTHER: Nothing.

FEMALE NEIGHBOR: Thank you very much.

MOTHER: Yes, yes.

Meanwhile, the GRANDFATHER, *in the bedroom, has found one of the* MOTHER's *little bottles of morphine and has injected a substantial dose into his arm. The* SON *accompanies the* FEMALE NEIGHBOR *to the door.*

The MOTHER *sits up.* SHE *grabs a walking stick. The* FEMALE NEIGHBOR *now realizes that the* MOTHER *is ill.*

SON: Don't move, Mom, I'll go with the lady to the door and then I'll take you to the bedroom.

FEMALE NEIGHBOR: Oh . . . you're not well?

MOTHER: But didn't I just tell you . . . ? Ugh, it makes no difference to you. Go ahead, goodbye.

FEMALE NEIGHBOR: (*Very concerned.*) Are you . . . sick?

MOTHER: Sick? (*Pause.*) I have cancer. (*Pause.*) Here. (*SHE touches her chest.*) Well, here . . . and who knows where else. Cancer. (*Pause. In a louder voice.*) Cancer . . .

SON: Mom, let it go.

MOTHER: Cancer, do you know what I mean? My son doesn't like me to say it, as if it were some kind of a sin that I had to be embarrassed about. But I don't care. (*Pause.*) I have a cancer this big, Madame, inside here. They wanted to take it all out of me, and they opened me up from here to here, and they looked inside, and they saw that it was so black that they closed it up immediately, and they didn't take anything out of me . . .

SON: Mom . . .

MOTHER: You see? He's already scolding me.

SON: I'm not scolding you.

MOTHER: Yes, you're scolding me.

SON: The doctor said . . .

MOTHER: Leave the doctor out of this, for once. (*To the* FEMALE NEIGHBOR.) The whole damn day carrying on: the doctor said this, the doctor doesn't want you to do that, the doctor thinks this would be better . . . I've had it up to here. So yes, Madame, I'm practically dead. How old are you?

FEMALE NEIGHBOR: I'm sorry.

MOTHER: How old are you?

FEMALE NEIGHBOR: You poor, poor woman.

MOTHER: I said how old are you?

FEMALE NEIGHBOR: Me? Fifty.

MOTHER: Well I'll never reach that age. (*To the SON.*) Go with her.

FEMALE NEIGHBOR: (*Pause.*) Madame.

MOTHER: What is it, now? Why are you looking at me that way?

FEMALE NEIGHBOR: I'm sorry. Such a good woman. I'm sorry.

The FEMALE NEIGHBOR *goes toward the* MOTHER *and suddenly gives her a hug, clumsily. The* MOTHER *makes an effort to contain her emotions. The* FEMALE NEIGHBOR *looks at her, her eyes fill with tears, and* SHE *goes running off. The* SON *looks at the* MOTHER *with a tension-filled gaze. The* FEMALE NEIGHBOR *has just done what* HE *has not done and cannot do.* HE *is embarrassed. In order to hide his shame,* HE *gestures toward the door through which the* FEMALE NEIGHBOR *has exited and brings his index finger to his temple as if to say: "this woman is crazy".*

MOTHER: (*Pause.*) How disgusting. Besides the stench that I'm giving off, that woman just left me completely impregnated with the disgusting odor of her cheap perfume. (*The* SON *moves closer to the* MOTHER *to help her walk.*) No! You pain! If I don't ask you, I don't want you to help me do anything, is that clear? I can make it to my room on my own. If you want to do something for me, tell your sister to bring a sponge and soap to my bedroom to clean me up. Or, no. No! Better yet, you do it. Unfortunately, you do these things better than your sister, too, and she finds it even more disgusting to touch me. Come on, clean me up right now. This stench of patchouli is making me nauseous. And spray all this with disinfectant.

The MOTHER *goes to the bedroom. The* SON *disappears through the door to the hallway. The* MOTHER *sees the* GRANDFATHER *in the bed with the syringe.* HE *is delirious and is singing.*

MOTHER: What are you doing in my bed? What is that? YOU'VE TAKEN MY MORPHINE AGAIN?!! Get out of here, you stupid old man! I plan to tell your son to either take you to the old people's home today or I'll inject you myself with twelve doses of this drug right into this vein in your neck to make sure you leave this goddamn world once and for all! It's not enough for you make things impossible for me for more than half my life; on top of that you have to ruin the four days I have left?! I told you to get out!! Get out!! This is my house, mine, mine!! You came here when your wife kicked off because she couldn't take you anymore, "I'll only stay here for a short time, to be near my beloved son" and it's been fifteen years!! You understand, you stupid old man? Fifteen years of putting up with your obsessions and cleaning the shit from your underwear! Get out!!! Pack your bags! You're going to . . . the old folk's home, to the old folk's home, right now to the old folk's home!!! (SHE *hits him repeatedly.*)

GRANDFATHER: I don't want to go to the old folk's home! Ha ha ha! I don't want to go there, and I won't go there! Hee hee hee!

MOTHER: GET OUT OF MY HOUSE!

GRANDFATHER: And I don't want to leave this goddamn world either, and I won't go! You'll go first, ha ha ha!

MOTHER: You evil, crazy, stupid, miserable man! Why do I have to die before you, you decrepit . . . , why?!! Why?!!

SHE *hits him each time with increasing rage until, exhausted,* SHE *sinks down in a sea of tears. The* OLD MAN *complains weakly and ends up falling asleep. The* MOTHER, *on the floor, grabs her legs and begins to rock back and forth. The* OLD MAN *snores loudly.*

Darkness.

SCENE 6

Twenty-first century.

The FATHER, *in bed.* HE *is snoring. In the living room, the* MAID, *dusting the furniture, with the* SON, *who is having coffee.*

SON: Is he still sleeping? (*The* MAID *nods.*) How long has he been like that?

MAID: Two days. Since your sister got here.

SON: Has he eaten?

MAID: No. Well, I think yesterday he got up in the middle of the afternoon and ate all the cookies in the pantry.

SON: Cookies? He shouldn't eat them; his glucose level will go up.

MAID: He says he doesn't care, that from now on he won't diet or take any more medication.

SON: Who bought him the cookies? You? (*Pause.*) But didn't I tell you . . . ?

MAID: I'm sorry. It's just that he likes them so much . . . If I don't buy them for him, he makes a face like this.

SON: Have you spoken with him?

MAID: About what?

SON: About my sister's arrival.

MAID: No. He doesn't talk to me about that.

SON: And what are we going to do.

MAID: I do what I can. (*Pause.*) How come he didn't tell you she was coming?

SON: Has my father ever talked to you about her?

MAID: Never.

SON: You find it strange that a father would never speak about a child of his that he hasn't seen for a long time, don't you?

MAID: Yes. Very. It's too bad. (*Pause.*) In my country, it would be impossible.

SON: Oh, really?

MAID: Even though they're far away, or dead. Not a day goes by that a father or mother doesn't speak about his or her children, about their parents, about their brothers and sisters, dead, or exiled to another country, or disappeared, and that they don't think about them. And there's not a day that they don't speak or don't want to speak with them. With the living and with the dead. It's a necessity. It's a richness.

SON: Right.

MAID: Well, I talk to my family every day. I only call them once a month. And I write them letters from time to time. When your father helps me. I'm so slow to . . . But I talk to them every day. *Every day.* Here. (SHE *touches her head.*) It makes me feel good. Because I know they listen to me. (*Pause.*) The richness of the poor is their love of family. And that's all we have but it has the greatest value. It doesn't give us anything to eat here (SHE *touches her stomach.*), but yes here (SHE *touches her heart.*), and one thing makes up for the other. That's what my parents taught me. And what the parents of my parents taught . . .

SON: Yes, yes, I get it.

MAID: Are you making fun of me?

SON: No. (*Pause.*) You're absolutely right. (*Pause.*) Do you have a lot of family there?

MAID: Six brothers, three sisters, my mother, twelve nieces and nephews and . . . cousins . . . wait . . . (SHE *begins counting on her fingers.*)

SON: Do you . . . Do you miss them?

MAID: More than I'd like.

SON: You've never gone back since you came here?

MAID: Last summer.

SON: Why didn't you stay there if you miss them so much?

MAID: They need the money I send them.

SON: Does it bother you to talk about these things?

MAID: A lot.

SON: Will you go back there to live?

MAID: When your father dies.

SON: Are you so sure?

MAID: Yes.

SON: And where will you get the money, then?

MAID: Don't you know?

SON: About what?

MAID: Your father prepared a will two months ago.

SON: And?

MAID: He'll be leaving me . . . He hasn't told you? (*Silence. The* SON *laughs.* SHE *is very serious.*) What do you find so funny?

SON: What you just said . . . Ha ha ha . . .

MAID: Your father loves me . . . I've been taking care of him for years . . .

SON: Yes, yes, of course . . . ha, ha, ha . . .

MAID: It's normal for him to do it, I would do it too..

SON: Yes, of course, me too . . . ha ha ha . . . ugh, ugh . . .

MAID: I don't see the humor in it. On the contrary, if I were you, I would be crying. A father that leaves his inheritance to a . . . a stranger . . .

SON: . . . And not to his son, right? Ha, ha, ha . . . yes, I should be crying . . . ha ha ha . . . ugh, enough, please, ha ha ha, ugh, I don't know what's gotten into me that I've had an attack . . . hee hee hee . . . ugh, I'm hysterical, ugh, ugh . . . (*Pause.*) Sorry. It's nerves. I'm sorry.

MAID: Laughing from nerves? Just like that, because?

SON: No, of course. I'm sorry. (*Pause.*) It's just that my father doesn't have anything. Any property. Not even this house. It's mine. It went directly from my mother to my sister and me. My father was just a non-paying tenant. When we became adults, I bought my sister's half from her. My father only has some savings and his pension. And no one will receive that when he dies. My mother died some . . .

MAID: He hasn't told you.

SON: (*Pause.*) I'm sorry you had to find out this way . . .

MAID: Me too, I'm sorry you had to find out this way . . .

SON: Huh?

MAID: I made your father promise that he would tell you days ago. Apparently, he hasn't. We got married three months ago. When he dies, I'll be his widow..

The SON *stops smiling. The* MAID *stops staring at him and exits. Silence for a while. The door at the entrance is heard. The* GRANDDAUGHTER *appears. Twenty years old.* SHE *carries a very elaborate bouquet of flowers.*

GRANDDAUGHTER: Hi, Dad. (*Pause.*) Where's my aunt?

SON: Inside.

GRANDDAUGHTER: Does she like flowers?

SON: Ask her.

The SON *leaves without looking at his daughter.*

GRANDDAUGHTER: Imbecile.

The DAUGHTER *appears through the hallway door.* SHE *is dressed in clothes that one would wear around the house. The* GRANDDAUGHTER *goes toward her and shows her the flowers.*

GRANDDAUGHTER: They're for you.

DAUGHTER: Thank you.

GRANDDAUGHTER: Do you like them?

DAUGHTER: Very much. I'm going to put them in water.

GRANDDAUGHTER: I'll do it.

DAUGHTER: No, let me do it. I'd like to.

SHE *exits, looking at the flowers and smelling them enthusiastically.*

GRANDDAUGHTER: Are you already set up in the bedroom?

DAUGHTER: (*From inside.*) Yes. I had to buy new sheets. The ones that were there were moth-eaten.

GRANDDAUGHTER: From not being used. They were closed up for so many years. Did the woman do a thorough cleaning for you?

DAUGHTER: (*From inside.*) Yes, yes she did. Too much. There's an artificial smell of pine disinfectant that hits you in the face. Since I left, no one has used it?

GRANDDAUGHTER: At least as far as I know, no. Do you feel at home?

DAUGHTER: No, not at all. I detested it then; imagine how I feel about it now. It's small and dark. Uncomfortable and . . . (*Entering.*) . . .depressing.

The DAUGHTER *arrives with the flowers in a vase and puts them on the dining room table. Once* SHE's *done this,* SHE *continues looking at the flowers, almost hypnotized.*

GRANDDAUGHTER: Are you feeling all right?

DAUGHTER: Yes.

GRANDDAUGHTER: What are you thinking about?

DAUGHTER: My own problems.

GRANDDAUGHTER: And your son?

DAUGHTER: Shopping. We've been in this city for two days, and I've hardly seen him. He's mesmerized by the number of stores with electronics and computers and things like that. That's all he thinks about. Yesterday he showed me a little machine this small, capable of storing I don't know how many songs. Although, don't ask me why he wants it if he doesn't like music. He likes noise. Chuku-pah, Chuku-pah, Chuku-pah. You tell me. Surely he does it to spend money. To spend *my* money on worthless rubbish. He doesn't like it, no, he loves it. Bringing about my financial ruin is his favorite pastime.

GRANDDAUGHTER: I wanted to meet the two of you so badly . . .

DAUGHTER: Oh, really? (*Pause.*) And I wanted to meet you, too.

GRANDDAUGHTER: Whenever your name came up in conversation with my father or with my grandfather, it was a taboo subject.

DAUGHTER: Right.

GRANDDAUGHTER: And I would think, I'm sure she couldn't possibly be as bad as they make her out to be.

DAUGHTER: They would say bad things about me?

GRANDDAUGHTER: Well, bad, bad . . . not exactly. But there was a kind of resentment. When they did talk about you, of course. If I weren't such a pain asking questions, I wouldn't even have known you existed. (*Pause.*) I think they've never forgiven you for leaving home that way.

DAUGHTER: What way? What do you know about it?

GRANDDAUGHTER: In fact, they never really finished explaining it to me.

DAUGHTER: What did they tell you?

GRANDDAUGHTER: That one day, you got up and left without saying a thing. Just after my grandmother's death. To go and live in a foreign country. With the man who later became your husband. And that's it.

DAUGHTER: Well yes. That's how it was.

GRANDDAUGHTER: Have you ever regretted it?

DAUGHTER: Ugh . . . So many questions . . . (*Pause.*) It's true, you are a bit of a pain, aren't you?

GRANDDAUGHTER: I like knowing things about people. And if they're members of my family, it's even better. Have you ever regretted it?

DAUGHTER: What do you think?

GRANDDAUGHTER: No, you haven't.

DAUGHTER: Why?

GRANDDAUGHTER: You were right to leave. Our family is . . . (SHE *stops talking.*)

DAUGHTER: What?

GRANDDAUGHTER: Is . . . Ugh, I can't find the exact word to define it . . .

DAUGHTER: Maybe there isn't a word to define it well. Or, maybe there is. (*Pause.*) A cancer?

Pause. The TWO WOMEN *look at each other intensely.*

GRANDDAUGHTER: What was my grandmother like? My father never talks about her.

DAUGHTER: He doesn't? (*Pause.*) She . . . was . . . (*Pause.*) It doesn't matter.

GRANDDAUGHTER: From what few photos I've seen . . . you look a lot like her, don't you?

DAUGHTER: No. I don't look like her at all.

GRANDDAUGHTER: (*Pause.*) I like you.

DAUGHTER: I like you, too.

GRANDDAUGHTER: I'm sure you'll get better. The hospital where you'll be undergoing treatment is the best there is.

DAUGHTER: That's why I'm here. To be cured. (*Pause.*) And nothing more.

GRANDDAUGHTER: And to meet me, right?

DAUGHTER: Yes. Maybe.

GRANDDAUGHTER: I feel like I've known you all my life.

DAUGHTER: Me, too.

Silence. The DAUGHTER *grabs a flower from the vase.* SHE *looks at the* GRANDDAUGHTER *and very slowly moves closer to her.* SHE *places the flower in her hair, near her ear. An instant of stillness as their gazes cross. Music from the apartment upstairs destroys the magic of the moment.*

DAUGHTER: Again? What jerks.

GRANDDAUGHTER: I love this music.

DAUGHTER: Who are they?

GRANDDAUGHTER: I don't know. They moved in just a couple of weeks ago. It seems like bunch of people are living there. Immigrants. I suppose someone has rented the apartment and is subletting it illegally to them. I hope no one reports them. We could use some life in this building, filled with zombies.

The doorbell is heard.

DAUGHTER: Isn't the maid around?

GRANDDAUGHTER: I'll get it.

DAUGHTER: Maybe it's my son. Your father only gave us one key, and I have it with me.

GRANDDAUGHTER: If you want, I'll give you one of mine. I have two.

DAUGHTER: No. This way I have him under control.

GRANDDAUGHTER: And why do you have to control him? He's not a ten-year-old . . .

DAUGHTER: Up here, he's even younger. Come on, go ahead and open it.

The GRANDDAUGHTER *goes to open the door. The* DAUGHTER *looks at the flowers and caresses them softly, as if* SHE *were recalling something. Voices and a scream are heard in the hallway. The* GRANDDAUGHTER *appears with the* GRANDSON, *who is accompanied—held up by the arm—by a* YOUNG MAN, *twenty-two years old and good looking, the neighbor from upstairs, an immigrant. HE speaks with a very slight accent. The* GRANDSON *has his entire face covered in blood. Behind them, silently, an eleven-year-old boy appears, the* ORPHAN.

DAUGHTER: What happened?

YOUNG MAN: He fell down the stairs.

GRANDSON: It's nothing . . .

YOUNG MAN: I think he broke his nose.

GRANDSON: I haven't broken anything. (HE *looks at the young man, who is holding him up, and tries to contain his rage.*) And let me go; I'm not an invalid. (HE *looks at the* DAUGHTER.) I'm not sick.

GRANDDAUGHTER: I'll go get some peroxide.

The GRANDDAUGHTER *takes the flower out of her hair, and it falls to the ground. The* GRANDSON *sits down on a chair. The flower remains at the feet of the* YOUNG MAN. HE *picks it up. When the* GRANDDAUGHTER *goes to look for the first-aid kit,* SHE *comes upon the* ORPHAN.

GRANDDAUGHTER: (*To the* YOUNG MAN.) Who is he . . . ?

YOUNG MAN: He's my . . . He lives with me. With us.

GRANDDAUGHTER: Hi.

ORPHAN: Hi. How are you?

The GRANDDAUGHTER *pats him on the head and exits. Meanwhile, the* DAUGHTER *has gone over to the* GRANDSON *and wants to examine where* HE *is bleeding.*

DAUGHTER: But how did it happen?

GRANDSON: It doesn't matter, leave me alone, I'm all right, really.

YOUNG MAN: We were going up behind him on the stairs. We saw how he was reading something and wasn't paying attention to the stairs and . . .

ORPHAN: . . . Babam! Puagh!

DAUGHTER: Let me see.

GRANDSON: Leave me alone already, you pain, damn it!

The GRANDDAUGHTER *appears with peroxide and cotton.* SHE *goes toward the* GRANDSON *and without saying anything to him, inspects his face. The* YOUNG MAN *does not stop looking at the* GRANDDAUGHTER *all the while. The* DAUGHTER *catches his eye.*

GRANDDAUGHTER: Let's see what's . . . Hold your head up. It's nothing, man! Just a second. (SHE *cleans the remaining blood from his face.* SHE *does it with skill and grace. When* SHE *has finished,* SHE *gives him a kiss on the cheek.*) Now, there you are.

YOUNG MAN: Next time I'll break my own nose.

GRANDDAUGHTER: Huh?

YOUNG MAN: So that you can take care of me the same way. (HE *extends the flower toward her.*) Put it back, it looked good on you. (HE *looks deeply into her eyes.*) Sorry if I looked at you strangely. It's just that the last thing I expected when I knocked on the door was that such a pretty girl with a flower in her hair would answer. (*Pause.*) The flower and the girl. (*The* GRANDSON *huffs and puffs, making fun of the* YOUNG MAN.) Did you take it out because you thought I would make fun of you? Well, on the contrary, I liked it. (HE *gives her the flower.* THEY *look at each other.*) Goodbye.

GRANDDAUGHTER: Do you live upstairs?

The YOUNG MAN *nods his head and goes toward the* ORPHAN. HE *looks at the* GRANDDAUGHTER, *sweetly.* SHE *blushes for a split second.* HE *says something to the* ORPHAN *in his native language and exits. The* DAUGHTER, *who has been watching the* YOUNG MAN *and the* GRANDDAUGHTER, *has a small fainting spell.*

DAUGHTER: No . . . No.

SCENE 7

Twentieth century.

In the living room, the MOTHER *and the* DAUGHTER. *The* MOTHER *is sitting with a blanket on her lap and a nice old book in her hands. The* DAUGHTER *is very tense.*

MOTHER: No.

DAUGHTER: Yes.

MOTHER: You're not going out today.

DAUGHTER: Who's going to stop me? You?

MOTHER: Of course.

DAUGHTER: I don't know how.

MOTHER: I'll block the door, if necessary.

DAUGHTER: Don't make me laugh. You can barely stand, you fart so much.

MOTHER: You're right about that. I can't stand it anymore. Who do you want to go out with? Your brother's friend?

DAUGHTER: What difference does it make to you?

MOTHER: Didn't what I told you do any good?

DAUGHTER: I don't know what you're talking about.

MOTHER: Have you gone to bed with him yet?

DAUGHTER: Yes.

MOTHER: Well, that's enough. Let's get things straight. This boy doesn't like you. Nor do you like him.

DAUGHTER: And if I told you we were getting married? Would that make you feel better?

MOTHER: No. On the contrary.

DAUGHTER: He's hinted about it.

MOTHER: That doesn't matter. You won't marry him. And if you do, too bad for you.

DAUGHTER: You don't understand anything.

MOTHER: Excuse me; you're the one who doesn't understand anything. Have you spoken to your brother about all this?

DAUGHTER: No. Why should I?

MOTHER: Don't you think you should tell him, to see what he thinks?

DAUGHTER: And what do I care what that subhuman idiot thinks?

MOTHER: Don't insult your brother.

DAUGHTER: Look who's talking. You haven't stopped calling him names since the day he was born.

MOTHER: That's different. I'm his mother.

DAUGHTER: And I'm his sister.

MOTHER: I do it for his own good.

DAUGHTER: Ha ha ha. Right. Well, I'm going to get ready, and I'm going out.

MOTHER: I said no!

DAUGHTER: You know what's the matter with you? You want me to tell you?

MOTHER: No.

DAUGHTER: You're jealous of me, you're envious and angry, pure envy, you would like to be like me and be able to do what I'm doing, going out and about, and being with people and attracting the attention of boys the way I do, and chatting with them and having a lot of wild fun, which is what I plan to do tonight whether you like it or not. Do you think I don't realize how you've been looking at me all these years? Since I got breasts and this waistline and this ass? Always looking me over with those witch eyes, cursing me, even though you might want to hide it. I so notice you doing it a lot! And it makes me so mad. You can't even imagine. I might actually enjoy it if a friend of mine were jealous, but you? My mother? I find it so disgusting that I haven't been able to tell anyone. The clothes you've bought me all these years and that you make me put on are an insult to my body and my face. Everything you want me to do or stop doing is to fuck things up for me, to shut me down inside, to convert me into an old hysterical woman like you. But I'm a lot smarter than you think, because I've always known where your disdain for me came from and the obsession you have with me. You can't stand the fact that a very pretty girl could have possibly come out of you!, and one that's much more attractive to men than you are. And even though you might think you can control me and that ultimately I'll say yes to everything out of respect for your illness, on the inside, I'm cursing you, and I don't give a shit about you, and I don't give a shit what you tell me, and I plan to do whatever I want, even if I have to do it over your dead body.

MOTHER: You've already done it. (*Pause.*) An old hysterical woman, me?

DAUGHTER: You're forty-four! Forty-four! It's not exactly the prime of life. *I'm* at the prime of my life. Me. You've already lived what you've had to live, and it's over. Leave everyone alone, and stop trying to control and fuck up our lives the way you always do, because we're doing what you neither did or dared do when you were young, even though you were dying to do it! Jealous bitch! I've had it with you!

MOTHER: I just want to help you.

DAUGHTER: Whaaaat?!

MOTHER: Make you open your eyes and understand . . .

DAUGHTER: Understand? Understand what? I already understand everything, Mom, everything. I know you make my life impossible because it angers you to think that you'll leave this world without having managed to make me a carbon copy of you. It terrifies you to die, thinking I will never be a continuation of you in any way. Times have changed. I'll go to college, and I'll become someone, and I'll choose my own friends and the men I'd like to be with, and I won't waste away the rest of my life in a dark old cave like this one, preparing meals and ironing shirts for a boring man and opening up my legs when he feels like it and cleaning the shit off the ass of the children that I didn't want to have.

MOTHER: At least I tried. (*Pause.*) Can I say something to you? Just one thing?

DAUGHTER: What?

MOTHER: Go to hell.

The MOTHER *refrains from looking at the* DAUGHTER, *opens up the book, and begins reading with feigned tranquility. The* DAUGHTER, *in a nervous attack, snatches the book and lifts it up in front of her* MOTHER's *face, as if* SHE *were going to hit her hard. The* MOTHER, *instinctively, protects her face with her hands. But immediately afterwards,* SHE *takes them down in cold defiance of her* DAUGHTER.

MOTHER: I dare you . . . Go ahead!

The DAUGHTER *lowers her hands and remains looking at the book, frustrated. The* MOTHER *puts out her hand and takes the book. The front door is heard. And the voice of the* FATHER.

FATHER: Hello? (HE *enters.*) Are you presentable?

MOTHER: What's up?

FATHER: I couldn't tell them no. I'm sorry. I hope they don't bother you too much. They're the little one from upstairs and his older brother.

DAUGHTER: What do they want, now?

FATHER: (*To the* MOTHER.) They've brought something for you. Should I let them in?

MOTHER: Fix me up a bit. And then, we'll talk for a while about your daughter. She wants to go out carousing tonight and I've prohibited it.

DAUGHTER: Carousing!

FATHER: You'll do what your mother says. You'll stay home.

DAUGHTER: I'll escape when you're all asleep.

FATHER: I feel sorry for you. If you do . . .

DAUGHTER: What are you going to do to me?! What! You think you can scare me?

MOTHER: Enough bickering! We have guests. They can hear you. How embarrassing! What do you want, to stoop to their level? A bit of manners, for the love of god! (*Silence.*) Let them in.

The FATHER *exits. The* DAUGHTER *and the* MOTHER *look each other in the eye and, neither of the two lets go of her gaze. The* FATHER *enters with the* BOY *and the* MALE NEIGHBOR, *a* YOUNG MAN *of approximately twenty years old, very good looking, although very poorly dressed. He speaks with an accent. The* BOY *carries a bouquet of red flowers in his hand.*

MALE NEIGHBOR: Hello, excuse us. My little brother was afraid to come on his own . . .

The DAUGHTER *looks at the* MALE NEIGHBOR. SHE *feels a chill. The* MOTHER *sees it. The* BOY *timidly moves toward the* MOTHER *with the bouquet of flowers in his hand.*

BOY: For you.

MOTHER: (*To the* DAUGHTER.) Go get a vase with water. (*To the* BOY.) Thank you.

BOY: You're welcome.

MOTHER: This wasn't necessary.

MALE NEIGHBOR: You have such a nice house.

MOTHER: You are the older son of the people upstairs?

MALE NEIGHBOR: Yes, yes.

MOTHER: The one . . . who uy uy uy?

MALE NEIGHBOR: Huh?

MOTHER: Never mind. (*Pause.*) I spoke with your mother the other day. I was complaining about the noise you were making. I haven't been able to get much rest because of it.

MALE NEIGHBOR: Is it our fault?

MOTHER: Yes.

FATHER: My wife . . . is in a delicate state, very delicate and . . .

MOTHER: It doesn't matter. Even if I were healthy. You make too much noise. And in our neighborhood we're not accustomed. I know you have customs that are very different from ours, and that when you scream, it doesn't necessarily mean you're fighting, and I understand it all very well and I accept it, that goes without saying, but you need to understand that you live here now, because you've chosen to do so for your own reasons, here you have things that you can't get in your homeland, so it's normal that you would have to adapt at least minimally to our customs so that we can live together. We are peaceful people, sensible and quiet, and we can't stand when people from the outside cause upheaval in our lives and destroy our peace and tranquility by taking advantage of our generosity and good will. Do you understand? (*To the BOY.*) You understand me, don't you, little one?

BOY: Yes, ma'am.

MALE NEIGHBOR: Good will?

The DAUGHTER *arrives with the vase.* SHE *goes toward the* MOTHER *and takes the flowers from her.*

MOTHER: (*To the BOY.*) They're beautiful flowers. (*To her HUSBAND.*) Bring me into the bedroom, please, I'm tired.

FATHER: As you wish.

The FATHER *helps the* MOTHER *up and accompanies her to the bedroom. The* DAUGHTER, *nervous, puts the flowers in the vase. A flower falls to the ground. The* MALE NEIGHBOR *reacts and picks it up. Without saying anything, making sure not to be seen by the* MOTHER *and* FATHER, HE *puts the flower in the* DAUGHTER'S *hair, next to her ear. The two exchange an intense gaze of desire. The* MOTHER *sees this and stops at the door to the bedroom.*

FATHER: What's the matter?

MOTHER: Nothing. (*Pause.*) Honey? You're going out tonight with your boyfriend, aren't you? (*To the* MALE NEIGHBOR.) My daughter. She's seventeen years old, but she thinks she already knows everything about life, ha ha ha!

The MOTHER *laughs cynically. The* FATHER *brings her into the bedroom. The* BOY, *frightened, moves close to his brother and pulls at his sleeve.*

BOY: Let's go.

The MALE NEIGHBOR *and the* BOY *go toward the door. When they are about to leave, the* MALE NEIGHBOR *turns, looks at the* DAUGHTER, *and winks at her. The* DAUGHTER *blushes suddenly, leaves the flowers alone, and disappears through the other door. The* MALE NEIGHBOR *smiles. The* BOY *pulls at him again to leave. The* MALE NEIGHBOR *gestures to his brother to wait.* HE *enters the living room, silently goes over to a bookcase where there is a box of cigars, opens it, and places two of them in his pocket. The* BOY *gestures to him not to do it. The* MALE NEIGHBOR, *playfully, grabs the entire box and puts it under his sweater, as if he wanted to take it with him.*

BOY: No! No!

The MALE NEIGHBOR *looks at the boy and laughs. He leaves the box where it was. The* BOY *stares at him and, for a few moments, a look of hatred toward his* BROTHER *can be seen in his face. His* BROTHER *makes a friendly gesture toward the* BOY *to undo the tension, and the* BOY *steps back to avoid contact with him. The* BROTHER *looks at him. The* BOY *is embarrassed and exits running.*

Darkness.

SCENE 8

Twenty-first century.

The door that connects the living room with the bedroom is closed. In the bedroom, we see the SON *with an open suitcase on the bed.* HE *takes clothing out of the closet and folds it. The* FATHER *is a few meters away from him, sitting with a bitter grin on his lips. In the living room, the* DAUGHTER *is reading. The* MAID *appears through the hallway door.*

MAID: There's a man here to see you. Should I let him in?

DAUGHTER: Who is it?

MAID: He doesn't want to say. He says he's come here just for a few days to do I don't know what, and that he's leaving tomorrow, and that it's urgent that he see you.

DAUGHTER: Let him enter.

The MAID *goes to let him in. The* DAUGHTER *fixes her clothes and her hair. The* MAID *enters, accompanied by the* MAN. *The* DAUGHTER *looks at him.* SHE *knows that* SHE *recognizes him from somewhere but still hasn't made the connection. The* MAID *looks at her.*

MAN: Hello.

DAUGHTER: Hello.

MAID: (*Pause.*) Well, I'm going to go finish preparing your things.

DAUGHTER: Huh?

MAID: Your clothes, to transfer them . . .

DAUGHTER: Oh, yes. Go ahead, go ahead.

MAID: Can I get you something to drink?

MAN: No, thank you.

MAID: As you wish. (SHE *exits.*)

MAN: (*Silence.*) You don't recognize me?

DAUGHTER: No.

MAN: Of course. The last time you saw me I was . . . like this. (HE *makes a gesture to indicate the height of a child.*)

DAUGHTER: (*Now* SHE *understands.*) And . . . and it was . . . there.

MAN: Yes! In that bedroom, if I recall correctly.

The DAUGHTER'*s face lights up.* HE *smiles at her.* SHE, *however, feels uncomfortable.* HE *realizes this.* THEY *do not want to let on.*

DAUGHTER: Have a seat. (*The two of them sit. The* MAN *holds a wrapped package in his hands. Pause.*) It's been many years.

MAN: Many.

DAUGHTER: What do you want?

MAN: How are you?

DAUGHTER: Fine. And you?

MAN: Fine.

DAUGHTER: I've been told that life has treated you well, hasn't it?

MAN: I can't complain.

DAUGHTER: Congratulations.

MAN: Although it has its ups and downs, you know.

DAUGHTER: Yes, of course. (*Pause.*) I've thought about you sometimes.

MAN: Oh, yeah? Thanks.

DAUGHTER: Yes. But you never looked like this.

MAN: Oh, no?

DAUGHTER: No. I imagined you with the same face as when you were . . . like this! (*Pause.*) What do you want?

MAN: And why were you thinking about me?

DAUGHTER: I don't know. When someone told me things were going well for you, I thought: I'm not at all surprised.

MAN: Why not?

DAUGHTER: Because despite . . . everything, I could tell, that you would be one of those people who is successful in life.

MAN: Ha, ha! I haven't been successful in life. If I began telling you about all my problems, I wouldn't finish until tomorrow.

DAUGHTER: Come on, Come on, right, right. (*Pause.*) How did you know where to find me? Who told you? Did you talk to my brother and he told you . . . ?

MAN: To your brother? No. I haven't seen him again, since. I don't live here. I only come here once in a while to give a seminar. And I never would have dared come by to see him without calling first.

DAUGHTER: He's in there. (*Pause.*) Don't you want to see him, too?

MAN: (*Pause.*) No. I've just come to see you.

DAUGHTER: (*Silence. Referring to somebody else.*) You've seen him, haven't you?

MAN: Yes. A week ago. I went to give a lecture at another university very close to where he's living. I didn't know. And I found him sitting in the front row with a frighteningly drunken look on his face. It'd been twelve or thirteen years since we'd last seen each other. Imagine how my lecture went.

DAUGHTER: The truth is, I could care less what he's . . .

MAN: I'm sorry to have to play this role, really. I'm sorry and I assure you that for me, it's also hard to swallow. (*Pause.*) When I finished the lecture, we got to talking. He told me that your youngest son had called to tell him that you were here, and that you weren't going to get out of this one. (*Pause.*) I didn't know you were so sick. (*Pause.*) I'm sorry.

DAUGHTER: And he asked you for money, of course. (*Pause.*) And you gave him some. (*Pause.*) And then what?

MAN: He seemed very moved. Really.

DAUGHTER: And that's it? (*Pause.*) Look, I know all too well how your brother gets moved. I've been indifferent to it for ten years. I don't even remember him. I don't give a shit what he says; I'm all too familiar with his scenes. By the way, how are his sons, who were also mine, unfortunately? Are they well? You know, don't you? I imagine he must talk about them. Or maybe not? The oldest, with drug problems, the other an alcoholic like him, and the other in the service, because it's the only place where they would have him. That's the result of the affection that your brother feels for me. So he sent you to tell me . . .

MAN: No one has sent me. I'm here because I want to be. I've never been anyone's lapdog. And especially not his.

DAUGHTER: Why have you come then?

MAN: They've inaugurated a new literature department just four blocks from here.

DAUGHTER: What?

MAN: I've just signed a contract to teach there during the next three years.

DAUGHTER: And?

MAN: I'd like you to convince your brother to sell me this apartment. I want to buy it.

DAUGHTER: What? (*Pause.*) And why don't you ask him? As far as I'm concerned you can do whatever you want with this apartment. It's his. Do you want it for yourself? Ask him, go ahead, he's right here. (SHE *gets up.*) If you want . . .

MAN: No. (*Pause.*) If he knew who I was he wouldn't sell it to me. He never liked me.

DAUGHTER: Oh, no? Maybe you're wrong about that. (*Pause.*) Why do you want this place?

MAN: (*A very tense pause.*) I can't tell you. I'm sorry. (*Pause.*) I can't tell you. I don't even know why.

DAUGHTER: (*Suddenly, with tears in her eyes.*) Is it . . . is it *a secret*, perhaps?

MAN: (*With an intense gaze, conscious that* HE *is reliving an important moment for himself, and also for her.*) Yes.

SHE *has to get up and move, so as not to burst into tears in front of him.* SHE *has just received an unexpected answer to a question that* SHE *had asked herself a long time ago and had completely forgotten . . .*

DAUGHTER: I'll do what I can.

MAN: Thank you. You can tell him, for example . . . that if he wants to sell it and leave it in good hands, to post some ads on bulletin boards at the university . . .

DAUGHTER: He won't want to sell it. My brother has never finished cutting the ties that still bind him to these walls.

MAN: Maybe not yet. But maybe . . . (HE *stops.*)

DAUGHTER: (SHE *holds back her tears.*) You're used to always getting your own way, aren't you? (*Pause.*) And on top of that, other people probably thank you and everything, don't they? That's what I call knowing how to get the most out of life, you know. (*Pause.*) I'm glad I got to see you.

MAN: Me too.

DAUGHTER: If you'll excuse me, I'm feeling a bit queasy and I have things to do.

MAN: Have I disturbed you?

DAUGHTER: No. (*Pause.*) Well, a little, yes, let's not kid ourselves. But that's OK. Things are moving around here inside me. It must mean I'm not completely dead, yet. I won't see you out, if you don't mind.

MAN: That won't be necessary. Goodbye.

HE goes toward her and gives her two kisses and a hug. They look into each other's eyes. And SHE, suddenly, gives him a smile. And an image of many years ago is transmitted from her eyes to his . . . HE slowly separates from her and goes toward the door. SHE leans on the table and sees the package that the MAN has left.

DAUGHTER: You've left . . .

MAN: No. (*Pause.*) It's . . . for you.

And HE leaves. Intrigued, SHE unwraps the package. It is an old hard-covered book, the same one that we had seen the MOTHER reading in the previous scene. The DAUGHTER has a strong sensation and goes out toward the hallway. Meanwhile, in the bedroom:

FATHER: No. I've spent my entire life in this bed and no one will move me from here. Much less that degenerate sister of yours.

SON: She's gravely ill, Dad. Today she begins chemo at the hospital. She needs a lot of rest, and she needs to be as comfortable as possible. This room is the best in the house. The doctor said . . .

FATHER: I don't give a damn what the doctors say.

SON: Well I don't give a damn what you say. Beginning tonight, you'll sleep in the servant's quarters, next to your little woman. I've already spoken with her, and she's getting the spare bed ready. I told her I'll take care of moving your clothes myself.

FATHER: Why did you say my "little woman"?

SON: Just drop it.

FATHER: She's not my little woman. Have some respect for you mother.

SON: For my mother? Who can remember her, now? Perhaps, you?

FATHER: Every day of my life. (*Pause.*) Well, not exactly every every day . . . but . . .

SON: You're talking nonsense, Dad. I don't know how you let yourself get so mixed up.

FATHER: Mixed up? With whom?

SON: Enough. It upsets me to talk about it.

FATHER: About what?

SON: HOW IS IT THAT YOU DIDN'T CONSULT WITH ME ABOUT MARRYING THAT WOMAN, YOU STUPID OLD JERK?! I WOULD HAVE CONVINCED YOU NOT TO, IMMEDIATELY!

FATHER: Oh. Is that it? Well, and why did I have to check with you? Am I not old enough?

SON: Enough? . . . TOO OLD!

FATHER: It made her happy, poor thing. What do you want? She didn't want to die an unmarried woman.

SON: She didn't want to die an unmarried woman?! And that's why she married you?! BUT HOW COULD YOU HAVE DONE SOMETHING LIKE THIS, YOU FOOL?! Don't you realize that she did it to obtain citizenship and get your money?

FATHER: What money? I don't have any! And she already had citizenship! She did it because she loves me.

SON: Oh, how romantic. And you love her too, right? That's why you treat her the way you do!

FATHER: She's been taking care of me and feeding me all these years. And offering me her affection without demanding anything in return. Something that you've never done.

SON: I never . . . ? (*Pause.*) Do you know why you're here, Dad? Do you know why you've never needed anything? Why you're so healthy and have such a clear head? Because I'm here. Because I've worked like a dog my entire life so that you could continue living in this house and pay all the doctors you needed and all the vacations you wanted and all the whims you asked me for, in addition to the salary of that woman, WHO'S NOW YOUR WIFE!!! I've been maintaining you all these years, since you retired early because of a depression at age fifty-five . . . AT AGE OF FIFTY-FIVE . . . AND BECAUSE OF A DEPRESSION, MY GOD . . . AND YOU NEVER STOP FUCKING CHEAP WHORES EVERY SATURDAY AND SUNDAY! AND I PAID FOR THEM TOO, ME, YOU KNOW, THE WHORES?! I must have even paid without knowing it was for the wedding gift you gave that woman, right? And meanwhile you were depositing your entire pension directly into the bank, each month of your fucking life, for more than twenty years, without giving me even a cent with the excuse that you were doing it to put aside some savings and ensure a future for yourself. BUT WHAT FUTURE, HELL, YOU'RE MORE THAN EIGHTY YEARS OLD!? That money, you greedy, egotistical, pig of a father, will go to help a poor family in some lost village in South America!!! DO YOU UNDERSTAND?!!! And if you were doing it for social convictions or a sense of justice, hey!, I would applaud you! I would be proud of you! I'm no financial genius, nor am I a genius when it comes to business, nor am I any sort of genius, that's why I've had to sweat and slave to make a small name for myself in my job and be able to maintain you all these years!! And that amounts to giving you nothing in exchange? I've given you too much. Too much, if I compare it with the affection I've received from you.

FATHER: But do you know why you did it? Because you were worried about what people would say. As usual. So everyone would say that you were a model son, in spite of being . . . the way you really are. You did it to keep me happy, and so I would let you do your own thing and not get involved in your life as . . . as . . . a coward. A COWARD! (*Pause.*) Not because you really cared.

SON: Enough.

FATHER: I'm asking you to please not move me from this bedroom. There are too many memories, son, too many things lived within these walls, you have to understand.

SON: You'll sleep in the bedroom at the end of the hallway. Enough already! And if you complain to me anymore, I'll sell the apartment and throw you and *your wife* out.

FATHER: Whaaaat? You'd be *incapable* of doing any such thing. (*Pause.*) You're too soft. All you have to do is imagine what your buddies and your colleagues at work would say when they find out you've kicked your father out on the street, and you'd die of shame. Because . . . for all your goodness, sensitivity, liberalness, and the like . . . no matter how you slice it, deep down, you're hypocritical, egotistical, overly proud and vain, and a shameless fool, who's getting old and doesn't know how to face a problem, as though he still wanted to hide behind his mother's skirt!

SON: (*Making a very violent gesture toward him.*) Why do you say that?

FATHER: (HE *becomes frightened and says with an inflated, comical tone.*) Huh? Why do I say what? (*Pause.*) Why are you looking at me that way? What's the matter? (*Pause.*) What did I say?

Music from the apartment above.

FATHER: Strangers, foreigners!

SON: Just what we need.

FATHER: They came from the hills and took our castles away.

SON: Huh?

FATHER: I'm just referring to those foreigners who are robbing from us what little remains that is truly ours. You know what I mean.

SON: She's not a foreigner. Like it or not, she's your daughter.

FATHER: Who ran off forty years ago with one of them, rejecting her family, her homeland, her language, and her own blood. That's not a daughter. It's bad enough that a bunch of these strangers have moved in here, but they continue leading an identical life to the one they lived there, listening to the same damned music, eating the same garbage, buying things at the same stores, of which there is every kind and I don't know how they let them, dressing the same way, giving off the same odors, and speaking the same language. They even have their own sacred places to pray just a few blocks away from here! She, on the other hand . . . not even a phone call, not even a postcard, not even a visit in forty years . . . I don't understand how she didn't miss all this. Not even when her four children were born did she do us the honor of a visit. And she appears at our door now with the news that she's dying. And you believe it, imbecile! What really happened is that her husband has left her, and he doesn't send her his pension, and she doesn't have a cent and wants to sponge off us for the rest of her life! (*Pause*) Well, off you, to be more precise.

SON: You don't know what you're talking about. (*The SON finishes putting all the clothing in the suitcase and closes it.*) There, that's it. All the clothes packed up. I'm going to take this suitcase to the other bedroom.

The SON picks up the suitcase and leaves the bedroom. The FATHER follows him. When HE arrives at the doorway between the bedroom and the living room, the FATHER stops and looks at the SON, who continues walking with the suitcase in his hand. The vision of the SON with the suitcase suddenly causes him to tremble.

FATHER: Wait. (*Pause.*) Son!

SON: (*Stopping and looking at him.*) What?

FATHER: Why did you put the clothes in the suitcase?

SON: Because they're easier to transport this way. So they won't wrinkle.

FATHER: Are you sure?

SON: Of course.

FATHER: Where are you taking them?

SON: To the bedroom at the end of the hallway.

FATHER: You're not tricking me?

SON: Dad . . . Did you not believe what I said before? (*Pause.*) You yourself . . .

FATHER: But . . . Where did you get that suitcase?

SON: From your closet. Why?

FATHER: It belonged to my father.

SON: To grandpa, yes. I remember it. (*Pause.*) So?

FATHER: (*Pause. His eyes seem to evoke a distant image.*) Nothing . . . nothing. My god!

The FATHER *is frightened. The* SON *exits with the suitcase through the door to the hallway. The* DAUGHTER *appears where the* SON *has just entered, loaded down with clean folded sheets and a bag.* SHE *comes face to face with the* FATHER.

DAUGHTER: And now, I'm robbing your bedroom from you. (*Pause.*) You'll hate me even more, won't you?

FATHER: No. (*Pause.*). When you were little you were my princess. Then . . . (*Pause.*) . . . maybe I did end up cursing you. For years. For many years. But hate you, hate you . . . well, a little bit, yes, let's not kid ourselves. When you left. (*Pause.*) . . . But now, you see. Just when you can no longer recall her face . . . boom!, she comes back! And she shoves me out of the place where I had decided to die, which is the place where *I* have slept and lived all my life, with the excuse that she is going to die before me and, what a coincidence!, on a whim she decides that it will be in that exact place. And I, since I'm an old fart who, according to them, doesn't matter, she doesn't even consult me, nor does she ask my opinion. They take all my clothes, they push me out whatever which way, off you go! If you don't like it, tough, and don't complain because there are a lot of people *like you* who are much worse off. And on top of that she tells me: "you'll hate me even more, won't you?"!! Well . . . what do you want me to say?! (*Pause.*) Yes!!! . . . (HE *exits and enters again.* HE *goes over to a piece of furniture, grabs the box and takes out a cigar.* HE *shows it to the* DAUGHTER.) It's just that it helps my nerves. Not a cent for your brother. And for that little woman, even less, understand?

The DAUGHTER *nods no, very serious.* HE *exits.* SHE *smiles.*

DAUGHTER: By the way, congratulations on your wedding!

SHE *waits for an answer, but does not receive one.* SHE *enters the bedroom and closes the door. As soon as* SHE *closes it, the* FATHER *pokes his head out from where* HE *has exited.*

FATHER: What? What did you say? (HE *sees that* HE*'s alone. Bitter.*) Thank you! (*Pause.*) Bah!

HE *takes a breath and sits down. The* MAID *enters, annoyed.*

MAID: Now, don't expect me to unpack your things from this suitcase on my own. Then you won't know where to find them in the closet and you'll drive me crazy! It's already happening!

FATHER: Right, right . . . (HE *draws closer to her and wants to touch her rear.*) Did you already put the pills in the draw of the new nightstand? (HE *slaps his hands.*) Oh . . . Are we still worked up? (*Pause.*) I've already told both of them, my little bird . . .

MAID: Both of them, no, because your son had no idea!

FATHER: But my daughter congratulated me and everything! Ask her, go ahead . . .

MAID: YOU DON'T EVEN TALK TO EACH OTHER!! (SHE *exits, muttering, in her maternal language: "but, mother of god, how could he have done this to me?!, and the embarrassment that he's caused me!!, of course I'm not surprised, after seeing how the members of this very "civilized" family treat each other, they seem like animals more than people . . .")*

FATHER: You stupid foreigner!

But HE *exits behind her like a puppy. Suddenly the* SON *appears in the same place, staring at the* FATHER. HE *takes a breath and shakes his head.* HE *crosses the living room and goes to the bedroom.* HE *opens the door. The* DAUGHTER, *inside, is trying to unfold a sheet, but it does not spread out properly. Her gestures are clumsy, very similar to those that the* MOTHER *made years earlier. Seeing the scene leaves him paralyzed.* SHE *notices him.*

DAUGHTER: You startled me. (*Pause.*) What happened? Have you seen a ghost?

*By the look on his face and his interior suffering (*HE *has made an effort to disguise his emotions upon opening the door and seeing his* SISTER *there, in that room), the* DAUGHTER *understands immediately: yes,* HE *has seen a ghost.* SHE *stops what* SHE *is doing and sits down on the bed.* SHE *looks at the* SON.

DAUGHTER: Do you want to sit down for a while and we can talk?

SON: No. I have work to do.

DAUGHTER: You still haven't been able to get over it, after all these years?

SON: Over what?

DAUGHTER: Over what? (*Pause.*) Over whom.

SON: (*Pause.*) She suffered a lot. (*Pause.*) And I wasn't . . .

DAUGHTER: I can't believe it! (SHE *laughs*.) You still haven't forgiven yourself for not being at her side, holding her hand, the night that she died? (*Pause.*) You're . . . (SHE *laughs*.) She was unconscious for days!

SON: No. She woke up. She spoke, and I didn't go to her, I couldn't . . .

DAUGHTER: You're hallucinating! (*Pause.*) Don't tell me that after so many years it still bothers you . . . ?

SON: I haven't talked with Dad about it, about that night, it's like it never existed. How was it? Why did you run off afterwards, without saying anything to us? What happened? (*Pause.*) Sorry, I have to go; in fact, I'm already late for work. I just wanted to know if you needed . . .

DAUGHTER: After she died, I tried to find you. I called you at the home of . . . of that friend of yours to tell you that you could come. But you weren't there. Where did you go?

SON: Somewhere and nowhere. I wandered the streets. I ended up sleeping on a bench in a train station. When the sun came up, I returned home. I hope she's dead, I thought. And, from the other side of the street . . . I saw you going out the door with a suitcase. Mom is dead. And she's leaving. I wanted to follow you and speak to you, and . . . But I didn't do it. I couldn't get out of my head the last thing you said to me. And I remained frozen as I stared at you as you were leaving, thinking: all that's left for me is Dad: how awful, only Dad.

DAUGHTER: The last thing I said to you was . . . that you too should be there when Mom died. That leaving would not be better for you. That's what you couldn't get out of your head? (*The* SON *indicates no.*) What, then? (*Pause.*) That night . . . (*Pause.*) When you left, it happened . . . it doesn't matter. I was there. I heard the sound of her breathing. It wasn't a human sound, it was . . . And suddenly, everything became silent. Afterward, I heard Dad vomiting, and I thought: it's happened. I . . . came in here and . . . (*Pause.*) She was dead. And her eyes were open. Very open. As if at the last moment she'd seen something . . . Something . . . important . . . Transcendental. And she was looking toward the door . . . (*A strangely pleasurable silence invades the space. Pause.*) She was looking at me. (*Pause.*) Yes. She was looking . . . at me. (*Pause.*) And I . . . I didn't feel anything. Nothing. (*Pause.*) I didn't feel . . . anything. And I thought to myself: it's over. Finally. (*Pause.*) And I closed her eyes. (*Pause.*) And, I don't mind admitting it: I felt better. Much better. (*Pause.*) That's it.

SON: That's it? So nothing happened?

DAUGHTER: Does that seem like nothing to you? She was already dead and she looked at me. Don't you understand? She looked at me . . . from there . . . from the other side. Maybe . . . she knew. Yes, of course, that must've been it, how is it that I didn't realize until now? . . . She knew.

SON: What?

DAUGHTER: That afternoon, down at the pharmacy . . . ha ha ha . . . that very afternoon . . . they told me that I was . . . (SHE *places her hand on her abdomen.*) Three or four hours before Mom died, funny, isn't it?

SON: Why didn't you tell me?

DAUGHTER: Why did I have to tell you? (*Pause.*) Of course. She looked at me because at that very last moment she knew. That I would have a child and then another and another and another. And that I would end up a fool for my entire life. Maybe she even knew that I would come right back here to die like her. They say you know everything when you go through to the other side of the looking glass, you know? What's a shame is not being able to come out and explain it. The mystery. I need very little to decipher it. I'm sorry. I won't be able to explain it to you. You'll have to wait a good many years, because you're a lot like Dad, you know? You'll see your sons and your grandsons in the grave, ha ha ha. Go on, go ahead, you said you were late.

SON: Do you need anything?

DAUGHTER: Nothing, thanks. (*Pause.*) Well, yes, one thing. (*Pause.*) I can't ask my son. Or, I don't want to . . .

SON: What?

DAUGHTER: Will you stay with me?

SON: Huh?

DAUGHTER: Until . . . the . . . end? (*Pause.*) Do you think you'll be able to do it, this time? (*Tense pause.*) I'm sorry, I have no right to ask. (*Suddenly, furious.*) Go on, go to work, I don't know why the hell you make me talk about these things, damn it! (*Pause.*) GET OUT, FOR CRYING OUT LOUD!! (HE *leaves.* SHE *grabs a pillow and beats it with almost hysterical, nervous gestures. The pillow falls to the floor.*) Shit!

Darkness.

SCENE 9

Twentieth century.

In the bedroom, the MOTHER *with the* SON. HE *is giving her a sponge bath. In the living room, the* FATHER *and the* DAUGHTER. HE *is reading the newspaper and* SHE *is giving herself a manicure. And then, a pedicure. Then,* SHE *tweezes her eyebrows as* SHE *looks in a small mirror. When* SHE *is finished,* SHE *does all kinds of touching up to her face,* SHE *squeezes a pimple, etc.* SHE *has a record player next to her and listens to The Beatles.*

MOTHER: (*To the* SON, *referring to how he is bathing her.*) Scrub a little harder!

SON: I don't want to hurt you.

MOTHER: You're not. Harder, I said!

SON: Like this?

MOTHER: What a weakling you are, boy. More, more!

SON: I'll scrub your skin off.

MOTHER: I don't care. Let it all come off. I want my skin to be glowing and perfumed. I can no longer wash out the decay that I have inside me; at least it shouldn't be noticeable on the outside. Ha ha! That's really the story of our lives, isn't it? Ha ha ha!

SON: What?

MOTHER: What I just told you.

SON: I don't understand you.

MOTHER: Right, of course. You never understand anything.

SON: I mean it.

MOTHER: All clean on the outside, but totally decaying on the inside, ha ha ha! Do you understand now or do I have to spell it out for you?

SON: No. It's not necessary.

MOTHER: And you'll be this way until you die. And that's all right.

SON: What?

MOTHER: Ugh, kiddo, you seem so dense!

SON: It's just that I don't know what you're referring to.

MOTHER: You, the perfect son, good grades at school, well bred, polite, sensible, always surrounded by serious books and never raising your voice, a true friend . . . If I had a daughter to marry off, you'd be the ideal son-in-law. But, of course, so much perfection is impossible.

SON: Do you want to be quiet?

MOTHER: Do you have a little girlfriend?

SON: If you continue to move like that, I won't be able to wash you.

MOTHER: Then stop washing and listen to me.

SON: But didn't you want to be clean and nice smelling?

MOTHER: I can never be clean, and no matter how much soap you use, as soon as I vomit and a huge wind escapes from me, I'll be stinking once again.

SON: Why are you so nasty?

MOTHER: Don't you ever fart?

SON: Please!

MOTHER: No. And that's your problem. You would never be capable of farting in public. But you do fart, like everyone else. Oh, no . . . You're one of those people who says he's never farted . . . But you don't fool me, you do fart, in bed, when everyone is sleeping. And the stench stays in your sheets and you love to smell it! Don't you? You love your own disgusting stench!

SON: I can't take anymore.

MOTHER: Listen to me.

SON: What.

MOTHER: Stop and look at me. (*Pause.*) If you want to be anything in life, listen to me. Don't be like your sister. She does the opposite from you; she goes around throwing stink bombs all around her and then wants everyone to believe that she's not the one who farted.

SON: Would you stop with this vile way of talking?

MOTHER: No. I won't stop until you listen to me.

SON: I'm listening to you.

MOTHER: But you don't understand me!

SON: Yes I do.

MOTHER: No! What am I talking about?

SON: That . . . that . . . I don't fart, no, that I do fart, that farts . . . ay enough!

MOTHER: You see? How's your friend doing?

SON: Huh?

MOTHER: Have you seen him lately?

SON: Hmm?

MOTHER: Answer me.

SON: Yes, we went to the movies yesterday.

MOTHER: Has he said anything to you?

SON: Anything, about what?

MOTHER: About your sister.

SON: Huh?

MOTHER: Don't you know that they've been going out together, alone, for the past few days? And that they're saying they want to get married? (*The* SON *suddenly turns pale.* HE *grabs the sponge and wants to wash her again.*) PUT THE SPONGE DOWN, DAMN IT! YOU SEE HOW YOU DON'T UNDERSTAND ANYTHING, IMBECILE? YOU THINK I DON'T REALIZE WHAT'S HAPPENING WITH YOU? I'M DYING, DEAR, I'M DYING, AND BEFORE I DO I WANT TO LEAVE EVERYTHING RESOLVED SO THAT NONE OF YOU WILL BE AS UNHAPPY AS I'VE BEEN IN THIS SHIT LIFE, DO YOU UNDERSTAND?! YOU THINK I HAVEN'T REALIZED WHAT YOU'RE ABOUT, DEAR? I GAVE BIRTH TO YOU, I BROUGHT YOU UP, I TRIED TO DO THE IMPOSSIBLE TO CHANGE YOU, AND I HAVEN'T BEEN ABLE TO. I FOUND OUT THE FIRST DAY I SAW YOU SECRETLY PLAYING WITH MY MOTHER'S PORCELAIN DOLLS WHEN YOU WERE TWO YEARS OLD! TWO YEARS OLD! TWO YEARS OLD!! (*Pause.*) Listen to me. There are a lot of rich girls willing to marry a good boy like you. Pick out the dullest and ugliest and marry her. If you want to be someone in life, get married. Give her a son. It won't be so difficult for you. All you have to do is turn off the bedroom light and let your imagination run wild, the way you do every night in your room, thinking about your friend, that's the kind of smelly farts I was referring to, you dimwit. And as far as he's concerned, stop seeing him. What I'm telling you is very important, do you hear me? Stop seeing him. And don't worry: your sister is not in love. She'll forget about him sooner than you think. Besides, something tells me your friend is going out with her to get closer to you. That's why it's so important for you to get far way from him. He's not the guy with whom you should be doing the things you dream about each night. Not with him, do you understand? He's a boy from a good family, Catholic, and you go to school together, you see each other too often. Everyone would realize and it would be an embarrassment for the families. Once you're married, your wife will let you go out with your friends to play cards on Saturday and Sunday afternoons. That's when you should do it. But only then, and with men you don't know; above all, not with that boy, do you understand?, with men you don't know and if they're foreigners or lowlifes like the people upstairs, and you have to give them money in exchange, so much the better. That way you won't be obliged to them in any way. That is if you want to do something worthwhile and not be taken for a fool all your life. If what you want is something else, go ahead. You decide. Do you understand, now? (*Pause.*) You don't know why I'm telling you all this, do you? (*Pause.*) You can go far in life. You have this flaw, which is very serious; but no other defects. Now, I should also say that you're no genius. Don't look at me that way. You're not. And if you didn't know it by now, now you know. You'll have to work hard to be someone, but you have a great deal of will, you're honest, and you do things well. Will you look at me and stop crying already? You come off as such a dimwit! (*Pause.*) In fact, that's what you are. (SHE *begins laughing. Suddenly, serious.*) I need to tell you something even more important. And I won't repeat it again: if you sell this house, I'll rise up from my tomb and I'll come for you, and I'll castrate you, do you understand? I'll cut off your balls and your dick, and I'll sew up your ass, you faggot, and then your life will really be over.

SON: Why . . . are . . . you saying these things to me?

MOTHER: Because you have to achieve everything I lost because of your father. Well, because of the foolish thing I did in marrying for *love*.

SON: I don't understand you.

MOTHER: I owe it to your grandfather. To my father. He was the second in a family of country folk. He arrived in this city with one hand in front and the other behind his back. And he married your grandmother, a rich girl from the upper part of the city. The typical story: they had a boy from a good family all picked out for her, she ran off with him, and they cut off her inheritance. Dad worked like a dog all his life to provide Mom with all the luxuries she had lost as a result of their marriage. And he managed to do it. Properties, plots of land, this apartment, the country house, and even servants. I was his little princess. Poor Dad. He died the day I turned eighteen. Some days earlier, he made me promise I wouldn't touch my inheritance. He said that the properties were . . . an eternal sign of his love for us. But a year later, I fell in love with your father. Or, I thought I was in love. The absence of my father was so unbearable for me that I attached myself to the first guy who gave me a flower. And he was the one. A good man like anyone else, but too honest to make a good living like he should have in the time we had. The war destroyed everything of ours, and to feed the two of you and make sure you had everything you needed . . . I had to sell everything. All the effort, all the work, Dad's sweat . . . ! Everything sold for a piece of bread and four beans! Everything but this house. Which not long from now will belong to you and your sister. I can't depend on her, but I can trust you. I owe a debt to my father and now you owe a debt to me. Do you understand?

SON: Mom . . .

MOTHER: Do you understand? (*The* SON *nods yes.* SHE *hugs him as hard as* SHE *can.*) WHAT I CAN'T UNDERSTAND IS WHY I HAVE TO DIE SO YOUNG, DEAR, I CAN'T UNDERSTAND IT . . . (SHE *cries.*) Go, I don't want you to see me this way . . . it's humiliating.

SON: Mom, please.

MOTHER: GO!

SON: I'll never sell this house, I promise.

MOTHER: The day you do . . .

SON: . . . you'll rise up from your grave and castrate me . . .

MOTHER: No. That's no way to talk, you idiot . . . (*Pause.*) The day you do . . .

SON: What?

MOTHER: The day you do . . .

Silence. The MOTHER *closes her eyes.* SHE *continues to pronounce, with a faint voice, "the day you do . . ." Suddenly,* SHE *becomes still. In the living room, the* DAUGHTER *is looking in a large mirror.* SHE *touches her breasts, her hips. The* FATHER *looks up from the newspaper and looks at her.*

DAUGHTER: What?

FATHER: Nothing. For just a moment . . . I thought I saw . . . your mother when we first met.

DAUGHTER: Was she pretty?

The FATHER *makes a gesture with his hand as if to say: "you have no idea." In the bedroom, the* MOTHER *remains still. The* SON *becomes frightened and extends his hand to touch her.*

SON: Mom . . . ?

Suddenly, the MOTHER *begins to snore noisily. A loud wind escapes from her body, under the sheets. The* SON *lifts them up and takes his hand quickly to his nose. The putrid smell is intolerable. His first reaction is disgust.* HE *gets up and feels a wave of nausea.* HE *takes a few steps back with his hand to his nose until he comes to a chair.* HE *sits down.* HE *remains dazed for few seconds and, then,* HE *looks at her and begins to cry in silence.*

Darkness.

SCENE 10

Twenty-first century.

The ORPHAN *boy from upstairs is sitting at the dining room table. The* FATHER *is standing, leaning on his walking stick, looking at him. The* MAID *appears.* SHE *comes from the kitchen with a tray with a drink and sandwich for the boy.*

In the bedroom, the DAUGHTER *is reading, very moved, the book that the* MAN *has brought her.*

FATHER: You smell, kiddo, you smell.

MAID: Come on, little one, go ahead, here, eat.

ORPHAN: No . . . no . . .

MAID: You don't have to beg; I know you're hungry.

FATHER: Get him out of here once and for all.

MAID: Shut up and go back to bed.

FATHER: Where did he come from?

MAID: I don't know. He was sitting on the staircase. I think he lives upstairs. You live upstairs, don't you, sweetie?

ORPHAN: Yes.

FATHER: He smells.

MAID: Not any more than you do. (SHE *places the tray in front of the* ORPHAN.) Come on, don't dawdle.

The ORPHAN *begins to eat, to devour practically everything on the plate. The* MAID *laughs. The* FATHER *is looking at her, entranced.*

FATHER: You would have liked to have children, wouldn't you?

MAID: (*Pause.*) You like it? Very good. Eat it all up and then you'll come with me and I'll make you a hot bath with lots of bubbles, all right?

ORPHAN: (*With his mouth full.*) Yes.

FATHER: You're joking, right? I will not have this boy put his dirty feet in my bathtub. He'll leave behind all the filth he has on him. He must be full of microbes. Don't you see? He must have fleas and everything! Let his own parents bathe him!

ORPHAN: (*With his mouth full.*) I don't have parents.

MAID: You don't? Who do you live with?

ORPHAN: With my aunt and uncle.

FATHER: And don't they bathe you? And don't they feed you?

ORPHAN: Yes. And I'm dirty because I was just playing football, OK? I take a shower every day.

FATHER: Yeah, right. On top of it all, a liar!

MAID: (*To the* ORPHAN.) Don't pay attention to him. He's an old man and he's not all there.

FATHER: I'm not all there? (*To the* ORPHAN.) She says I'm not all there! That I'm crazy in the head! And look who's talking! This crazy woman I took off the street! I gave her a roof, an education, food, clothing, I taught her my language and my customs, and for what? So that she can end up telling me that I'm crazy in the head!!! (*The* ORPHAN *begins to laugh, looking at the* FATHER.) What are you laughing at?

ORPHAN: At you. (*To the* MAID.) You're funny.

FATHER: Funny? What's so funny?

ORPHAN: You. You get mad and act silly.

FATHER: Wait until I give you a good one with this hand, and then we'll see if you still feel like laughing. But you've got to be kidding? Are you making fun of me, kid? (*The* ORPHAN *laughs even more. The* FATHER *moves closer to him with his hand in the air.*) Look . . .

MAID: (*Stopping him.*) Hey! Hey! Enough, come on, enough already! What a way to behave, mother of god! Go on, leave us alone and go to your room.

FATHER: I don't feel like it. (*To the* ORPHAN.) And I can't go back to my room because my son kicked me out. An old man, like me. You tell me. And he's buried me in a cave without windows, at the end of the hallway, like an old piece of junk, you know, little one?

ORPHAN: (*Offering him his food.*) Do you want some? (*To the* MAID.) I think he's so mad because he's hungry.

FATHER: I'm in a bad mood because I don't know what the hell you're doing here, kid. Isn't it enough that you have to torment us with your music and your noise and your smells, then on top of that you have to come into our houses and rob us of what little we have left? This is the height of . . .

ORPHAN: Eat some, mister, it's really good.

FATHER: What is it?

ORPHAN: Sausage.

FATHER: (HE *moves closer to the* BOY, *dying of hunger.*) Sausage?

MAID: Hey! He can't eat that! His cholesterol level!

FATHER: Oh, shut up already and don't curse! Give me a bite, kid.

ORPHAN: What's cholesterol?

MAID: An ugly thing in the blood that makes old people die. And we don't want him to die, do we?

ORPHAN: Noooo . . .

MAID: So, he can't eat sausage. (SHE *slaps the* FATHER*'s hand, which he had extended toward the sausage sandwich.*)

FATHER: You think I'll die because of a little nothing bite, evil woman? (*To the* ORPHAN.) She has me on a diet, and she's a pain in the ass.

MAID: And that's why he's healthy and active.

FATHER: And starving. I think about food all day long. I even dream about it. You witch!

ORPHAN: Don't insult her, mister, she doesn't want you to die.

FATHER: Oh, really? At this rate, I won't die because of cholesterol; I'll die of famine.

ORPHAN: Of fam . . . ?

FATHER: Of hunger!

ORPHAN: My parents died of hunger. (*And automatically,* HE *takes a bite of the sandwich.*) Mmm . . .

Suddenly, silence. The MAID *pats the* ORPHAN *on the head and exits. The* FATHER *sits down at the table without taking his eyes off the* ORPHAN.

FATHER: (*Referring to the sandwich.*) Do you like it?

ORPHAN: Yes. Come on, go ahead, have a bite of this cholesterol, it's great. I won't tell her. But just one, OK?

FATHER: Thanks. (HE *grabs the sandwich and takes a bite.*) Mmm . . .

ORPHAN: Good, huh? (*The* FATHER *nods. Pause.*) Your wife is very pretty. You love her a lot, don't you? (*The* FATHER *maintains a lost look. Pause.*) Don't you?

FATHER: What wife? . . .

ORPHAN: Oh, you have more than one? . . .

FATHER: Huh? My wife . . . died many years ago . . .

ORPHAN: And was she as nice as this one you have now?

FATHER: (*With his thoughts confused, filled with memories.*) Come on, finish eating and go on home, kid. And tell them not to make so much noise and not to turn up the music so loud, if they don't want me to call the police. Fools! (*Serious, about to cry.*) My daughter is . . . sick and she can't get any rest, and because of all of you, she'll be leaving this world before it's time, like her . . . mother. I'm going to see if she's all settled in *my* bedroom . . .

HE *gets up with difficulty and goes to the bedroom, slowly, startled, taken by the memories. An unreal atmosphere imbues the scene.*

Without a clear transition, we move from the twenty-first to the twentieth century.

The DAUGHTER, *in the bedroom, is now the* MOTHER. *She's reading her old book, which we have seen earlier. The* FATHER, *old, upon crossing the threshold, has magically become younger (an imperceptible change in the actor). In the dining room, the* ORPHAN *is the boy, sitting at the table, eating.*

MOTHER: Have you given him a snack?

FATHER: Yes.

MOTHER: When he's finished, ask him to come in here.

FATHER: What's with you and this kid?

MOTHER: I like him. I feel sorry for him.

FATHER: Sorry?

MOTHER: Yes.

FATHER: Why?

MOTHER: He doesn't feel loved.

FATHER: How do you know?

MOTHER: I know.

FATHER: What's brought this on, now?

MOTHER: If he were my son . . .

FATHER: You have two sons.

MOTHER: That's just it.

FATHER: And you love them.

MOTHER: Oh, do I?

FATHER: Yes.

MOTHER: If you say so. (*Pause.*) Come here.

FATHER: Do you want me to give you an injection?

MOTHER: Later. Come here.

FATHER: What do you want?

MOTHER: To talk.

FATHER: About what.

MOTHER: I want you to promise me something.

FATHER: What?

MOTHER: That you won't remarry.

FATHER: Please . . .

MOTHER: That you will never love any other woman.

FATHER: But why . . . ?

MOTHER: Even if you live to be a hundred.

FATHER: You know perfectly . . .

MOTHER: Promise me.

FATHER: I promise.

MOTHER: What. (*Pause.*) Say it, all the words.

FATHER: I will never fall in love with any other woman. I won't remarry. I've only loved and will only love you. Even if I live to be a hundred. (HE *cries and sits on the bed.*) Why are you doing this to me? Why? Why are you doing this to me? (*Pause.*) I won't be able to go on with this family and this house without you, I won't be able to . . .

MOTHER: Yes you will . . . (*Pause.*) But remember what you promised me.

In the living room, the GRANDFATHER *enters through a door. HE sees the boy sitting and eating.*

GRANDFATHER: What is this boy doing here eating my cookies?!!! Did I give you permission to eat?!! I didn't, did I?! Get out of here, you thief!!! On top of it all they come into our house without asking our permission, and they take our food! You've got to be kidding . . . ! Go on! Get out of here!!

MOTHER: (*To the* FATHER.) Go tell your father to leave the child alone. He's my guest, and this is my house, and I've given him permission to eat as many cookies as he wants. And tell him to leave the *cookies* and go prepare the *suitcases*. Since you didn't dare take care of it, I did it. I called the old people's home. They're expecting him tomorrow. I want to die in peace. Once I'm buried, you can bring him back here, if you want. If your kids will let you. Because from that day on, this house will be theirs. (*Pause.*) I'm sorry.

The FATHER *goes to the living room and realizes that the* GRANDFATHER *has been listening on the other side of the door to everything that the* MOTHER *has been saying.* HE *grabs the* BOY *and takes him into the bedroom, closes the door, and remains staring at the* GRANDFATHER. *The* SON *enters the bedroom silently and goes toward the bed. The* MOTHER *hands the book to him.*

MOTHER: (*To the* BOY.) This . . . is for you.

The BOY *grabs the book, excitedly, and remains staring at it.*

Darkness.

PART TWO

SCENE 1

Twenty-first century.

In the bedroom, the DAUGHTER *and the* GRANDDAUGHTER *near the bed. The door between the bedroom and the living room is open. In the living room, the* SON *reads the newspaper, and the* GRANDSON *plays with a laptop computer. The* MAID *appears with a tray and breakfast.*

MAID: I'll leave it here? There's more coffee in the kitchen if you want.

SON: Thanks. (*Pause.*) What's my father up to?

MAID: What do you think he's up to? Going around complaining. (SHE *exits.*)

In the bedroom, the DAUGHTER *feels slightly faint and sits down on the bed.*

DAUGHTER: (*To the* GRANDDAUGHTER.) Close the door.

GRANDDAUGHTER: Are you all right?

MOTHER: Yes, yes. Close the door.

The GRANDDAUGHTER *gets up and goes toward the door.*

SON: (*To the* GRANDSON.) You're not eating?

GRANDSON: I'm not hungry.

SON: (*To the* GRANDDAUGHTER, *who is closing the doo.r*) Why are you closing it?

GRANDDAUGHTER: She asked me to.

SON: Is she OK?

GRANDDAUGHTER: She says she is.

The GRANDDAUGHTER *closes the door. In the living room, the* SON *serves himself some breakfast without taking his eyes off the* GRANDSON'*s computer.*

SON: What are you doing?

GRANDSON: What difference does it make to you?

GRANDDAUGHTER: (*To the* DAUGHTER.) Why do you want me to close the door?

DAUGHTER: So that my son doesn't see me . . . (*Pause.*)

GRANDDAUGHTER: Doesn't see you . . . how?

DAUGHTER: Crying. (*Pause.*) I don't want him to see me this way . . . it's so humiliating. (SHE *cries.*) I don't know why I've asked you here. (SHE *looks at the* GRANDDAUGHTER *and caresses her face.*) Or maybe I do . . . I hope all of you, when I'm no longer here . . . (*Pause.*) I haven't been able to . . . (SHE *cries.*)

SON: (*To the* GRANDSON.) Eat something, come on.

GRANDSON: I'm not hungry.

SON: You have to eat. How can you sit at the computer so early in the morning without anything in your stomach?

GRANDSON: And why not?

The SON *observes the* GRANDSON. *The scene seems familiar to him. The* FATHER *enters, silently, in his pajamas. He stands behind his* SON, *who is eating and does not see him. In the bedroom, the* DAUGHTER *calms down.*

DAUGHTER: I'm sorry . . . I've frightened you. It's nothing. I'm all right. It's just . . . it's just that today I'm beginning another set of treatments, and I'm scared. That's all.

FATHER: Good morning!

SON: Oh!

GRANDSON: Hey! Hi, grandpa, I didn't see you!

SON: You scared me! (HE *looks at him.*) You don't look so good!

FATHER: I couldn't sleep all night. And when I finally did fall asleep, I had a terrible nightmare. (*Pause.* HE *looks at the door to the hallway to see if the* MAID *is there.*) She can't hear me, can she? (*Pause.*) I dreamt that your mother rose up from her grave and wanted to kill me for betraying her memory. (*The* SON *looks at him, surprised. The* FATHER *looks at the food that the* SON *is not eating.*) Hey, you stupid fool! Are you planning on eating any of that or what?

GRANDSON: (*Cordially.*) It's all for you, grandfather! Come on, sit down here and eat, you need it, you don't look so good! You'll see how it'll put you in a better mood. Come on, I'll help you. Come on, grandpa, be good and open your mouth.

The FATHER *sits and the* GRANDSON *gives him something to eat, which the* FATHER *devours. The* SON *contemplates the* FATHER *and the* GRANDFATHER *with a dazed look. As if time had played a bad trick on him. Darkness.*

SCENE 2

Twentieth century.

In the bedroom, the FATHER *is finishing packing a suitcase with all the* GRANDFATHER*'s clothing. The* GRANDFATHER *is standing, with a trench coat folded over his arm, a hat in his hand, and an umbrella.*

GRANDFATHER: Sometimes my mind goes and I do stupid things, but it really won't happen again . . .

FATHER: Quiet, Dad.

GRANDFATHER: We've lived together for so many years, son, I have too many memories within these walls, you can't do this to me . . .

FATHER: This has never been your house; it's not my fault if you never realized it. I have.

GRANDFATHER: But . . . they mistreat people in those places, and they let them die like animals . . . I . . . if you leave me there, I'll die tonight. (*Pause.*) You don't have feelings . . .

FATHER: Please! It's hard enough for me; don't muck things up anymore . . .

GRANDFATHER: It's her, isn't it? That whore . . . Ohhh . . . Ohhh . . . Where is she? She's locked herself in the bathroom, so she doesn't have to see me go?

FATHER: Enough . . .

GRANDFATHER: . . . so she doesn't have to feel guilty and feel like a bad person? Well she is, she is, she always has been and she's converted you into a puppet!

FATHER: Enough . . .

GRANDFATHER: . . . and she's made my life impossible all these years, and now she won't be able to go in peace if she doesn't see me miserable! BUT EVEN IF THAT BITCH LOCKS ME AWAY IN AN INSANE ASYLUM, I'LL TAKE MANY YEARS TO DIE AND SHE ALREADY HAS ONE FOOT IN THE GRAVE, AND THAT'S ENOUGH, GOD ALWAYS BRINGS JUSTICE!!!

FATHER: ENOUGH, ENOUGH, THAT'S IT! (HE *closes the suitcase violently and grabs it.*) Let's go.

GRANDFATHER: Don't put your hands on me, you reckless fool! I can go without you dragging me. I still have a little bit of dignity left, not like you, you wimp!

The SON *looks at him defiantly. He opens the door to the living room and goes toward the hallway with the suitcase in his hand. The* GRANDFATHER *looks at him, and a shiver goes up his spine, as though in his mind, time had stopped for a few moments.*

GRANDFATHER: Wait! (*Pause.*) Son!

FATHER: (HE *stops.*) What?

GRANDFATHER: Why am I only taking one suitcase?

FATHER: It'll only be for a few months, or a few weeks.

GRANDFATHER: Are you sure?

FATHER: Of course.

GRANDFATHER: Where are you taking me?

FATHER: To a nice place outside the city.

GRANDFATHER: You're not tricking me?

FATHER: What's wrong? Why do you have that look on your face?

GRANDFATHER: And if I don't come back?

FATHER: (*Pause.*) Let's go.

GRANDFATHER: Shouldn't I take the photo album, too?, and the ones I have framed in the bedroom?, and the gifts your mother gave me? My cufflinks, my hats, and my ties?, and the box where I keep my cards?, and my mother's trunk?, and the pillows you bought me for my back?, and the canary?, who will feed him, who will take care of him, I should take him with me with the cage and everything, shouldn't I?

FATHER: I'll bring you everything little by little when I come visit you.

GRANDFATHER: Then tomorrow bring me . . .

FATHER: Dad. I won't come every day.

GRANDFATHER: Oh, no? Why not?

FATHER: (*Pause.*) It's too far. And besides I want to be . . .

GRANDFATHER: Here for her, right? (*Pause.*) Of course, of course. I understand. (HE *cries.*)

FATHER: What's wrong, now?

GRANDFATHER: (*Pause.*) Nothing . . . nothing. My god! . . . (*Pause.*) Let's go.

The SON *takes the suitcase and walks toward the door. The* GRANDFATHER *looks at him and has a very strange feeling.* HE *knows that* HE *will never return to this house. And that the image of the* SON *walking toward the door with the suitcase will survive . . . perhaps not with him. But perhaps it will. As though it were the memory of a future moment. This time, though, the* FATHER *(his* SON*) does not disappear with the suitcase through the door to the hallway, toward an interior bedroom . . .*

. . . But rather through the door to the hallway, toward the outside. Toward the disappeared and the forgotten.

The GRANDFATHER *feels as though his body were breaking inside.* HE *adopts a dignified pose and begins walking toward the door. At that moment, the* MOTHER *appears, very pale, through the door to the hallway.*

MOTHER: You hate me. Don't you?

The GRANDFATHER *stops at the hallway door and does not turn around.*

GRANDFATHER: What . . . do you want . . . me to say to you? (*Pause.* HE *turns slowly and looks at her.*) Yes.

Darkness.

SCENE 3

Twenty-first century.

In the bedroom, the DAUGHTER, *in bed.* SHE *has her eyes closed and her hands on her belly. At her side, sitting in a chair, reading, is the* SON. *In the living room, the* GRANDSON *with a laptop computer, and the* GRANDDAUGHTER, *sitting in front of him, with her arms crossed. While* THEY *talk,* HE *does not stop looking at the screen and typing all the while on the computer. The door that connects the two bedrooms is open.*

GRANDDAUGHTER: (*To the* GRANDSON.) Listen. I don't understand how you can be here playing Pac-Man with this piece of tin with your mother in there feeling the way she does.

GRANDSON: What's the matter? Your father is in there. She probably prefers his company to mine. She's seen too much of me. They haven't seen each other for forty years. They must have a lot to talk about, don't you think?

GRANDDAUGHTER: You're such a cynic.

GRANDSON: What?

GRANDDAUGHTER: You didn't even go with her to the hospital . . .

GRANDSON: She didn't ask me to.

GRANDDAUGHTER: It was horrible. When we got home, she vomited on the staircase landing. I thought she was going to die.

GRANDSON: It's the fifth time she's had these treatments. She survived the other four without a problem. She was bald within three days, and after a while, she had hair again. I'm sure she'll make it through this time. She's stronger than anyone.

GRANDDAUGHTER: She doesn't seem that way to me.

GRANDSON: Because you don't know her.

GRANDDAUGHTER: Maybe I know her better than you.

GRANDSON: Listen, leave me alone, don't you see I'm busy?

GRANDDAUGHTER: And your brothers?

GRANDSON: What?

GRANDDAUGHTER: Why aren't they here? Did you let them know?

GRANDSON: Why do I have to let them know?

GRANDDAUGHTER: Why do you think?

GRANDSON: Look, girl, I don't know where they are, understand?

GRANDDAUGHTER: You don't see them?

GRANDSON: Not for years.

GRANDDAUGHTER: Why?

GRANDSON: What difference does it make to you. Get out of here, do you mind?

GRANDDAUGHTER: I don't feel like it. Liar. Give me their phone numbers, I'll call them myself, if you don't want to do it.

GRANDSON: I don't have any numbers for them.

GRANDDAUGHTER: I don't believe you.

GRANDSON: Well, then don't believe me. And even if I had their numbers, what would you tell them?

GRANDDAUGHTER: The truth. That your mother is dying.

GRANDSON: And you think they would come?

GRANDDAUGHTER: Of course.

GRANDSON: Ha ha ha.

GRANDDAUGHTER: You think it's funny?

GRANDSON: You think they would respond by telling you: "oh, how terrible, we're on our way"? "your mother is dying" . . . ha ha ha. Look, girl, the phrase "I'm dying" I haven't stopped hearing every day of my life for the past ten years, when they removed her first tumor, get it? I don't deny I was affected by it the first time. I was nine years old, and she had just separated from my father, with all the shit that that entailed. I couldn't choose like my brothers, and the judge made me stay with her. A huge mess. Then, the damn cancer thing . . . But why the fuck am I explaining this to you? Get out of here.

GRANDDAUGHTER: Why did your brothers choose to go with him.

GRANDSON: Because my mother is a fucking whore.

GRANDDAUGHTER: Oh, really?

GRANDSON: Yes.

GRANDDAUGHTER: And your father is a saint? (*Pause.*) He used to hit her. Didn't he?

GRANDSON: I don't remember.

GRANDDAUGHTER: She told me about it the other day.

GRANDSON: Well, if she told you about it, then it must be true.

GRANDDAUGHTER: And you still defend him?

GRANDSON: Get out of here, damn it!

GRANDDAUGHTER: Why won't you look me in the eye?

GRANDSON: Because I don't fucking want to.

GRANDDAUGHTER: You're a fool. Your mother is in there, suffering, and you haven't even looked her in the eye or asked her how she's doing, if she needs anything . . .

GRANDSON: She doesn't need anything, and much less from me. And you don't know anything about it, girl, anything at all about my life to justify this Teresa of Calcutta act. My mother had me because that drunken, sadistic, abusive ass of a father of mine wouldn't let her have an abortion, understand? As long as I can remember, that's what I've heard throughout my entire life. So if I owe anything to anyone it's to him, even though he hasn't seen me for ten years and doesn't remember who I am, and even though when they lived together, he hit her, abused her, and gambled away her part of the inheritance of this fucking house when she sold it to that fu . . . to your father. If it were up to her, I wouldn't exist, girl. I have nothing to say to that woman. And the "I'm dying" routine, she's used it all these years to keep me from running away from her house and to blackmail me and treat me like a slave and take advantage of me. OK, now you know everything. Are you happy?

GRANDDAUGHTER: No.

GRANDSON: In fact, come to think of it, you people should understand perfectly, you know?

GRANDDAUGHTER: Why?

GRANDSON: From what she's told me, your father has also had his problems, ha ha ha . . . (HE *makes an obscene gesture.*)

GRANDDAUGHTER: And you think it's caused a single problem for me? Well no.

GRANDSON: That's what you think.

GRANDDAUGHTER: I said no.

GRANDSON: And that old fart, the little friend who lives with him, what do you call him? Mom, too?

GRANDDAUGHTER: I call him by his name. I call my mother Mom.

GRANDSON: And all four of you have dinner together once a week? You, Mom, Dad, and Dad's little boyfriend?

GRANDDAUGHTER: Not once a week, but once a month, we do.

GRANDSON: Oh, you're so modern . . . so proper, tolerant, and oh so European, yeah, right!

GRANDDAUGHTER: I don't know what your deal is. My mother suffered a very big depression when it happened. But with Dad, above all, they've always been friends . . .

GRANDSON: Right, because anything else . . . (HE *laughs.*)

GRANDDAUGHTER: . . . And she got over it. Because they talked. (*Pause.*) They talked for real. Without screams or ulterior motives, or saying one thing when you mean to say another. And my dad loves her. In his own way. But he loves her.

GRANDSON: I would have busted his face a long time ago, that faggot of a father. And his boyfriend's, too. Both of them.

GRANDDAUGHTER: Coming from you, I believe it.

GRANDSON: Don't exaggerate, girl. Even though you pretend to be so modern and tolerant and you are so kissy and friendly with the guy who your father gives it to up his ass and dirties his dick with his shit, although, since they're such old farts, they must just do it after they've seen some porno with some young guys giving each other blow jobs . . . , you don't fool me, girl, you're in the same situation as me.

GRANDDAUGHTER: At least he has someone to give it to up the ass. It must be a lot more fun than getting off every day in front of the computer screen, looking at tits on the internet. Now that is really sad.

GRANDSON: You're in exactly the same situation as me, girl.

GRANDDAUGHTER: In what situation?

GRANDSON: In hell. In no place. Where we were before we were born. Hell. Call it what you want. We exist by mistake. Neither you nor I should be here. If your father and my mother's lives hadn't been a complete fucking lie, neither of us would have been born. Son-of-a-bitch fucking lie. Ha ha ha. We wouldn't have been born.

GRANDDAUGHTER: You're crazy.

GRANDSON: Less than you are.

GRANDDAUGHTER: And scared to death.

GRANDSON: What?

GRANDDAUGHTER: Scared.

GRANDSON: Ha ha ha. Scared? Scared of what, girl?

GRANDDAUGHTER: Of being left without the only thing that you're sure of in your *fucking shit* of a life: your mother, even though you hate her. Because now, yes, it's true that she's dying.

GRANDSON: I won't be so lucky.

The GRANDDAUGHTER *touches a button and disconnects the computer.*

GRANDDAUGHTER: Now, that's it!

GRANDSON: Are you an imbecile or what!!!

GRANDDAUGHTER: Excuse me, but I think everything you've just said is a bit much!! Now, leave this damn thing alone and go in and see your mother and ask her how she's feeling.

GRANDSON: Stupid, everything I was doing has been deleted! Will you leave me alone for once and stop sticking your nose where it doesn't belong, girl?!

GRANDDAUGHTER: If you call me girl one more time I'll smash your face in.

GRANDSON: Go on, go suck the dick of the neighbor upstairs and let him stick his tongue up your ass and maybe you'll calm down.

The GRANDDAUGHTER *slaps him in the face. In the bedroom, the* DAUGHTER *opens her eyes and looks at her* BROTHER, *who stops reading and moves closer to her.*

SON: (*To the* PEOPLE *in the living room.*) Will you please be quiet? (HE *goes to close the door.*) What's going on in here? (*Silence.* HE *goes to close the door.*)

DAUGHTER: No, don't shut it! Let me . . .

Suddenly, the GRANDSON *and the* GRANDDAUGHTER, *in the living room, become the* SON *and the* DAUGHTER *in the twentieth century. In the bedroom, the twenty-first century, the* DAUGHTER *is looking in the direction of the living room. The* SON, *attentive to her needs, is not looking at the* YOUNG PEOPLE. *It is as though only* SHE *were reliving the scene. In the living room, the twentieth century, the* DAUGHTER *argues with the* SON.

DAUGHTER: You say I shouldn't stick my nose where it doesn't belong? He asked me to.

SON: That's a lie. You're the one who follows him around.

DAUGHTER: Because he likes me.

SON: No!

DAUGHTER: And what do you know?!

SON: You won't marry him!

DAUGHTER: Then go tell him. It was his idea.

SON: I don't believe it.

DAUGHTER: And why shouldn't I marry him?

SON: You would make a fool out of him. You think I haven't realized how you look at other guys on the street? And the neighbor upstairs?

DAUGHTER: What? What does that have to do with anything?

SON: You only want to marry him because it would be comfortable. And later on, you can do whatever the hell you want. And also because you'd have the perfect excuse to get away from this house without causing a scandal. But you don't love him. Once you're married, you'll cheat on him with the first fool that gives you a flower. (*Looking upstairs.*) With that son-of-a-bitch, for example . . .

DAUGHTER: You're an imbecile. Just because I'm nice to the neighbor, you think . . . ?

SON: Nice? Come on, girl, don't make me laugh. I see how you eat him alive with your eyes when he comes down the stairs. And he realizes it and plays the game. Careful he doesn't make you a victim of his conquests one of these days, because he's really on the hunt. Nice and charming but look at his family. A bunch of pigs, illiterate people, involved in corrupt businesses, you can only imagine where they got the money to be able to rent an apartment in this neighborhood. And on top of that, they come here to destroy our lives, they move into our houses without asking us and fuck around with our sisters! And you flirt with him every chance you get?! And you tell me what you'll do later, pregnant from a guy like that. The shame of the family.

DAUGHTER: Coming from Dad or Mom, I could care less. But you?!

SON: Stop seeing my friend. I don't want you to hurt him by making him think you like him when it's not true. And if you want to go to bed with the guy upstairs, do it, but far away from home. And when Mom is dead. That way, you'll save her the grief that would have killed her before it's time for her to go. Wait until she's dead, and then, get the hell away from here. There you can fuck whoever you want. But don't get us involved. And certainly not . . . him. He's *my* friend, do you understand? *Mine* . . . (*Pause.*) I . . . I . . . I have too much respect for him to let him be made a fool of for the rest of his life, having to put up with a whore like you in his house. And if he's hinted he wants to marry you, it's only because . . . because . . .

HE *cries. The* DAUGHTER *now understands.* SHE *goes over to her* BROTHER *and slaps him in the face.*

DAUGHTER: I swear to you on what you love most, on your soul mate, if that's what you want to call him, or maybe I should swear on his little ass?, that I won't say another word to you as long as I live. How do you think I feel, now, huh, imbecile?! The two of you were using me to . . . Disgusting. Not what the two of you might do when you're alone, no. What you've done to me. I'm sorry. From now on I no longer have a brother. (*Pause.*) Faggot.

Silence. One could hear a pin drop. The DAUGHTER *in the bedroom seems to have witnessed a scene from her own memory. We return to the twenty-first century. The* DAUGHTER *and* SON *in the living room are once again the* GRANDSON *and* GRANDDAUGHTER. *The* GRANDSON *types away at the computer at a frenetic pace, and the* GRANDDAUGHTER *does not take her eyes off him. In the bedroom, the* DAUGHTER *grabs her* BROTHER's *hand and looks into his eyes.*

SON: (*To the* DAUGHTER.) Do you want something?

The DAUGHTER *nods yes.* SHE *wants to say something and* SHE *cannot speak.* SHE *turns her head to one side and vomits violently. The* GRANDDAUGHTER *goes to the door of the bedroom. The* SON *sits up and goes to his sister's side.* HE *grabs her hand and her head and helps her finish vomiting.*

SON: (*To the* GRANDDAUGHTER.) Bring a bucket with water and a mop.

GRANDDAUGHTER: (*To the* GRANDSON.) Your mother just vomited. Don't drag your ass off the chair, no, it's not necessary. (SHE *exits through the door to the hallway.*)

DAUGHTER: Help me.

SON: What do you want?

DAUGHTER: To go to the bathroom to clean myself up. (*The* SON *helps her off the bed. Her clothing is covered in vomit.*) Does it disgust you?

SON: No.

DAUGHTER: You were always such a hypocrite.

SON: Don't say anything now, all right?

The SON *grabs the* DAUGHTER *and takes her into the living room. The* GRANDDAUGHTER *makes noise inside. The voice of the* MAID *is heard.*

MAID: (*From inside.*) What's going on?

GRANDDAUGHTER: (*From inside.*) I can't find the mop!

MAID: What?

GRANDDAUGHTER: Where the hell is the mop? I need it right now!

Clamor from the movement of things is heard, pots, buckets, etc., as they fall to the ground.

VOICE OF THE GRANDDAUGHTER: Shit! But what is all this? Who stores things in a closet like this?! Shit!

VOICE OF THE FATHER: Would you mind being quiet and not making noise, you're not letting me take my nap?!!

VOICE OF THE MAID: I'm coming!

VOICE OF THE FATHER: On top of it you condemn me to this lousy bedroom!

VOICE OF THE MAID: Be quiet and get back in bed, you pain!

The SON *and* DAUGHTER *are crossing the living room. The* SON *looks at the* GRANDSON, *who makes an effort to hide the impression caused by seeing his* MOTHER *in this state.*

SON: Do you want to accompany your mother to the bathroom while I fix all that?

DAUGHTER: I can go myself, let me. You're disgusted by me, but, on top of things, he hates me. (SHE *goes toward the* GRANDSON; SHE *puts her hand on his head and leans on him, crying.*) Right?

GRANDSON: If you say so . . .

DAUGHTER: (*To the* SON.) I'm a hysterical woman and I'm doing it to get attention. (*To the* GRANDSON.) That's what you think, right?

GRANDSON: If you really felt bad you wouldn't waste your energy insulting me.

DAUGHTER: And if this is the last thing I want to do in my damn life? Die insulting you?

SON: Enough, please!

The DAUGHTER *goes, all alone, toward the hallway door.* SHE *moves, leaving behind remains of vomit and excrement on the floor. The* SON *remains staring at the* GRANDSON.

GRANDSON: What's the matter.

SON: Is it so hard for you to treat her like a sick person? (*The* GRANDSON *gets up and goes to exit.*) Where are you going?

GRANDSON: What difference does it make to you?

SON: Don't talk to me that way, young man, I'm not your father, and I'm not your mother either.

GRANDSON: Ugh, I don't need this! (*Pause.*) What do you want, to teach me a lesson in morals? Go to hell!

The GRANDSON *gets up to leave and slips on a drop of the* MOTHER's *vomit and excrement. The* SON *looks at it and cracks a laugh. The* GRANDSON *gets up, however* HE *can, upset, with tears of rage in his eyes. The* GRANDDAUGHTER *appears with a bucket of water and a mop. Behind her, the* MAID.

GRANDSON: How disgusting. I hate you! I hate you all!

GRANDDAUGHTER: What are you doing, on the floor, now?

GRANDSON: Forget about me, OK?! (HE *exits running.*)

MAID: Where is he going? His mother is ill. Doesn't he have any sense of shame? (SHE *turns and looks at the* GRANDDAUGHTER. *Referring to the bucket and the mop.*) Give it to me; this is for me to do.

GRANDDAUGHTER: No. I'll do it.

MAID: (*Forcing with the bucket.*) No, no, go to her, she needs someone at her side, I'll clean up.

FATHER: (*Appearing at the door.*) Would you mind telling me who's in the bathroom, who won't let me in to take a piss? Have you also prohibited me from taking care of my own necessities or what?! What do you want, you want me to piss in my pants?!

SON: Dad, please go back to your room and leave us alone.

MAID: Will you give me the bucket already?

GRANDDAUGHTER: I said no! Go with grandpa and help him get back to bed.

SON: I'll do it. (*To the* FATHER.) Go on, get out of here. All we need now is for you . . . (SON *and* FATHER *exit.*)

MAID: What a house, my god, what a house. So little respect for each other, and what fools you are for not daring to speak with your hearts instead of obsessing so much about your ridiculous fears and stupidities. A bunch of egotistical, dishonest fools who should look each other in the eye more often and much less in the mirror. Like this boy, who just left, pretending to be oblivious. I'm willing to bet anyone he's crying on the street corner, covering his face, ashamed at himself for not being able to say a single nice word to his mother before she passes on to a better life, as if it were so difficult! My god . . . when one of my cousins writes me in a letter that she envies me for living here, I'm totally convinced that she has no idea what it's like. "What's Europe like?, Nice, isn't it?" Yes, nice, very nice. When you look at it from the outside, like a tourist. But inside . . . that's what it is. (SHE *lowers her head and points to the vomit and excrement.*)

GRANDDAUGHTER: Yes. (*Pause.*) Yes.

MAID: Excuse me . . .

GRANDDAUGHTER: Excuse us, please.

MAID: I'll clean that up. May I? (SHE *grabs the bucket again, but the* GRANDDAUGHTER *does not let her and resists.*) May . . . I?

GRANDDAUGHTER: As far as you're concerned, I'm also like them, aren't I?

MAID: I don't know. I don't know you well enough to . . . (*Pause.*) I don't know you well enough. (*Pause.*) But no. You're . . . (*Pause.*) Anyway, we'll talk about it later, right now I have to . . .

GRANDDAUGHTER: No. (*Pause.*) The two of us will take care of it together.

MAID: All right, let's go.

Between the GRANDDAUGHTER *and the* MAID, THEY *clean up what remains on the floor. Then* THEY *go into the bedroom and begin to mop. As they do so,* THEY *begin hearing noises coming from above. First running, then banging and screams, each time louder and more abundant. The* MAID *and the* GRANDDAUGHTER *stop mopping and look up toward the ceiling. The* DAUGHTER *enters the living room and goes to the bedroom. SHE has cleaned herself up a bit, but the expression on her face is not good. SHE also looks up. The screams become more intense. Without a doubt somebody is being beaten.*

DAUGHTER: What's going on?

MAID: Nothing good. I'm going to look out the window in my bedroom and see if I can see anything. (SHE *exits through the hallway door.*)

DAUGHTER: I can't take it anymore, for the love of god . . .

GRANDDAUGHTER: After, I'll go up and see . . .

DAUGHTER: Don't get involved. Those people are . . . I don't want them to hurt you

GRANDDAUGHTER: Should I help you into bed?

DAUGHTER: What is happening to us? . . .

Suddenly, we return to the twentieth century.

Now the DAUGHTER *is the* MOTHER, *and the* GRANDDAUGHTER *is the daughter. The banging and screaming upstairs continues, but the voices of the neighbors are much more present. The* FEMALE NEIGHBOR *is heard screaming, asking for help, crying, and begging. At times, there are terrible thumps against the floor and walls, accompanied by the bellowing and terrifying voice of the* FEMALE NEIGHBOR's HUSBAND, *who, completely drunk, is beating her. In the bedroom, the* MOTHER *and* DAUGHTER *listen, petrified by all the clamor and commotion.*

DAUGHTER: Should we do something?

MOTHER: We shouldn't get involved.

DAUGHTER: Where's Dad?

MOTHER: He went to the old people's home with your brother to bring some things to your grandfather.

DAUGHTER: I'll call the police.

MOTHER: No!

DAUGHTER: That man is crazy, Mom, can't you hear it?

MOTHER: It's their problem.

DAUGHTER: Their problem?! How can you be so lacking in compassion, for the love of god! He's beating her to death!

MOTHER: And what do you want, for him to kill us, too? (*The doorbell rings insistently, and the voice of the* BOY *is heard, asking for help. The* DAUGHTER *goes to open it.*) Don't open it!

The DAUGHTER *goes to open it.* SHE *enters immediately with the* BOY, *who is crying and sobbing. The* MOTHER *gets up, grabs her walking stick, and goes into the living room. Upon seeing the* BOY, SHE *is touched with emotion and changes her attitude.*

DAUGHTER: Calm down, calm down . . .

BOY: Help me, please . . .

DAUGHTER: What's going on?

BOY: My . . . father . . .

DAUGHTER: How is your mother?

BOY: She has blood on her . . . A lot of blood . . . please . . .

DAUGHTER: And your brother?

BOY: He's not there . . . Go get him, please . . .

DAUGHTER: Do you know where he is?

BOY: At the bar.

DAUGHTER: Which bar?

BOY: The one with the pool tables.

DAUGHTER: I'll go look for him.

MOTHER: You're not leaving here. (*To the* BOY.) It's all right, little one. You'll see how everything will get better. (SHE *goes toward the hallway, supporting herself with the walking stick.*)

DAUGHTER: Where are you going?

MOTHER: I'll be right back. Watch him.

The MOTHER *exits through the hallway door. The* BOY *starts crying again and the* DAUGHTER *does not know how to console him.*

BOY: (*After a pause.*) I hate them . . . I hate them . . . all . . . (*Pause.*) I hate . . . my . . . family.

Suddenly, upstairs, silence. The MOTHER *appears with the* FEMALE NEIGHBOR, *whose face is covered in blood and whose eyes are swollen.* SHE *is sobbing and muttering a series of incomprehensible words.*

MOTHER: Calm down, calm down, sit down here . . .

FEMALE NEIGHBOR: Close . . . close . . . you didn't close the door . . . !

The DAUGHTER *jumps in to help the* MOTHER *and the* FEMALE NEIGHBOR *The* BOY, *petrified, goes to a corner and crouches down.*

MOTHER: (*To the* DAUGHTER.) No, no. Close the door. And then call the police.

DAUGHTER: It's too late.

In effect, the female neighbor's HUSBAND *has just appeared at the door in a completely drunken state.* HE *looks around without comprehending anything.* HE *stutters some words, under his breath, in his own language, in a very low voice.* HE *moves toward his* WIFE, *who, instinctively, lets out a suffocated scream and covers her face with her hands. The* BOY *screams with full force. The* MOTHER *positions herself between the* HUSBAND *and the* FEMALE NEIGHBOR. *The* DAUGHTER *gazes at her* MOTHER *with a mixture of admiration and awe.*

MOTHER: Get out of my house immediately. We've already called the police. They're on their way.

HUSBAND: Huh?

The HUSBAND, *suddenly, seems as though* HE *is awakening from a dream.* HE *looks at his small son and goes toward him. The* BOY *becomes frightened and wants to step back, but the wall impedes him from doing so.*

MOTHER: You want to hurt him, too? Your son? (*Pause.*) Leave him alone.

HUSBAND: Huh? Don't . . .

MOTHER: Look at him, look at him. (SHE *grabs the* HUSBAND *by the arm. The* DAUGHTER *begins to move closer to her. The* MOTHER *gestures for her to leave her alone.*) Do you think he'll ever be able to forgive you, for what you've done? And it's not the first time, is it?

DAUGHTER: Mom, please . . .

FEMALE NEIGHBOR: Madame . . . leave him alone . . . he'll hurt you . . .

MOTHER: He won't hurt me. (*Looking into the* HUSBAND's *eyes and grabbing him firmly by the arm.*) Will you? (*Pause.*) Get out.

The HUSBAND *undoes himself from the* MOTHER's *grasp.* HE *wants to say something, but his bewildered state impedes him from doing so. It seems as though* HE *is about to have another attack of violent rage, but automatically, the* MOTHER *moves closer to him and gives him a strong slap in the face. The* HUSBAND *reacts and suddenly lets go of whatever anger* HE *was feeling.* HE *looks at his* WIFE *and* SON. *It seems as though* HE *is about to burst into tears and shrink in size. The* MOTHER *does not take her eyes off his. Upon seeing her gaze, the* HUSBAND *steps back, as though* HE *were frightened.* HE *exits. The* MOTHER, *suddenly, comes out of her defiant pose and begins to tremble with fear and apprehension. Silence.*

MOTHER: (*To the* DAUGHTER.) Close the door. (*The* DAUGHTER *closes the door and immediately returns.*) Call a doctor. While we wait, clean her wounds with peroxide.

DAUGHTER: And the police?

FEMALE NEIGHBOR: No!! No, not the police, no, please, they won't help a thing . . .

DAUGHTER: What?

FEMALE NEIGHBOR: It's not the first time . . . you must forgive him . . . he always gets like this when he drinks . . . but he's . . . he's . . . (SHE *stops speaking.*)

MOTHER: He's a good man. That's what you meant to say, isn't it?

FEMALE NEIGHBOR: He's my husband . . . my husband . . . until death do us part . . . God wanted it that way . . . You're a good woman, and god will help you for what you have done for me. Thank you, thank you.

DAUGHTER: But . . . ? You need to press charges . . .

MOTHER: (*To the* DAUGHTER.) Don't get involved. (*To the* NEIGHBOR.) God won't help me, Madame. Neither me nor you. He's abandoned us. And you don't have to thank me for anything. I didn't do it for you. I did it because it was a question of . . . decency. (SHE *looks at the* BOY. *Then her* DAUGHTER, *who cannot hide a strange sense of admiration for what* SHE *has just done. To the* DAUGHTER.) Cotton and peroxide, so her wounds don't get infected.

The DAUGHTER *exits through a door. The* FEMALE NEIGHBOR *cries,* SHE *looks over at her little* SON *curled up on the floor in a corner and extends her arms toward him, crying all the while, so that* HE *will come to her. The* BOY *gives his* MOTHER *a severe look and shakes his head no.*

MOTHER: (*To the* FEMALE NEIGHBOR.) Leave him alone. He's frightened.

The DAUGHTER *enters with a small first-aid kit.* SHE *goes over to the* FEMALE NEIGHBOR. SHE *saturates a piece of cotton with peroxide and cleans the remaining blood from the* FEMALE NEIGHBOR's *face. The* BOY *covers his face with his hands. The* MOTHER *moves closer to the* BOY. SHE *wants to calm him down.*

MOTHER: Will you come with me to the bedroom, little one?

The BOY *looks at her and nods yes.* HE *gets up and takes the* MOTHER'*s hand.* THEY *go toward the bedroom. Simultaneous dialogue.* MOTHER *and* BOY*, in the bedroom.* FEMALE NEIGHBOR *and* DAUGHTER*, in the living room.*

DAUGHTER: (*Passing the cotton over the wounds of the* FEMALE NEIGHBOR'*s face.*) Am I hurting you?

FEMALE NEIGHBOR: No. *He* hurt me.

MOTHER: (*To the* BOY.) Sit down next to me. You and I need to talk. (SHE *sits down on the bed and sits the* BOY *down next to her. Pause.*) How are things at school? Do you like it?

BOY: Yes.

MOTHER: Do you get good grades? (*The* BOY *nods yes.*) Good? Or very good?

BOY: Very good! I'm . . . first in the class! Anyway, one of the best!

MOTHER: Ah, and look at how you say it! (*Pause.*) No. You shouldn't do that.

BOY: Huh? What?

MOTHER: It doesn't matter if you're first or not. You should never say it. Even if it's true. You don't have to boast or brag. It doesn't look good. At all. You could hurt a lot of people who might not be as smart as you, but it's not their fault.

BOY: What does "boast or brag" mean?

MOTHER: What you just did. Act overly proud. How do you young people say it? "Show off"? (*Pause.*) Don't do it, that's all. Let the mediocre people do it. "I'm this, I'm that . . ." Bah. And what difference does it make? Does that make you happier? No, right? What makes people happy is being able to do something well. Whatever it may be. Wherever you may come from. A house, a child, a family, a job, a drawing, a bridge, a book, whatever. And enjoy yourself while you're doing it. And that's it. (*Pause.*) You won't do that again, will you? (*Pause.*) "I'm first in my class!" . . . Well, you have some hidden faults. Like everyone. You'll need to control them. You understand what I mean, right?

BOY: I don't know.

MOTHER: Yes. You've understood me. I know you have. I asked you if you get good grades, knowing perfectly well that you do. Just to see how you would react.

BOY: And how did you know? Did my mom tell you?

MOTHER: No. Because it's written all over you face.

BOY: What?

MOTHER: Well . . . just that. That . . . you're a good student. (*Pause.*) A smart boy.

DAUGHTER: Are you sure you don't want to press charges against your husband? I can help you. I have a friend. His father is a good lawyer . . .

FEMALE NEIGHBOR: It's over.

DAUGHTER: No, it's not. (*SHE wipes the cotton once again over her face.*) Has he been . . . hitting you for a long time?

FEMALE NEIGHBOR: Thank you.

DAUGHTER: Has he been hitting you for a long time?

FEMALE NEIGHBOR: You are all so nice.

DAUGHTER: Will you answer me? How long has he been hitting you?

FEMALE NEIGHBOR: Yes, yes.

DAUGHTER: Not "yes, yes," no. I'm asking you a question.

FEMALE NEIGHBOR: Don't call anyone. Not even the doctor, please. The last time, he asked me questions and I told him I had fallen . . .

DAUGHTER: Down the stairs, right?

FEMALE NEIGHBOR: Yes, yes.

DAUGHTER: Don't you realize that one of these days he may kill you?

FEMALE NEIGHBOR: Yes, yes. (*Standing up.*) I have to go. Can you let my son know?

DAUGHTER: You don't understand me, or you don't want to understand me?

FEMALE NEIGHBOR: Yes, yes. Let him know, please.

The DAUGHTER *stands up and begins to go toward the bedroom.*

MOTHER: (*To the* BOY.) Can I tell you . . . a secret?

BOY: Me? Why?

MOTHER: Because you're a good boy and I know you won't tell anyone. Right? (*The* BOY *nods his head yes.*) Very good. This is my secret: I would have liked very much to have a son like you.

BOY: And . . . and me to have a mother like you.

MOTHER: Ha, ha . . . I'm not so sure about that . . .

BOY: What I told you is also a secret.

MOTHER: So don't tell anyone else.

The MOTHER *kisses the boy on the forehead.* SHE *cannot contain her emotion and hugs him with all her strength just at the moment when the* DAUGHTER *enters through the door. Upon seeing the scene, the* DAUGHTER *remains paralyzed. The* MOTHER *sees the* DAUGHTER *and suddenly undoes the embrace.*

DAUGHTER: She wants to leave.

MOTHER: Fine. (SHE *looks at the boy.*) Will you think of me, sometime? (*The* BOY *looks at her and nods yes.*) Now, go on.

The BOY *separates himself from the* MOTHER *and goes toward the* DAUGHTER. *When* HE *reaches the door,* HE *turns and looks at her.*

BOY: My mother says you are very sick. You won't die, will you?

MOTHER: (*To the* BOY, *but looking at the* DAUGHTER.) Yes, I will die. But like you and like her and like everyone else. I might go a little bit earlier than I would like, but that's all.

BOY: But I don't want you to die.

MOTHER: Remember our secret. And don't tell it to anyone. Never. All right?

The BOY *nods yes and then looks at the* DAUGHTER. *The* DAUGHTER *is very tense, filled with mixed emotions toward her* MOTHER. *The* FEMALE NEIGHBOR *pokes her head in the doorway.*

FEMALE NEIGHBOR: You're really, very, very nice. Yes. (*Pause.*) Yes.

SHE *grabs the* BOY *by the hand,* THEY *cross the living room and exit. The* DAUGHTER *remains alone in the bedroom, looking at the* MOTHER, *who is lying in bed.* SHE *has a worried expression on her face. As though* SHE *cannot get out of her head the image of her* MOTHER *embracing that strange and foreign child with a tenderness that* SHE *does not remember having ever received from her.* SHE *cannot make sense of it. Perhaps many years will have to pass before* SHE *is able to . . .*

DAUGHTER: What secret? (*Pause.*) What secret? (*Pause. Yelling.*) What was the secret?!

MOTHER: It doesn't matter to you, and it doesn't interest you. And calm down, you seem awfully upset. (*Pause.*) Did she have any serious wounds?

DAUGHTER: No. But the gashes he gave her will be noticeable for months.

MOTHER: She'll say she slipped and fell down the stairs.

DAUGHTER: She already said it.

MOTHER: It doesn't matter. She'll say it again. And they'll advise her to go to the eye doctor, and no one will ask any questions. And for the entire week, at the hairdresser's, that's all they'll talk about. By the way, I won't be able to go there anymore. Look at these ends. I want you do go to my hairdresser and tell her . . .

The doorbell rings.

DAUGHTER: Again? Who is it now?

MOTHER: Don't open it.

The DAUGHTER *crosses the living room and opens the door. The* MOTHER *gets up and adjusts the bedroom door so as not to close it completely and spies on the scene through a crack in the doorway. In the living room, the* DAUGHTER *enters with the* MALE NEIGHBOR.

MALE NEIGHBOR: Where is my father? Where is he?! You didn't see where he went, which direction?

DAUGHTER: No. Will he be back?

MALE NEIGHBOR: Not now. He's too much of a coward. He didn't do it in front of me because he's scared of me, he can't go up against me anymore. He must've gone to his brother's house. He'll stay there for a few days and then come home like a battered dog. Like the other times. That son-of-a-bitch.

DAUGHTER: But . . . can't you press charges?

MALE NEIGHBOR: My mother won't let us.

DAUGHTER: And you can't convince her?

MALE NEIGHBOR: Me? That's her problem. She shouldn't have married him.

DAUGHTER: You have so little love for your parents . . . ?

MALE NEIGHBOR: And you for yours?

A very tense silence. The DAUGHTER *and* MALE NEIGHBOR *exchange a glance filled with desire. The* MOTHER, *behind the bedroom door, bears witness to the encounter, to the communion of these two characters. But . . . is it really the* MOTHER, *in the twentieth century, who is watching what is happening at this moment? Or . . . ?*

DAUGHTER: My father has never lifted a hand to my mother once, nor to my brother, nor to me. The screams and blows I may have received from my mother, perhaps I deserved them. Because, I'm a stupid, selfish girl, who's never known what she wants in life. I have a lot of problems with my parents. A lot. But don't compare them to yours, please. Your mother, a dumb slob, cowardly, and shitting with fear; your father, a drunken wife-beater; your sisters, just like your mother; and the little one, more shy and scared than a . . .

MALE NEIGHBOR: Don't mess with him, he's different.

DAUGHTER: Yes, maybe, but the rest . . . Really, don't compare your family to mine. I won't allow it.

MALE NEIGHBOR: Oh. I'm sorry. I thought you were the rebel in the family. The modern one.

DAUGHTER: I am.

MALE NEIGHBOR: Oh, really? Well, just now you seemed like one of those goody-two-shoes with the little socks and pigtails, who goes to parochial school and gets good grades in every class to please her mommy and daddy.

DAUGHTER: Oh, really? Well you're wrong. I fail almost every class.

MALE NEIGHBOR: But . . . what's your deal?

DAUGHTER: You don't believe me?

MALE NEIGHBOR: No.

DAUGHTER: Oh.

MALE NEIGHBOR: All right then . . . go ahead, prove it to me.

DAUGHTER: Prove it to you? Why?

MALE NEIGHBOR: Because I said so.

DAUGHTER: That's not an answer. Why do I have to prove it to you, huh? Give me one reason.

MALE NEIGHBOR: Because you're dying to.

DAUGHTER: I'm dying to what?

MALE NEIGHBOR: To prove it to me . . .

DAUGHTER: To prove . . . what, I can't even remember? Ha ha ha. (*Pause.*) What . . . ha ha ha . . . what do I have to prove to you, let's see?

MALE NEIGHBOR: Well . . . for example . . . how far . . . in your rebellion are you willing to go . . .

DAUGHTER: What do you think?

MALE NEIGHBOR: I don't know. I only know how far *I* am willing to go. About you, I know nothing . . .

DAUGHTER: That I'm a rebel, you know that.

MALE NEIGHBOR: And modern?

DAUGHTER: And you, how far are you willing to go? Come on, tell me if you think you know so much.

MALE NEIGHBOR: We weren't talking about me just now.

DAUGHTER: And why shouldn't we?

MALE NEIGHBOR: Because I'm sick of talking. Aren't you?

DAUGHTER: No. Never. I love to talk.

MALE NEIGHBOR: Me too. But not now.

DAUGHTER: Well if you don't want to talk . . . what then?

Their faces are already beginning to move within a dangerous distance. SHE *is becoming excited. The* MOTHER *(or is it the* MOTHER, *exactly . . . ?) in the bedroom has been experiencing, for a while, a kind of interior conflict. When the lips of the* DAUGHTER *and the* YOUNG MAN *move closer,* SHE *cannot stand it any longer and violently opens the door. The* YOUNG MAN *instinctively takes a step back, and the* DAUGHTER *lets out muffled scream.*

DAUGHTER: Oh!

MOTHER: (*Or* DAUGHTER?, *to the* DAUGHTER *[or to herself . . . ?]*) No!
    Don't do it. (*To the* MALE NEIGHBOR.) Get out. Get out of here.

A very tense silence. The YOUNG MAN *looks at the mother and disappears. Suddenly, the walls of the house seem to fade away for a few seconds. We see only the* TWO WOMEN, *face to face. Staring at each other. The space between them is instilled with magic, for a few instants. An entire lifetime—past, present and future—flows like the water of an enormous river, from one fleeting gaze to the next. Everything locked in a state of suspension. The* MOTHER *looks at the* DAUGHTER *and thinks: "do you understand now?" The* DAUGHTER *from the twenty-first century looks at herself forty years earlier, in the same position as the* MOTHER *at that time, with death already approaching, equally inevitable for her, and* SHE *appears frightened. Perhaps,* SHE *thinks: "yes, mother, I understand . . ." And it is now, forty years later, when* SHE, *too, is able to comprehend the transcendence of the moment.*

The magic is abruptly interrupted by some noises upstairs that immediately transport us into the twenty-first century. The DAUGHTER *and the* GRANDDAUGHTER *listen to the noise of the neighbors. Suddenly, silence. The* TWO WOMEN *remain in a state of anticipation. The doorbell rings.*

DAUGHTER: No! Don't do it!

GRANDDAUGHTER: Huh?

DAUGHTER: Don't open it.

GRANDDAUGHTER: Why?

DAUGHTER: I'm sure it's him.

GRANDDAUGHTER: Him, who?

DAUGHTER: Listen to me, don't open it!

GRANDDAUGHTER: You're delirious, auntie.

DAUGHTER: I'm not delirious. I still have several days left before I lose my mind. Several!

GRANDDAUGHTER: But you're very weak. Lie down in bed. It's all right.

The GRANDDAUGHTER *goes to open the apartment door. The* DAUGHTER *gets up to spy on the scene from behind the bedroom door. The* GRANDDAUGHTER *enters the living room with the* MALE NEIGHBOR. *But* HE *is also accompanied by the little* ORPHAN, *who carries a box in his hands.*

YOUNG MAN: I came with my . . . (HE *searches for the right word.*) . . . nephew, who's come to apologize for something bad that he did. (*Pause.*) Right?

ORPHAN: (*With the box in his hands.*) Yes. I came . . . I came to . . . to give this back . . .

DAUGHTER: But, what . . . ?

YOUNG MAN: He's not finished yet. (*Silence. To the* ORPHAN.) You're not finished, right?

ORPHAN: No, I'm not finished. I also . . . I also wanted to . . .

YOUNG MAN: . . . "say" . . .

ORPHAN: Say . . . (*It's difficult for him.*) . . . I'm sorry . . . (*Very quickly.*) . . . for taking such a nice box from your house without asking permission for me to take it, and now I'm giving it back to you, and I wanted to say I'm sorry, I'm sorry, I'm sorry. (HE *hands the box to the* GRANDDAUGHTER.)

GRANDDAUGHTER: But what is this? I don't understand anything, really . . .

YOUNG MAN: This . . . (*Pause.*) . . . nice little boy . . . is the son of some cousins of my father's sister-in-law. They died, and now he's living with me. I'm trying to teach him some manners, but it's difficult. He's been going to school, here, for years, and he was bounced around from one relative to the next until I finally got custody of him, legally and everything, but the memories of that place and his family situation still affect him a lot. He's been coming down to your place with the excuse that your grandfather is so nice, and he likes him a lot. And he's been stealing things. First, nothing special: papers, a spoon, a bottle of Coke, but last time . . . he took this.

ORPHAN: I didn't steal it, I just took it so I could paint it again, since it's very old, and then I can give it to the grandfather as a gift!

YOUNG MAN: But how do you expect to give it to him as a gift if it's already his? Come on, just keep quiet!

ORPHAN: But if I paint it, the picture is mine and that's the gift!

YOUNG MAN: Quiet!

GRANDDAUGHTER: But . . . But . . . it's really OK that he took it . . . (SHE *laughs.*) . . . It's an old cigar box and no one uses it anymore . . . (*To the* BOY.) Keep it, I'm giving it to you. And you can paint it with pictures that you invent yourself, if you like. I'm sure it'll look a lot nicer.

The GRANDDAUGHTER *gives him the box, still laughing. The* BOY *grabs the box and goes over to a corner, caressing it as though it were some sort of treasure. Suddenly, the cheerful gaze of the* GRANDDAUGHTER *meets that of the* MALE NEIGHBOR. *There are sparks . . . But, unexpectedly, a dark cloud passes by her face and SHE adopts a glacial, anguish-ridden expression.*

GRANDDAUGHTER: What was that noise?

YOUNG MAN: Huh?

GRANDDAUGHTER: Those horrible noises that you were making a little while ago, upstairs.

YOUNG MAN: I don't understand.

GRANDDAUGHTER: Did you hit him?

YOUNG MAN: Huh?

GRANDDAUGHTER: The boy. I heard a lot of shrieking. Did you hit him? (SHE *moves rapidly toward the boy and grabs him.*) Listen to me, listen up and tell me the truth. Did he hit you?

ORPHAN: No.

GRANDDAUGHTER: No?

ORPHAN: No, really.

The GRANDDAUGHTER *examines the* BOY'*s skin and arms.*

YOUNG MAN: What are you doing? Leave him alone! You're scaring him! Hey! HEY!!! (*The* GRANDDAUGHTER, *instinctively, slaps him in the face.* HE *grabs her firmly by the arms.*) I've never hit anyone. Do you understand? Anyone, not even when I was a boy and used to play on the street. Would you mind not accusing me just because of the prejudices you have about us? Who just hit who?! (HE *lets go of her abruptly. To the* BOY.) Let's go. (HE *goes toward the door.*)

GRANDDAUGHTER: You've never hit anyone? Well, from the way you just grabbed my arm no one would ever know it.

The YOUNG MAN *stops in his tracks and looks at her.* HE *then looks at the* ORPHAN *and whispers something in his ear, indicating for him to leave them alone. The* ORPHAN *smiles at the* GRANDDAUGHTER *and nods his head as if to thank her for the box and exits, nervous and happy. The* YOUNG MAN *and the* GRANDDAUGHTER *are standing, face-to-face. The* DAUGHTER *continues to spy on them with increasing fascination.*

YOUNG MAN: Listen, I know that at your house you're not going through a very good time. From what the boy tells me. He talks a lot about your family whenever he comes back from his visits. About the grandfather and the nice woman who lives with him and who also keeps house. About you and the other woman who arrived a few days ago with the son who's nasty to everyone, except the grandfather. About your entire strange, sick family. And the boy is fascinated. Of course, it's the element of difference. I swear, I haven't been hitting him. I was only teaching him a lesson. I had to do it. You don't know what he's like, this kid. The noises you heard were because he was running around the house like he was having some kind of nervous attack, filled with rage, and he was behaving like a wild animal, throwing chairs on the floor, kicking the furniture, flinging things in my face. *He* was the one who was making all the noise and who was hitting me. NOT ME. I swear. He told you I didn't hit him. He told you in all honesty, right? (*Pause.*) Right? Did he tell you, yes or no?

GRANDDAUGHTER: Yes, he told me.

YOUNG MAN: And you don't believe him? (*Pause.*) Or me, either? Why? (*Pause.*) Because I wasn't born here?, in your country?, in your land?, in your city?, in your nice little bourgeois neighborhood?, in your house, in your own bed? *You* just smacked *me* in the face, look, I should have some kind of mark here because it stings like hell, look! (HE *moves his face close to hers. Pause.*) And what are you accusing me of, let's see, what? Of being violent? Of mistreating a minor? You know what? (HE *moves his face even closer to hers and says in a low, very sensual voice.*) Go to hell.

Their lips are about to meet. Unexpectedly, the YOUNG MAN *begins to weep in silence. The* GRANDDAUGHTER *caresses his cheek, softly and moves her lips closer to his. The* DAUGHTER, *at the other end of the bedroom, can no longer contain herself and opens the door.*

DAUGHTER: (*In a low voice.*) No! Don't do it!

But the GRANDDAUGHTER *and the* YOUNG MAN *neither hear nor see her. The attraction between them is overpowering. Now, neither the* DAUGHTER's *pleading, nor anything in the world, can stop it. The* DAUGHTER *remains still and witnesses, frightened and moved, the physical consummation of her niece's amorous attraction to the* MALE NEIGHBOR. *(Or, of her own attraction to the* MAN *who not long after would become her husband . . . ?) The kiss between the* GRANDDAUGHTER *and the* YOUNG MAN *is very sensual and passionate. The* DAUGHTER *watches them and senses a brutal rupture within her own body. The scene that* SHE *is observing has nothing romantic about it; rather, it is crude and sordid. The contact between the* TWO YOUNG PEOPLE, *so sudden and passionate, awkward and lewd. Without taking her eyes off them,* SHE *takes a few steps back, enters the bedroom, closes the door, and lets herself drop to the floor, slowly, with her back propped up against the door.* SHE *remains crouched on the floor, with a strange glow in her eyes.* SHE *doesn't cry.*

Darkness.

SCENE 4

We are in the twentieth and the twenty-first century. Indistinguishably.

Time and characters are intermingled. The walls, floor, ceiling, doors, and furniture of the house seem out of focus. Or liquid. In the bedroom, the MOTHER-DAUGHTER *lies in agony. At her side, seated, the* FATHER-SON, *holds her hand. In the living room, the* SON-GRANDSON *is seated, staring off into the void. The* DAUGHTER-GRANDDAUGHTER *is separated from him, nibbling on her nails, and peering at him out of the corner of her eye.*

MOTHER-DAUGHTER: *(To the* FATHER-SON, *very weak, opening her eyes.)*
    How many days have I been like this?

FATHER-SON: Shhh.

MOTHER-DAUGHTER: Tell me.

FATHER-SON: Don't speak . . .

MOTHER-DAUGHTER: Two days? Three? A week? A year? I've lost all
    track of time.

FATHER-SON: Why do you want to know? What difference does it make?

MOTHER-DAUGHTER: How long have I gone without leaving this bed?

FATHER-SON: Four weeks.

MOTHER-DAUGHTER: So many? (*Pause. SHE looks at her* HUSBAND-BROTHER.) My legs aren't responding. I can't, can I? (*The* FATHER-SON *does not say anything.*) There, that's it. (*Pause.*) Right? (*Pause.*) Don't lie to me, please. (*The* FATHER-SON *lowers his head, trying to contain his tears.*) It's OK. I'm fine. I don't know what dosage you've given me, but I'm fine. I mean, nothing hurts me.

SHE *is overcome by a violent and very unpleasant coughing fit. Unintentionally,* SHE *wets the bed. The* FATHER-SON *reacts immediately. First sitting down at her side, then grabbing her sturdily by the shoulders and grasping her hands when* SHE *beckons to him. Once* SHE *has calmed down, the* FATHER-SON *looks at the sheets and moves slowly away from her.* HE *removes with a cloth the remaining vomit and mucus from her chin.*

FATHER-SON: Better? (SHE *nods yes.*) I'm going to get help.

MOTHER DAUGHTER: No. Wait. Give me some water.

The FATHER-SON *picks up a glass and gives her some water, in small sips. The* MOTHER-DAUGHTER *closes her eyes. In the living room, the* DAUGHTER-GRANDDAUGHTER *moves toward the* SON-GRANDSON.

DAUGHTER-GRANDDAUGHTER: Don't you want to go in? (*The* SON-GRANDSON *shakes his head no.*) Me neither.

SON-GRANDSON: I can't take all this. I don't know what we're doing here. What are we waiting for? I can't stand it. (HE *cries.* HE *gets up.* HE *goes to exit.*) Enough!

DAUGHTER-GRANDDAUGHTER: (*Grabbing him.*) You think if you leave, it will get better?

SON-GRANDSON: Let me go, damn it! (HE *exits, quickly.*)

DAUGHTER-GRANDDAUGHTER: Where are you going?! And, if
   something happens and you're not here . . . ?

SHE *does not obtain a response. The* GIRL *is anxious. After a few seconds, the*
NEIGHBOR-YOUNG MAN *appears in the living room.*

MALE NEIGHBOR-YOUNG MAN: I ran into him in the doorway and he
   didn't even say hello.

DAUGHTER-GRANDDAUGHTER: He's very upset. Even though he may
   not want to recognize it. She'll leave him with an unbearable emptiness.
   (*Pause.*) He's frightened.

MALE NEIGHBOR-YOUNG MAN: And you?

DAUGHTER-GRANDDAUGHTER: Me? (*Pause.*) I don't know. (SHE *lowers
   her head, very pale.*)

MALE NEIGHBOR-YOUNG MAN: (*Moving closer to her.*) But I'm here . . .

DAUGHTER-GRANDDAUGHTER: Yeah.

MALE NEIGHBOR-YOUNG MAN: . . . and with me, you'll be better off.

DAUGHTER-GRANDDAUGHTER: Oh, really?

MALE NEIGHBOR-YOUNG MAN: Really.

HE *grabs her by the arms.* SHE *is trembling like a leaf. Meanwhile, in the bedroom, the*
MOTHER-DAUGHTER *grabs the* FATHER-SON *by the arm and pulls him
closer.*

MOTHER-DAUGHTER: Listen. (*Pause.*) What have we done wrong?

FATHER-SON: Huh?

MOTHER-DAUGHTER: What have I done wrong?

FATHER-SON: I don't understand you.

MOTHER-DAUGHTER: I was supposed to ask you to forgive me for something, but now I can't remember what it was. Tell me what I've done wrong . . .

FATHER-SON: Nothing.

MOTHER-DAUGHTER: (*Looking toward the living room.*) Who's there, over there? (*SHE wants to sit up to look toward the door.*) Who's there?

FATHER-SON: Be quiet, please. And don't move, it's worse . . .

MOTHER-DAUGHTER: (*Suddenly, grave.*) Who . . . are they?

Suddenly, a gust of air traverses the house, from the living room to the bedroom. The MOTHER-DAUGHTER *makes an effort to breathe. SHE grabs the* FATHER *nervously and tries to look toward the doorway. In the living room, the* DAUGHTER-GRANDDAUGHTER *and the* MALE NEIGHBOR-YOUNG MAN *are gazing into each other's eyes. Pause.*

DAUGHTER-GRANDDAUGHTER: I'm pregnant.

Everything comes to an abrupt halt. The MOTHER-DAUGHTER *looks at the* FATHER-SON *with a new expression on her face, as if, suddenly,* SHE *were plainly conscious of the situation of doubling that is at work. The* FATHER-SON *does not seem to understand her expression and desperately grabs her hand.*

MOTHER-DAUGHTER: (*To the* FATHER-SON.) Who are you?

Silence. In the living room, the MALE NEIGHBOR-YOUNG MAN *is left bewildered by what the* DAUGHTER-GRANDDAUGHTER *has just said to him.*

DAUGHTER-GRANDDAUGHTER: (*To the* MALE NEIGHBOR-YOUNG MAN, *serious.*) What will we do?

MALE NEIGHBOR-YOUNG MAN: Now is not the time to talk.

DAUGHTER-GRANDDAUGHTER: When, then?

MALE NEIGHBOR-YOUNG MAN: (*After a pause.*) Later.

DAUGHTER-GRANDDAUGHTER: Later? (*Slowly, as though* SHE *were mesmerized.*) Forty years from now, perhaps?

MALE NEIGHBOR-YOUNG MAN: No. Later. When . . . (HE *looks at the door.*)

The MOTHER-DAUGHTER *clutches the* FATHER-SON *with greater force.*

MOTHER-DAUGHTER: And me? . . . Who am I?

FATHER-SON: I don't understand you.

MOTHER-DAUGHTER: Which one of them . . . ? Who am I?

FATHER-SON: Be quiet, please. Everything's OK. I'm here with you. I won't leave you.

In the living room, the MALE NEIGHBOR-YOUNG MAN *moves closer to the* DAUGHTER-GRANDDAUGHTER. *At first,* SHE *expresses rejection. Her gaze takes off toward the bedroom, where the* MOTHER-DAUGHTER *lies, delirious, in an unbearable and resounding state of agony. The death (of her aunt, of her mother, of herself some years from now . . . ?) on the other side of the door . . . In front of her . . . what is there? Who is this* MAN *who is embracing her and whom* SHE *is attracted to with such intensity that it almost makes her want to kill him?* SHE *feels powerless and attempts to make it apparent to him by the expression on her face.*

DAUGHTER-GRANDDAUGHTER: (*To the* MALE NEIGHBOR-YOUNG MAN.) It's OK. We'll talk about it . . . later.

In the bedroom, the MOTHER-DAUGHTER *is having difficulty breathing.*

MOTHER-DAUGHTER: I'm very tired.

FATHER-SON: Then close your eyes and go to sleep.

MOTHER-DAUGHTER: Should I? Sleep? I feel unclean. I smell awful. (*Very weak.*) You don't mind seeing me like this?

FATHER-SON: No. (HE *gives her a delicate kiss on the forehead.*) Go to sleep.

In the living room, the MALE NEIGHBOR-YOUNG *man moves his lips closer to hers and kisses her. A brief kiss, followed by an infinite embrace. In the bedroom, the* MOTHER-DAUGHTER *seems to see their embrace perfectly. Everything fades away, once again. But this time, with an overwhelming force. We only see, floating magically in the space, the* DAUGHTER-GRANDDAUGHTER, *embracing the* MALE NEIGHBOR-YOUNG MAN *and forming a single body, and the* MOTHER-DAUGHTER *dying, accompanied by her* HUSBAND-BROTHER *and looking in the direction of the* YOUNG COUPLE. *Suddenly, the* MOTHER-DAUGHTER *lets out a piercing desperate sound, the result of not being able to breathe for several seconds. The* FATHER-SON *does not know what to do. HE can only hold her tightly. With an unpleasant hoarseness, a strong and raucous sound, a grunt filled with liquid that emerges in spasms from her lungs and suddenly inundates her mouth, SHE stops breathing definitively. SHE remains with her eyes open and with an indescribable expression. A deep exhalation, filled with gases and viscous fluids, abruptly emerges from her body. And SHE remains definitively immobile. Immediately, the* FATHER-SON *leaves her side, retires to a corner, and begins to vomit. All of a sudden, the* DAUGHTER-GRANDDAUGHTER, *in the arms of the* MALE NEIGHBOR-YOUNG MAN, *looks toward the door. SHE leaves him and makes her way slowly toward the bedroom.*

The open eyes of the MOTHER-DAUGHTER *seem to focus abruptly on the eyes of the* DAUGHTER-GRANDDAUGHTER. *The gaze that travels from one woman to the other, unexpectedly, seems to materialize, beyond the limits of time and space. An imperceptible ray of light magically unites the eyes of one with those of the other. Three women and eight different gazes in only two bodies:*

The dead MOTHER *sees her* DAUGHTER, *in the twentieth century; and the* DAUGHTER *sees her* MOTHER . . .

The dead DAUGHTER *sees her* NIECE, *in the twenty-first century; and the* NIECE *sees her* AUNT . . .

But also . . .

The dead MOTHER, *in the twentieth century, sees her* GRANDDAUGHTER *in the twenty-first century; and the* GRANDDAUGHTER *sees the* GRANDMOTHER *that* SHE *never met . . .*

And, still more . . .

The dead DAUGHTER *in the twenty-first century sees herself, forty years earlier, reencountering herself at the most decisive moment in her life; and the* DAUGHTER *in the twentieth century sees herself and watches her own death, in the same place that the* MOTHER, *forty years later . . . And, then, all of them seem to understand a mystery that up until then was hidden or impenetrable.*

Immediately, the weak glow, which unites their eyes and makes their gazes materialize, intensifies abruptly to such a degree that it invades the entire space within tenths of a second and ends by bursting with a brutal explosion of absolutely blinding luminosity.

As if, surprisingly, we were somehow witnessing the origin of the universe.

And suddenly, darkness.

EPILOGUE

Twenty-first century.

We see the walls, the doors, the ceiling, the windows of the apartment. But it is completely empty.

There are only two chairs or stools and a package. HE *has just moved in. The* MAN *finds himself face to face with the* SON, *at a distance.*

SON: That's it. (*Pause.*) It's all yours.

MAN: Yes.

SON: Well. If you have any problems with the place, you can call me at this
       number . . . (HE *moves closer and hands him a card.*)

MAN: (HE *takes it.*) If I have a problem, I'll take care of it, don't worry.

SON: Of course. (*Pause.*) Well, good-bye. (*Pause.*) Oh, why didn't you want to
       tell me who you were, the day that we saw each other again for the first
       time? Were you afraid I wouldn't sell you the house?

MAN: Yes.

SON: Well, you were wrong. (*Pause.*) I recognized you from the very first instant. (*Pause.*) I'm happy to have seen you again.

A silence. The SON *gives him a serious look,* HE *picks up a last package and exits without looking at the apartment.* HE *leaves the door open. The* MAN *looks around the house.* HE *does not know what to think.* HE *sits down. The* ORPHAN *enters, silently.* HE *carries the cigar box in his hands, painted with vibrant colors.*

ORPHAN: Have they left, already?

MAN: Huh? Oh . . . Yes. Who are you?

ORPHAN: I live upstairs. I came to bring this to the grandfather. It's his. Well, she told me that she would give it to me to keep, but . . .

MAN: She?

ORPHAN: Yes, she, his . . . his . . . granddaughter. My uncle's . . . friend. But I don't want it. It belongs to the grandfather.

MAN: Then, give it to her, and she'll give it to him.

ORPHAN: She left some days ago. The day after that woman died. And she didn't even say good-bye to me.

MAN: And you don't know where she went?

ORPHAN: My uncle said very far.

MAN: And they're not friends anymore? (*The* ORPHAN *shrugs his shoulders and makes an expression that leads him to believe that* HE *does not know.*) Will she come back? (*The* ORPHAN *makes another expression, as if to say: "I don't think so."*) Well. So, what should we do?

ORPHAN: I don't know. I have to give this to the grandfather. And I don't know how I'll be able to, if I don't know where he is.

MAN: I know his son, and he can tell me.

ORPHAN: Oh, then you can give it to him!

MAN: But maybe he won't want it.

ORPHAN: Of course he will. The grandfather still sneaks a cigar sometimes
. . . (HE *laughs. The* MAN *laughs, too.*) Here. It's full, see? If you want to
smoke one. (HE *opens the box slightly.*) Real Cubans. I bought them.

MAN: You?

The MAN *looks at him in disbelief.* HE *moves toward the* MAN *and gives him the box.
The* MAN *looks at it.* HE *opens it.* HE *is fascinated. It is as though an entire lifetime
were inside it.* HE *puts his hand inside.* HE *takes out a cigar and sniffs it.* HE *roles it in
his fingers.*

MAN: I don't like cigars, I'm sorry. But they do smell good. (HE *looks at the
box and returns the cigar to its place.*) Did you paint it? (*The* ORPHAN *nods yes.*)
How . . . *cool!* Much nicer than it was.

ORPHAN: Oh, you've seen it before? (*Pause.*) How come? Did you also live
here?

MAN: No. (*Pause.*) But I'm going to live here now.

ORPHAN: Oh. Then we'll see each other.

MAN: Yes. (*Pause.*) Wait. Just a minute. Come here, closer. Sit down next to
me. You and I should talk. We're going to be neighbors from now on.

ORPHAN: I promise I won't play the music too loud!

MAN: No, that's not what I want to talk about. Come here.

A silence. The ORPHAN *looks at him.* HE *smiles and moves closer to him. The* MAN
*feels a chill. The memory of a very similar moment already lived suddenly impregnates the
emptiness of the walls. But it does not bother him; on the contrary,* HE *begins to laugh.*

ORPHAN: Why are you laughing? What have I done?

MAN: Nothing. Come here, sit. (*The* BOY *does. Pause.*) How are things at school? Do you like it?

ORPHAN: Yes.

MOTHER: Do you get good grades? (*The* BOY *nods yes.*) Good? Or very good?

ORPHAN: Very good! I'm . . . one of the best in the class!

Pause. The MAN *looks amazed. Suddenly, the boy, who is nervous, looks at him differently.*

ORPHAN: Can I tell you a secret? (*Pause.*) It's a lie! I'm not doing well at all! It's an awful school! It's filled with stupid kids who stare at me! And I'm mad that I have to go there!! It's awful and I hate it. (*Pause.*) I hate it, I hate it, I hate it . . . ! ! !

The ORPHAN *runs out. The* MAN, *unexpectedly, breaks into laughter. But then,* HE *has another thought and remains very serious.*

The end.

Barcelona, Map of Shadows

Lluïsa Cunillé

Lluïsa Cunillé

Photo: courtesy of the playwright

Lluïsa Cunillé and *Barcelona, Map of Shadows*

After participating for three years in the dramaturgy seminars conducted by José Sanchis Sinistera at the Sala Beckett, Lluïsa Cunillé began a prolific career in playwriting and active collaboration with other Catalan theatre professionals. Her first play, *Rodeo* (*Roundabout*), was staged in 1992 at the Mercat de les Flors and was awarded the Calderón de la Barca Prize; the same year she co-founded the Hongaresa Theatre Company with Paco Zarzoso and Lola López. The numerous plays that soon followed established Cunillé as one of the most individual voices in contemporary Catalan and European theatre. Works such as *Libración* (*Libration*) and *La cita* (*The Meeting*) show an unmistakeable kinship in their minimalist dialogue and sense of menace or enigma. Cunillé has habitually identified her characters only generically (Woman 1, Woman 2, etc.), which contributes to the air of mystery surrounding them. Although critics acknowledged the unconventional appeal of her theatre, audiences have been polarized in their reception, some simply mystified and others awaiting the next play with anticipation. The playwright herself has remained aloof from journalistic or academic analysis of her work, while being closely involved in the staging and interpretation of her plays.

Responding to a commission from director Toni Casares in 2004 to create a work in which the city of Barcelona figured prominently, Cunillé wrote *Barcelona, mapa d'ombres* (*Barcelona, Map of Shadows*), an atypical script in which character development is fundamental and lives are poignantly intertwined in Barcelona's unique ambience and geography. The production at the Sala Beckett received warm critical praise and the work received the City of Barcelona Prize for best play of the season. Two years later it was filmed by Catalan director Ventura Pons, with a cast headed by famed actors Núria Espert, Rosa Maria Sardà, and Josep M. Pou. In 2006 Cunillé wrote another surprisingly atypical play, revealing a decided bent for ironic humor in a postmodern sequel to Ionesco's absurdist classic *The Bald Soprano*. This twenty-first century continuation of the lives of Ionesco's characters is a scintillating romp in which the title character does indeed command the stage, albeit in a McDonald's restaurant. *La cantant calba al McDonald's* (*The Bald Soprano at McDonald's*) had its premiere at the Teatre Lliure in January 2006 in a double-bill with a revival of the Ionesco play. Her Pirandellian "re-reading" of the classic Spanish zarzuela *El dúo de la Africana*, in collaboration with director Xavier Alberti, proved to be one of the most acclaimed productions of the Teatre Lliure's 2006-2007 season. Cunillé was named playwright-in-residence at the Teatre Lliure in 2007, and new works will be staged yearly over the next four seasons. The first of these productions, *Après moi, le deluge*, focuses on a meeting in Kinshasa, Congo, between a western businessman and an African who communicates from off stage through an on-stage woman interpreter. Critics were virtually unanimous in their praise for the play's timely theme and Cunillé's distinctive structuring.

Although set in the present, *Barcelona, Map of Shadows* encompasses lifetimes, and in a coda flashes back to the sad day in 1939 when Barcelona was occupied by the troops of the Franco-led uprising against the Spanish Republic. It was the day that initiated a thirty-five year period in which Catalan language and culture would be suppressed and a shadow would indeed fall over the vibrant city. In its five self-contained scenes, the play focuses on the relationships of a retired doorman (He) from the Liceu Opera House and his wife (She) as they inform three lodgers (Woman, Young Man, and Foreign Woman) in their large apartment that they must leave the rooms that have become their homes. The eviction will bring uncertainty as they lose the one secure refuge in their lives.

The elderly man is dying of cancer and his cherished memories are from his life at the historic theatre. He retells his favorite anecdote—assisting the famed opera singer Maria Callas retrieve her pet dog after it strayed onto the Rambla. The story varies in the retelling, and how much may be fiction is uncertain. As the play progresses, we also learn that he is a cross-dresser and that during his years at the Liceu he frequented the wardrobe room to dress up in operatic attire, changing gender, identity, and time in the process.

All of the action takes place during a radio broadcast of Puccini's *La Bohème*, and the duration of the play and the opera broadcast are virtually identical. In the most poignant moment in the play (Scene 2), the Wife recites tenderly in Italian a passage from the final act of the opera to a young boarder, a mediocre soccer player, whose life already seems hopelessly failed. In the fourth scene, a new character from outside the confines of the apartment appears as the wife sits in the shadows listening to the final act of the opera broadcast. It is the Doctor, the wife's younger gay brother and, unknown to the world, also her son. While this element of incest may seem more appropriate to Greek tragedy, Cunillé makes it a credible part of her tapestry of Barcelona society. Although the play is rich in intertextuality and allusions to specific places, cultural artifacts, and events in Barcelona, it remains totally accessible to non-Catalan audiences accustomed to the multifaceted, allusion-filled plays of Tom Stoppard. The characters may have only generic identifications, but they become increasingly individual as their stories unfold. Cunillé has observed them with notable clarity, defining their personal conflicts, revealing their pasts, and deftly creating personal identity in their varied manners of speech and deportment. *Barcelona, Map of Shadows* proved to be a culminating point in Lluïsa Cunillé's career, and it seems likely to endure as one of her finest and most defining achievements.

MPH

Núria Espert in *Barcelona, un mapa* (2007), Ventura Pon's film version of *Barcelona, Map of Shadows*.
Photo: courtesy of Ventura Pons

Barcelona, mapa de sombras, Teatro Valle-Inclán, Madrid.

Photo: courtesy of the Centro Dramático Nacional

BARCELONA, MAP OF SHADOWS

by

Lluïsa Cunillé

Translated by

Marion Peter Holt

TRANSLATOR'S NOTE:

As its title suggests, this play is about a city and its culture as well as six characters who inhabit it. There are numerous references to places in Barcelona, some more familiar than others. It is essential that these names not be Hispanicized: Liceu Opera House (not Liceo), Passeig de Gràcia (not Paseo), etc. For a few of the less familiar places such as the MACBA and the Estació de França I have substituted generic descriptions but placed the specific names in brackets for the benefit of directors who may chose to retain them. The action of the play takes places during a radio broadcast of a peformance of Puccini's *La Bohème*, beginning early in Act I of the opera and ending as the final chords meld with the remembered radio speech made by the commander of the Nationalist forces to the defeated city on 26 January 1939. It is essential that the actors be familiar with the music and story of *La Bohème* since the progress of the broadcast parallels the unfolding of the play's five scenes. The actress who portrays "SHE" must also fully understand the meaning of Mimí's words when SHE sings them as a kind of lullaby to the YOUNG MAN in Scene 2. This is probably the most poignant moment in the play (as it is in the opera). In Lluïsa Cunillé's original text, Scenes 1, 2, 4, and 5 are in Catalan, but Scene 3 is in Spanish because the FOREIGN WOMAN is a Latin American immigrant who is not yet completely fluent in Catalan. The difference in her background is, I believe, apparent in her dialogue in English and it could be counterproductive to impose an accent to underscore that difference. I have left the song of the Barcelona soccer team, Barça, in Catalan, since it is the YOUNG MAN'S "aria," so to speak, and transcends its basic function for fans of the soccer team. The remembered speech of the victorious Francoist general that ends the play has been translated, with the pomposity and irony intact.

CHARACTERS

HE

SHE

WOMAN

YOUNG MAN

FOREIGN WOMAN

DOCTOR

1

An untidy room of an old apartment in Barcelona's Eixample. It's night.

WOMAN: Have you come to ask me to leave again?

HE: This time I came to beg you to go.

WOMAN: If only I could give you the Sagrada Familia or the Cathedral made of toothpicks, something as impressive as your patience. I've only been a persistent person, persistent but not patient.

HE: You don't owe me anything. We're at peace.

WOMAN: Don't speak as if you had no other choice besides living in the Eixample, where souls are mean and small as cat-holes.

HE: I'm ill, and I can't let myself hide it or pretend what I don't feel.

WOMAN: Then you can let yourself be sincere. How wonderful and how awful at the same time. What could I give you that's really adequate . . . (*Searches in a box.*) I have it. I'll give you this photograph.

HE: Who is it? I don't recognize him.

WOMAN: His name is Juan Rubio Macías, and when they took this picture, he was dancing over the body of his mother, whom he'd previously murdered.

HE: Why?

WOMAN: Why? Madness, clear thinking, who knows. It happened long ago. It's for you.

HE: I don't want it.

WOMAN: Don't refuse my gift. It's the last thing of value I have.

HE: Will you leave then?

WOMAN: I've always left before they threw me out. The fact is I'm losing my touch.

HE: Can I sit down?

WOMAN: No chair is what it seems. As you know.

HE *sits down.*

HE: And what about your students?

WOMAN: They're not what they seem either. Actually they're all a bunch of vampires who suck my blood, and once they've gorged themselves and sucked the last drop, they leave me and never come back.

HE: Why is it that you and I have never really talked?

WOMAN: People only really talk when they have nothing to lose, or when they're about to die, and they usually say things of little interest.

HE: Lately I've been dreaming about war. Especially about the day war ends.

WOMAN: Do wars ever end? They overlap but they never end.

HE: Then we're really talking today?

WOMAN: Certainly we are.

HE: Why today?

WOMAN: Maybe because I have nothing left to lose and you are dying.

HE: Do you feel sorry for me?

WOMAN: No. And what about you, do you feel sorry for me?

HE: No.

WOMAN: This moment calls for music. Let's see if we have any luck.

The WOMAN *turns on the radio and we hear the first act of Puccini's* La Bohème *already in progress.*

HE: *La Bohème.*

WOMAN: You know it?

HE: I worked for thirty-five years as a doorman at the Liceu Opera House. I retired the year it burned.

WOMAN: Then you must know who really burned it.

HE: I wasn't there that day.

WOMAN: Isn't it a bit strange that no one was there that day?

HE: I don't know. I don't like to look back.

WOMAN; You don't like to look back and I, on the other hand, don't like to look ahead.

HE: Is that why you're hiding?

WOMAN: Who told you I'm hiding?

HE: You seldom go out, and when you do it's at night.

WOMAN: All cities are more bearable at night than in daytime. However, in Barcelona only tourists and delinquents are in the streets at night. Some nights I stop in front of the apartments my son built and I look at the windows where there's light and the blinds are up, and I watch the people who live inside. I don't know any architect, including my son, who has had the courage to do something like that. My son's specialty is chamfers, so he has no choice other than working in Barcelona, but when he leaves work he flees as quickly as he can from the city before nightfall.

Pause.

HE: I can't close my eyes at night. I'm afraid of dying in my sleep. (*Pause. The* WOMAN *turns off the radio.*) Why did you turn it off.

WOMAN: Nobody should be talking when Callas is singing.

HE: Did you know that I met Callas? It was the same year I started working at the Liceu. An admirer had given her a puppy, and apparently it got loose on the Ramblas. When she got to the Liceu, all upset, she made me promise I'd find it for her. I spent more than two hours up and down the Ramblas looking for the puppy but I didn't find it. So when I got back to the Liceu I shut myself up in a workroom until Callas had left.

WOMAN: You didn't hear her sing?

HE: I didn't want her to see me. I've never been able to disappoint anyone.

WOMAN: And what about me? Doesn't it bother you at all to throw me out after all this time?

HE: My wife and I want to be alone these last months I have left. And we've decided not to rent any rooms to anyone else.

WOMAN: If I go now, I'll lose the last students I have left.

HE: You'll find others.

WOMAN: I don't think so. People have lost faith in the French language as much as they have in God. If it occurs to anyone to pray now they do it in English. Didn't you know that?

HE: I stopped believing in God during the war, when I heard the bombs exploding. The more ruins there were the less I believed in God. Praying would be hypocritical now.

WOMAN: "Ô mon semblable, ô mon maître, je te maudis!"

HE: What did you say?

WOMAN: It's a verse by a French poet.

HE: So why don't you give English classes?

WOMAN: Because I don't know enough, and I don't like it either. English is the ideal language for writing telegrams. French is something totally different. I even gave French classes in bars, when I had a lot of students and bars were a slice of life, and not just a place where people went to drink and pass the time. Those bars started a lot of people on the road to ruin. Bars today are utterly inoffensive.

HE: I'm sorry I never smoked or drank. Never to have done something I could blame my illness on now. I can't even blame someone else, because most of the people I knew have already died or live far away. I don't have anyone left except my wife.

WOMAN: Do you love her?

HE: My wife? Yes, a lot.

WOMAN: And you must also love Barcelona.

HE: Yes, I've always lived here.

WOMAN: "Un uomo singulare e universale."

HE: What?

WOMAN: Women are never called unique or universal. It's assumed that women must be loved simply because they're women.

HE: The truth is my wife scared me a bit when I first met her.

WOMAN: Scared you?

HE: At least I'm happy to die before her. I wouldn't know what to do all by myself. (*Pause.*) Pardon, but it's only that the doctor told me I'm not to hold in farts and belches. It's the first time a doctor said something like that, and it's also the first time I've gone to a psychiatrist. I used to go once a month to Social Security but since they only prescribed sleeping pills I stopped going.

WOMAN: How long did each session with the psychiatrist last?

HE: About five minutes, and I've never taken the pills he prescribed.

WOMAN: If you like, I can give you the address of a good psychiatrist I know.

HE: No need.

WOMAN: I assure you he's very good. He saved me a few times.

HE: Is he very expensive?

WOMAN: All psychiatrists are expensive. But I don't know if he has his office at the same place. We lost contact quite a while ago. Like so many others he also began in antipsychiatry and ended up in the most orthodox psychiatry, but he's very good.

HE: Thanks, but if he's very expensive I wouldn't be able to pay him, even less so now that we'll be alone and will only have the money from my pension.

WOMAN: Are you sure?

HE: About what?

WOMAN: That you don't want the psychiatrist's address.

HE: No. I only need for you to tell me for sure the day you'll be leaving. I have to know it tonight.

WOMAN: It won't be easy for me to find a room like this.

HE: There are many people who rent rooms.

WOMAN: But not one where they'll also let me give classes. And this time I want an elevator so it won't be so hard when I have to go out and, besides, my students will have one excuse less for not learning French.

HE: Then why don't you rent an apartment?

WOMAN: Can you imagine this kind of mess in an entire apartment? No, one room is quite enough for me.

HE: Have you always lived in rooms?

WOMAN: And the home of friends. But I stopped living there when they began to have grandchildren.

HE: And you can't go to your son's house?

WOMAN: My son and I can't bear each other for more than an hour. With him I committed the error of being completely sincere from childhood and I didn't hide my weaknesses from him. He's never forgiven me for it. Since he was a child I'd take him to walk with me around Barcelona. Those days I liked to photograph abandoned factories and empty lots. Maybe that's why wide, empty spaces cause him to panic like all bad architects. The only thing we both have always agreed on is that every time we walk in front of the Sagrada Familia we feel an urge to scream.

HE: You don't like the Sagrada Familia?

WOMAN: Perhaps the question should be phrased in reverse. Does the Sagrada Familia like us? If I were the Sagrada Familia I would also start screaming seeing all that's around me, and unable to run away from it.

HE: You could move from Barcelona.

WOMAN: I did spend long periods away, but I always came back. And now nothing can spare me the final transformation, the one that will make Barcelona definitively a city interchangeable with any other self-satisfied western capital.

Pause.

HE: If you want I can help you get all this together.

WOMAN: No need. I'd thought I'd throw it all out.

HE: The magazines too?

WOMAN: Whenever I move I say I'm throwing everything out and I end up saving it all.

HE *picks up a magazine and reads the cover:* Nasti de Plasti.

WOMAN: Do you want it?

HE: It's very old.

WOMAN; The older they are the less the words inside resemble what people do today.

HE: I've never collected anything. There's never been anything I liked enough to keep it for long. My wife has kept a diary since childhood. Shortly after we married she told me I could read it if I wished, but I told her there wasn't any need to. She's never mentioned it again.

WOMAN: I wrote a book a long time ago.

HE: Are you a writer?

WOMAN: In those days a lot of people wrote a book, only one, and then we spent years telling everyone what an effort it had been.

HE: And what was it, a novel?

WOMAN: Yes, a novel absolutely unclassifiable today like all the ideas in it. I wanted to be an author of ideas and not of feelings, but people have always been partial to feelings more than ideas, and fundamentally they're right, ideas sooner or later become dated, feelings on the other hand, however crude they may be, never go out of date.

HE: What was it about?

WOMAN: Novels of ideas are like detective novels or science fiction, they can't be explained in a few words.

HE: And don't you write any longer?

WOMAN: My best quality has always been to retreat in time.

HE: I could give you a plot if you wish . . .

WOMAN: For a novel?

HE: Yes. But you'd have to promise me not to publish it while my wife's alive.

WOMAN: It's an interesting proposition.

HE: You promise then?

WOMAN: If the promise of someone like me is of any use to you, I promise.

Pause.

HE: Forget it, it's silly. It wouldn't be of any use to you.

WOMAN: What?

HE: My idea.

WOMAN: The best ideas are useless but they can grow to be quite lovely.

HE: No, it's all the same.

WOMAN: Then you won't tell me?

HE: No.

WOMAN: Pity. It's been a long time since anyone told me anything interesting. All the people I know are too busy for anything interesting to happen to them.

HE: What about your students?

WOMAN: They're the busiest of all. They want to learn French just to be able to read travel guides and menus of expensive restaurants in London or New York.

HE: You shouldn't scold them.

WOMAN: Scold them?

HE: It can be heard in the dining room sometimes.

WOMAN: What can be heard?

HE: The way you scold them.

WOMAN: I don't scold them, we are having a disagreement. Some are the children of old friends of mine, from the time we escaped to Paris with hardly any money in our pockets but a lot of ideas in our heads. Now their children have a lot of money in their pockets and few ideas in their heads. They all want me to teach them right off how to pronounce "merde" in French, but they have no interest in learning the appropriate moments to say it, and that's why we have disagreements. You can only shout "merde" when you're caught in traffic or drop oil on your necktie or when you step in dog shit.

HE: I don't know any foreign language and I've never travelled very far.

WOMAN: I envy you.

HE: Me? Why?

WOMAN: Because you fart whenever you please.

HE: If I weren't sick I wouldn't do it.

WOMAN: Why don't you go with me tonight?

HE: Where?

WOMAN: For a stroll.

HE: A stroll?

WOMAN: For a while.

HE: No, it's very late.

WOMAN: We can go now.

HE: No. I can't.

WOMAN: But you'll go another day, won't you?

HE: Why do you want me to go for a stroll?

WOMAN: No special reason. You find reasons for strolling while you're strolling.

HE: I walk very slowly now and I tire quickly. We couldn't go very far.

WOMAN: It doesn't matter.

HE: Besides, it's hard for me to climb stairs, and I don't want to leave my wife alone at night.

WOMAN: "Voici le soir charmant, ami du criminel." Everything I think or say lately seems to be what I've already heard or read some place.

HE: I've hardly read anything. I dropped out of school to go to work.

WOMAN: At the Liceu?

HE: No. I went to the Liceu later.

WOMAN: In all those years you must have heard many operas.

HE: Bits and pieces. I never heard one complete.

WOMAN: You recognized *La Bohème* right away.

HE: I didn't recognize it. My wife told me they were broadcasting it tonight. She likes opera a lot.

WOMAN: And you don't?

HE: When we met I told her I liked it and once we were married I didn't dare tell her the truth. And now it's too late, right?

WOMAN: Too late?

HE: To tell her the truth.

WOMAN: I don't know. I've never bitten my tongue in time, which is why no one ever invites me out anymore.

HE: My wife and I don't go out much either. We no longer fancy going out.

WOMAN: From time to time some old friend who's just got a divorce calls me or some other one who's feeling nostalgic for the past. But I don't see them because I don't want to end up feeling sorry for them, or even worse, they end up feeling sorry for me. My son is like them more and more, it's as if I were seeing him ten years from now. Then I try to imagine myself ten years from now, and frankly I can't. I try to imagine myself in some concrete spot or walking along some street but I'm not anywhere.

Pause.

HE: I haven't always lived in the Eixample, I used to live in Poblenou. My father was from Murcia, and a crane crushed his head while he was working. It's strange because during the war he didn't want us to go to the shelters. My mother and I had to hide under the stairs.

Pause.

WOMAN: For years I had a room near the cemetery, but when they started building the Vila Olímpica I moved to the Raval, I stayed there a good while until the speculators turned up again and the joggers. They arrive almost at the same time. It's inevitable. Before, when someone ran down the street you could be sure he had a good reason. The police were after him or he was late for his wedding. The act of running has lost all transcendence. (*Pause. Turns off the radio. Pause.*) Fortunately, Callas isn't singing.

Pause.

HE: Then will you leave tomorrow?

WOMAN: So soon?

HE: Monday then?

WOMAN: Monday.

HE: It can't be after Monday.

WOMAN: "Avalanche, veux-tu m'emporter dans ta chute?"

HE: I'll throw everything out if you wish, but don't forget to tell your students not to come back here.

WOMAN: I think I'll have them all take a stroll and I'll spend a while just translating cookbooks and do-it-yourself guides. There's no better way of becoming reconciled to the world than cooking and hobbies.

HE: Why don't you ask some of your old friends for work?

WOMAN: I've worked for editor friends, business friends, and even politician friends. All of them are well-off now and ready to give me work in memory of old times or to sooth their consciences, which add up to approximately the same thing. But after a while I've left them and gone back to French classes. Basically it's vanity, I like myself more when I'm teaching French. It's a matter of being photogenic. It's like Juan Rubio Macías, who was surely never so photogenic as in this photograph, dancing naked over his mother's corpse.

HE: (*Looking at the photograph.*) Why is he completely naked?

WOMAN: Maybe to feel more authentic.

HE: More authentic?

WOMAN: Isn't that what stripping nude is all about?

HE: I don't know.

WOMAN: Haven't you ever felt the need to undress so that people would really look at you?

HE: I don't think so. (*Long pause.*) Sometimes at the Liceu as a young man, I disguised myself in secret. I liked to go to the wardrobe room and try on clothes. There were all kinds of costumes, from every period.

WOMAN: Did you do it alone?

HE: If anyone had seen me, they'd have fired me on the spot.

WOMAN: So no one has ever seen you in disguise?

HE: No.

WOMAN: Would you have liked for them to see you?

HE: I don't think so.

Pause. Lights down.

2

A very tidy room in the same apartment. The same night. The YOUNG MAN *is stretched out on the bed and is only wearing walking shorts.* SHE *is standing. There is a television turned on without the sound. There is a pistol on the night table.*

SHE: You're not going out tonight?

YOUNG MAN: No.

SHE: You weren't training today?

YOUNG MAN: I hurt my knee

SHE: What's wrong with it?

YOUNG MAN: Monday they have to make an x-ray.

SHE: You won't be able to play on Sunday?

YOUNG MAN: No.

SHE: How did you do it?

YOUNG MAN: Running, by myself.

Pause.

SHE: Which knee is it?

YOUNG MAN: This one.

SHE: Does it hurt?

YOUNG MAN: It bothers me.

SHE: Have you told them at work?

YOUNG MAN: Not yet.

SHE: And have you told them you're moving on Monday?

YOUNG MAN: I won't be able to go on Monday. I'll have to wait a few days. Until I find someone to lend a hand.

SHE: Then which day will you go?

YOUNG MAN: I don't know. Next Friday maybe.

SHE: Maybe?

YOUNG MAN: It takes a lot of going up and down stairs.

Pause.

SHE: It makes me nervous to know there's a pistol in my house.

YOUNG MAN: There are no bullets in it, it's not loaded.

SHE: It's all the same. (*The* YOUNG MAN *opens the drawer of the night table and puts the pistol in it without closing it. Pause.*) Won't someone miss that pistol?

YOUNG MAN: I'll return it tomorrow.

SHE: Aren't you afraid they'll fire you?

YOUNG MAN: I'll surely leave before they throw me out. They're very short of help but they don't pay very well.

Pause.

SHE: Why don't you call your wife?

YOUNG MAN: My wife?

SHE: To help you . . . with moving.

YOUNG MAN: It's been a while since I've talked with my wife. They've told me she's going out with another guy now.

SHE: Really?

YOUNG MAN: He drives a taxi. I'd intended to take his cab one night, have him drive me all over Barcelona, and when time came to pay I'd take out the pistol and give him a little scare.

SHE: And did you intend to do it tonight?

YOUNG MAN: No. Not tonight.

Pause.

SHE: (*Looking at the television.*) And the sound?

YOUNG MAN: I turned it off.

Pause.

SHE: Barça's playing tonight, right?

YOUNG MAN: It's an old game. I can't stand the voices of the sportcasters. They don't know a thing about soccer.

Pause.

SHE: I don't see you.

YOUNG MAN: Who?

SHE: Aren't you playing?

YOUNG MAN: I never got to play on Barça's first team.

SHE: My husband and I said we'd go see you play one day and we still haven't gone. (*Pause.*) You play on the Europa team, right?

YOUNG MAN: No. I play with Jupiter now.

SHE: Jupiter. Now I'll remember. (*Pause. SHE sits in a chair.*) You keep your room very tidy. I've never seen such a tidy room. (*Pause.*) Did you hear all the commotion this afternoon? When it's not Gaudí year it's Dalí year, or whoever. All that noise makes me nervous . . . (*Pause.*) Do you know that I've never climbed all the way up in the Sagrada Familia? The fact is for years I haven't gone to a museum or an exposition the way I used to. When I was young the museums were empty, there were no guards. Anyone could grab a painting or a piece of sculpture and carry it home.

YOUNG MAN: Most of the museums are still empty.

SHE: Really?

YOUNG MAN: People would rather steal in the shopping malls. That's where everyone is now.

SHE: Do you work in a shopping mall now?

YOUNG MAN: I go from one place to another.

SHE: Do you have a lot of work?

YOUNG MAN: We can't keep up with the demand for security guards. As the rich get richer they're afraid someone will rob them of all they can't spend.

Pause.

SHE: Have you seen my husband tonight? He went out and still hasn't come back.

YOUNG MAN: We spoke a while.

SHE: And what did he tell you?

YOUNG MAN: He asked me when I was leaving. He asked me three times.

SHE: Did he tell you that you have to go?

YOUNG MAN: No.

Pause.

SHE: I went to the bullfights this afternoon.

YOUNG MAN: Huh?

SHE: When I was a girl I went out with a boy who liked bullfights and he used to take me. At home I didn't tell them I was going to bullfights because they wouldn't have let me. And in fact I'd never gone again until today.

SHE: Did you enjoy it?

SHE: Not at all. I left before the last fight. (*Pause.*) Doesn't it happen to you, you've stopped doing something or seeing someone with no reason at all? All of a sudden? It's like losing your place in a book you're reading and then putting it aside and never picking it up again. Sometimes I think if I'd had sisters I'd be able to watch what they're doing and that way I'd know if I'd made a big mistake or not.

YOUNG MAN: I've never missed having brothers and sisters.

SHE: My father wanted a son desperately and when he saw that what he had was a daughter he ignored me and took refuge in his factory. For years I wanted to be a boy for him, and when I accepted the fact that I'd never be one, I only wished someone would set fire to his factory and my father would finally pay me a little attention. And then my brother was born.

Pause.

YOUNG MAN: And your mother? Did she give you any attention?

SHE: My mother was utterly hopeless. When she got married, she erased her personality. She would walk through the house afraid of stepping on the tiles or making the wall paper fall off. She did everything my father said and I soon lost respect for her.

YOUNG MAN: People only respect what they're afraid of.

SHE: I can also respect what I admire.

YOUNG MAN: Did you admire your father?

SHE: No. I loved him and that was it.

YOUNG MAN: I've only admired a few soccer players and now not even them. I find soccer more and more boring.

SHE: So do you watch it?

YOUNG MAN: It's the only thing I understand. I know when they're doing good or doing bad. Who's good or hopeless.

SHE: Is this game good?

YOUNG MAN: No, it's lousy. Besides, they've cut the dead spots when nothing's happening. I wish I could do the same with my life, don't you?

SHE: Do what . . . ?

YOUNG MAN: Cut out the times when nothing interesting is happening. But then almost nothing would be left.

Pause.

SHE: How old are you now?

YOUNG MAN: Me? Thirty-one.

SHE: I'm sixty-seven, and I'd like to be thirty years younger. Thirty-seven is the ideal age for a woman. One's not too young or too old either. It's still not too late to change, to do new things.

YOUNG MAN: And what's the ideal age for a man?

SHE: I don't know. I'd have to be a man to know that.

YOUNG MAN: I'd say fifteen.

SHE: So young?

YOUNG MAN: At least that was my ideal age.

SHE: You're still too young to know.

Pause.

YOUNG MAN: (*Looking at the TV.*) That was offside. Didn't you see it?

SHE: What's offside? (*Pause.*) What's . . . ?

YOUNG MAN: It's when the most advanced attacking player, at the moment a team member passes the ball, finds himself nearer the rival goalkeeper than the last defender. It's a little difficult to understand.

SHE: No. I get it.

YOUNG MAN: Really?

SHE: Yes.

YOUNG MAN: I believe it's the first time you've asked me anything about soccer.

SHE: What you ought to do is look for a job you really like and try to keep it.

YOUNG MAN: I always think that someone else can do what I'm doing better than me.

SHE: There's always someone who's better than all of us.

YOUNG MAN: In soccer when there's someone better than you he's the one who plays and you stay on the bench.

SHE: But soccer's not life.

YOUNG MAN: That's the same thing my wife used to say. No, she said it in reverse, she said life wasn't soccer. But for sure she's with someone better than me now.

SHE: You mean the cab driver?

YOUNG MAN: Who knows, maybe you've found someone better than me for this room and that's why you're throwing me out.

SHE: I told you why you have to go.

YOUNG MAN: I could stay in the front room, the one by the door, and you wouldn't even see me.

SHE: If you have to hide from us there's no point in your living here.

YOUNG MAN: You can pretend I'm not here.

SHE: I can't pretend I don't see you. (*Pause.* SHE *looks at the TV.*) Who won?

YOUNG MAN: In these old games Barça always wins.

SHE: My father was a Barça supporter. He went to the playing field almost every Sunday. Even after he had lost everything he didn't stop going. In that respect it was as if nothing had happened.

YOUNG MAN: (*Sings the Barça team song softly.*) "Tot el camp, és un clam. Som la gent blaugrana, tant se val d'on venim, si del sud o del nord. Ara estem d'acord, estem d'acord, una bandera ens agermana. Blaugrana al vent, un crit valent, tenim un nom al cel companys: Barça, Barça, Barça."

SHE: Why don't you change the channel?

YOUNG MAN: What do you want to see?

SHE: I can't stay, I have things to do. (*SHE gets up.*)

YOUNG MAN: Stay a while longer . . .

SHE: It's late.

YOUNG MAN: Just a bit . . .

SHE: Wouldn't you rather go to sleep?

YOUNG MAN: I'm not sleepy.

SHE: I still have to eat . . .

YOUNG MAN: Please . . . stay. Just a moment.

SHE: All right. I'll stay a moment.

Pause.

YOUNG MAN: Aren't you going to sit down?

SHE *has a moment of doubt and then sits down again. Pause.*

SHE: And the sound?

YOUNG MAN: When the commercials are over, I'll turn it up.

Long pause.

SHE: My husband is very late.

YOUNG MAN: Are you afraid he won't come back?

SHE: Why shouldn't he come back?

YOUNG MAN: I don't know.

SHE: We were supposed to listen to the opera together.

YOUNG MAN: What opera?

SHE: The one they broadcast on the radio. It's already started. Callas is singing. (*Pause.*) Did you know that my husband and I met at the opera? Once when it was raining, at the Liceu entrance, my cousin and I were waiting to catch a taxi to go home, and we looked so bored to him that he began to tell us how he had met Callas, the only time she came to sing at the Liceu. Apparently, a puppy she was carrying got loose on the Rambla and he found it for her. That's the first time we spoke, but we didn't really get acquainted until two or three years later.

YOUNG MAN: Your husband asked me to show him how to load the pistol.

SHE: Today?

YOUNG MAN: Yes.

SHE: And did you show him?

YOUNG MAN: I told him I didn't have any bullets.

SHE: He's more afraid of guns than I am. I'm more used to them.

YOUNG MAN: Have you ever fired a pistol?

SHE: Never, never . . . But my grandfather had a pistol. He bought himself one during the labor uprisings. He was afraid that the workers would lynch him, or something of the sort. In short, the pistol ended up at the back of a wardrobe, and my cousins and I would sneak it out to play with.

YOUNG MAN: Do you know how to load a pistol?

SHE: No, and I don't want to know. And what I'll do is lock it up until it leaves here.

SHE *gets up, goes over to the open drawer. It appears that* SHE *is going to take the pistol, but what* SHE *finally does is close the drawer. Pause.*

YOUNG MAN: Nobody wants a pistol in plain sight but everybody wants to have their money protected so's not a penny gets lost between the armored truck and the vault at the bank.

SHE: I didn't know you went to banks too.

YOUNG MAN: You can tolerate a nightstick in your house but a pistol's too much for you. Your husband's not so hypocritical.

SHE: My husband's ill. It's better to leave him alone.

YOUNG MAN: When you rented the room to me I thought you only wanted to have a guard in the house, someone to keep you from being afraid at night.

SHE: You're hardly ever home anymore. You're always out.

YOUNG MAN: At the company they think I live at my mother's house. They don't like for their guards to live alone or have marital problems.

SHE: You told them you lived at your mother's house?

YOUNG MAN: At first you treated me as if I were your son. You were even ready to waste a Sunday morning to come see me play. But it's better you haven't seen me because from the second division on down nobody really plays soccer. What we all do is kick the ball or the legs of the other team the same way, with the same mean temper.

SHE: I don't know a thing about soccer, and I don't like it either. Until you came to live here I didn't know anyone who liked it, not even my father. A lot of Sundays when he said he was going to see Barça play what he really did was go find himself a whore. At home we all knew it. Going to see Barça meant going to see a whore.

YOUNG MAN: Maybe that's where your husband has gone tonight.

SHE *slaps the* YOUNG MAN. *Pause.*

SHE: Did I hurt you? (*The* YOUNG MAN *takes her hand and lifts it to his lips and then to his cheek. Pause.*) I can't be your mother. I had a daughter.

YOUNG MAN: And where is she?

SHE: She died in the most stupid way. A bus ran over her on the Passeig de Gràcia a long time ago, one of those buses that ran in the wrong direction against the traffic and killed so many people. My husband almost lost his mind. He's never gone back to the spot and doesn't know that those buses are running in the wrong direction again.

Pause.

YOUNG MAN: This is her room?

SHE: My daughter's? Yes, it was. But now it's a room for renters, and next week it will be a guest room, only a room for guests. (*Pause.* SHE *withdraws her hand.*) Now it's better for you to go to sleep.

YOUNG MAN: I can't.

SHE: Does your knee hurt?

YOUNG MAN: I have insomnia.

SHE: Do you want a sleeping pill? My husband has them by the handful.

YOUNG MAN: Don't go yet. Stay a bit longer, until I fall asleep.

SHE: I'll stay until you close your eyes.

YOUNG MAN: Stay here, beside me.

SHE *sits on the bed.*

SHE: Lie back. (*The* YOUNG MAN *lies back and* SHE *turns off the TV.*)

YOUNG MAN: Don't turn it off.

SHE: Do you sleep with the television on?

YOUNG MAN: Yes. (SHE *turns the TV on again*) Do you know what the worst part about being on the night shift is?

SHE: What . . . ?

YOUNG MAN: The last hour before your shift ends. It's the longest hour and the one when you hear the strangest sounds.

SHE: What kind of sounds?

YOUNG MAN: The rest of the night you hear normal sounds but in that last hour you hear things that are never heard, as if in that hour your ears can hear everything. Even people.

SHE: What people?

YOUNG MAN: Voices of people . . . who aren't there.

SHE: Sometimes I hear voices too, but I don't listen to them. When I hear them, I start singing.

YOUNG MAN: Singing?

Pause.

SHE: Close your eyes.

YOUNG MAN: I can't.

SHE: Yes you can.

YOUNG MAN: But don't go yet.

SHE: I'm not going. (*The* YOUNG MAN *closes his eyes. Pause.* SHE *sings a passage from the fourth act of Puccini's* La Bohème.) "Sono andati? Fingevo di dormire/ perché volli con te sola restare./ Ho tante cose che ti voglio dire./ O una sola ma grande come el mare,/ come il mare profunda ed infinita . . . / Sei il mio amor . . . e tutta la mia vita."

Long pause. The YOUNG MAN *still has his eyes closed.* SHE *gets up slowly, opens the table drawer without making a sound and takes the pistol firmly in her hand. Lights down.*

3

A very small room. It is the same night. HE *is asleep seated in an armchair. In his lap* HE *has the photograph the* WOMAN *gave him. The* FOREIGN WOMAN *turns on the light, looks at him a moment as* HE *sleeps, then goes over to him, picks up the photograph, looks at it, and puts it down again. Then* HE *wakes up. The* FOREIGN WOMAN *is five months pregnant.*

FOREIGN WOMAN: Are you all right?

HE: Yes, I'm sorry. (HE *sits up and puts the photograph in a pocket.*)

FOREIGN WOMAN: No, don't get up.

HE: Sit down, sit down. You must be very tired.

FOREIGN WOMAN: (*Sits in the armchair.*) Thanks. (*Takes off her shoes and* HE *puts them aside.*) It doesn't matter, leave them there.

HE: Shouldn't you have stopped working by now?

FOREIGN WOMAN: I'll last till next month. I already move slowly, like a scorpion going backwards. (*Smiles. By the chair there is a fish bowl with two fish, and* SHE *begins to feed them very carefully.* SHE *has one finger bandaged.*)

HE: What happened?

FOREIGN WOMAN: They sharpened the knives today and I cut myself, it's nothing. Were you waiting for me?

HE: Yes, but I fell asleep. (*Pause.*) Your shoes are very pretty.

FOREIGN WOMAN: Do you like them? They were a gift. (SHE *takes a fan from her bag.*) Look what else they gave me. The best Spanish invention. The bad part is I can't use it at work. There's a big exhaust fan in the ceiling that doesn't do much except mess up my hair.

HE: Summer in Barcelona is very oppresive. And unfortunately these apartments have too few windows.

FOREIGN WOMAN: Do tell.

Pause.

HE: Do you need me to help you on Monday?

FOREIGN WOMAN: Monday?

HE: To move.

FOREIGN WOMAN: No. Some friends have promised to come.

HE: Are they the same ones who were supposed to come last Monday?

FOREIGN WOMAN: These friends work very hard, and they're only coming to do me a favor.

HE: Do they work in the restaurant too?

FOREIGN WOMAN: No. In Mercabarna. They load trucks with the spoiled fruit. They throw out so much food here. It really pisses me off. (*Pause. Looking at the fish.*) Why do you suppose they never bump into each other?

HE: I don't know.

FOREIGN WOMAN: Even though the fish bowl's as tiny as my room; that's why I bought them.

HE: They're very pretty . . .

FOREIGN WOMAN: Since I can't tell them apart I didn't give them names.

Pause.

HE: If your friends can't come Monday, I can look for someone to help you.

FOREIGN WOMAN: I didn't know you only rented this apartment.

HE: You didn't?

FOREIGN WOMAN: Your wife told me.

HE: Yes, for more than thirty years.

FOREIGN WOMAN: I never talked much with your wife. Lately I've realized that with my belly like this, all swollen up, people open their hearts to you easier.

Pause.

HE: And what else did she tell you . . . my wife.

FOREIGN WOMAN: She asked if I'd come visit sometimes.

HE: She did?

FOREIGN WOMAN: But I don't know if she really meant it. I promised to call first. She also asked me if I had many friends in the neighborhood.

HE: We used to know everyone around but now we don't even know the neighbors in the building.

FOREIGN WOMAN: That's exactly what your wife said. Look . . . now I'm going to have more time to learn Catalan, so use it when you speak to me from now on and that way I'll get used to it.

HE: But do you understand it?

FOREIGN WOMAN: In the restaurant I understand everything. Of course, I hardly ever leave the kitchen. The funniest word for me is the one that means crawfish. It makes me laugh.

HE: Will you keep on working at the same place?

FOREIGN WOMAN: And where do you expect me to work . . . ? Nobody's offered me anything better. Would you believe it, a couple of days ago a woman stopped me in the street and asked me if I wanted to work for her. It surprised me because I won't be good for much before long. So, acting like I wasn't interested, I played detective. And do you know what she really wanted?

HE: No.

FOREIGN WOMAN: For me to give her the baby when I had it. She said it in a different way but I knew right off which way the wind was blowing.

Pause.

HE: Do you know what you're going to name the baby?

FOREIGN WOMAN: I've been thinking about it a lot but I still haven't decided. One day I get up and think that the first name I hear will be it, but then I don't dare.

HE: You must be very careful. Don't let your mind wander for a moment, especially when you're crossing the street, and look in both directions. (*The* FOREIGN WOMAN *smiles.*) What's the matter?

FOREIGN WOMAN: That's what you said to me the first day I came here.

HE: Really?

FOREIGN WOMAN: Then I thought you were saying it so I wouldn't notice how tiny the room was.

HE: I didn't want to rent it, but my wife . . .

FOREIGN WOMAN: It's so tiny you can't ever forget you're in it, not even in the dark.

HE: I didn't think you'd stay so long . . .

FOREIGN WOMAN: I didn't either but as you can see it stuck to me like a shell. (*Pause.*) If you're going to stay a while you'd better sit down. (*After a moment of doubt* HE *sits in the only place anyone can sit, on the bed.*) The bed's comfy at least.

HE: Yes.

Pause.

FOREIGN WOMAN: Look me in the eyes. Don't treat me like all the . . .

HE: All the who . . . ?

FOREIGN WOMAN; For someone to look you in the eye here you have to at least cut your finger or fall down in the street.

HE: Have you ever fallen down?

FOREIGN WOMAN: No, but sometimes I have the urge to fall so that they'll help me up and ask me if I hurt myself.

HE: Now, with the baby, you must be very careful.

FOREIGN WOMAN: Yes, you already gave me that advice. (*Pause.*) What name would you give the baby?

HE: I don't know.

FOREIGN WOMAN: What if I called him "crawfish?" (*Pause.*) I was joking.

HE: Of course.

FOREIGN WOMAN: I asked your wife too.

HE: Asked what . . . ?

FOREIGN WOMAN: A name for the baby.

HE: And what did she say?

FOREIGN WOMAN: That she didn't know either. Here when people don't want to answer they say they don't know, and when they don't know they say they don't want to answer.

HE: If you wish, I'll think of a name and tell you.

FOREIGN WOMAN: Are you sure?

HE: If I think of one I will.

Pause.

FOREIGN WOMAN: Why have you never asked me who the baby's father is?

HE: Uh, well, I thought you'd probably tell us if you wanted to.

FOREIGN WOMAN: What if I told you it's yours?

HE: Mine?

FOREIGN WOMAN: You're not going to tell me you didn't ever think so.

HE: It was only once, and since I'm ill.

FOREIGN WOMAN: It was the night you told me you were sick.

HE: If you hadn't been here, I don't know what I would have done that night.

FOREIGN WOMAN: I was very sad that night too because they'd kicked me out at work and hadn't even paid me.

HE: You didn't tell me that. I thought you'd done it out of pity, because you felt sorry for me.

FOREIGN WOMAN: Yes, it was that too. I don't want to deceive you. First I thought of having an abortion, I talked with some friends and they all said I should, and that besides you were old and the baby could be retarded. But I finally decided I wouldn't, that with a child I wasn't going to feel so alone.

Pause.

HE: Have you told my wife?

FOREIGN WOMAN: That the baby's yours? For what . . . ?

HE: I don't know . . .

FOREIGN WOMAN: Did your wife ever eat anybody?

HE: Huh . . . ?

FOREIGN WOMAN: Did you ever see her eat anybody?

HE: No . . .

FOREIGN WOMAN: So why are you so afraid of her?

HE: I'm not afraid of her. I don't want to make her worry any more than she already does.

FOREIGN WOMAN: Yes, the truth is she's very worried about you now. (*Pause.*) I think I'm going to leave the fish bowl and the fish for you.

HE: No. Take them with you. They're yours.

FOREIGN WOMAN: I'll leave them for you to remember me by. They're a gift.

HE: Thanks.

FOREIGN WOMAN: Don't give them too much to eat each time or they'll burst.

Pause.

HE: Do you know yet in which hospital you'll have the baby?

FOREIGN WOMAN: Why do you want to know?

HE: I don't know . . .

FOREIGN WOMAN: Before, when you didn't know the baby was yours, you never asked me, never showed any interest.

HE: It's because I was always already in bed when you came home . . .

FOREIGN WOMAN: But tonight you waited up just to tell me to get busy packing my suitcases. But I guess your wife told you to.

HE: No. Well, yes, it's because she had to go out . . . and I also wanted to know if things were all right.

FOREIGN WOMAN: For who?

HE: You.

FOREIGN WOMAN: Well you've seen that I'm OK.

HE: Yes.

FOREIGN WOMAN: And what about you, are you OK?

HE: Yes . . .

FOREIGN WOMAN: Truly?

HE: I get tired more than before but I'm fine.

FOREIGN WOMAN: Does it hurt a lot?

HE: No. Not much.

FOREIGN WOMAN: I'm scared that it's going to hurt when the baby comes out. Nothing ever really hurt me much, not even a wisdom tooth. I don't know if I can stand it.

HE: Sure you can.

FOREIGN WOMAN: Probably not.

HE: During the war, I thought I wouldn't be able to endure it any more and finally, you could say, I got used to it . . .

FOREIGN WOMAN: I told you one day that I didn't want you to talk to me about the war or dead people . . .

HE: I wasn't going to talk just about that. (*The* FOREIGN WOMAN *interrupts him.*)

FOREIGN WOMAN: In my house everybody used to talk about the dead, day and night talking about dead people. There's nothing that smells worse than a wake.

HE: Yes, it's true.

FOREIGN WOMAN: If you were little, you could escape and play in the street, but when you grow up you have to go a lot farther.

HE: They shouldn't force anyone to go to a wake.

FOREIGN WOMAN: Did I say they forced me to go? Did I say that?

HE: No, but I thought . . . (*The* FOREIGN WOMAN *interrupts him again.*)

FOREIGN WOMAN: Having to live in a tiny room like this, that's what I'm forced to do. Working all day in a kitchen, roasting from the heat, that's something else I'm forced to do.

HE: That's true.

FOREIGN WOMAN: Don't just agree with me the way you do with your wife. I'd rather you argued with me. (*Pause.*) Why don't you disagree with me, for Christ's sake!

HE: I don't have anything to disagree with. There's nothing I disagree with . . .

FOREIGN WOMAN: Then better you not say anything. Don't pay any attention to me. I didn't mean that. But sometimes it's better to get angry and fight back than agree with everybody.

HE: That's true.

FOREIGN WOMAN: You're hopeless.

Pause.

HE: Do you want me to go?

FOREIGN WOMAN: Your wife also asked me my new address, but I avoided the question and didn't tell her.

HE: Naturally.

FOREIGN WOMAN: When somebody starts asking things they want to know more and more until it all gets too complicated.

HE: Yes . . .

FOREIGN WOMAN: Where I'm from women who ask a lot of questions and the ones who speak the gospel truth end up alone their whole lives.

HE: I've never told the truth for sure and I've never been alone.

FOREIGN WOMAN: It's not the same with men. Men always have a woman some place.

Pause.

HE: Have you always told the truth?

FOREIGN WOMAN: I was never that brave.

HE: We could do something. I ask you a question and you ask me another.

FOREIGN WOMAN: Why . . . ?

HE: To tell the truth.

FOREIGN WOMAN: The gospel truth?

HE: Yes.

FOREIGN WOMAN: What do you want to ask me?

HE: No. You ask first.

FOREIGN WOMAN: I'd rather you ask me first.

HE: All right. (*Pause.*) Why didn't you tell me before that the baby was mine?

FOREIGN WOMAN: Because you waited up for me tonight. If you'd waited up before, I'd have told you then.

HE: Only because of that?

FOREIGN WOMAN: I never thought of asking you for money, but I would have told your wife.

HE: Of course.

Pause.

FOREIGN WOMAN: Now can I ask you a question without feeling embarrassed?

HE: Yes, yes . . .

FOREIGN WOMAN: Who's the man in the photo?

HE: What photo . . . ?

FOREIGN WOMAN: The one you put in your pocket before.

HE: That's what you want to ask me?

FOREIGN WOMAN: I felt curious.

HE: (*Takes out the photograph.*) It's a gift. Someone gave it to me today.

FOREIGN WOMAN: Is he a friend of yours?

HE: No. He's someone who killed his mother and started dancing on her.

FOREIGN WOMAN: On his mother?

HE: Do you want to see it? Though the light's not very good.

FOREIGN WOMAN: I saw it before.

HE: Oh. (HE *puts the photograph away.*)

FOREIGN WOMAN: And why did he kill her?

HE: I don't know. I imagine he went insane.

FOREIGN WOMAN: Then you don't know him?

HE: No. It happened a long time ago.

FOREIGN WOMAN: So why did they give it to you?

HE: Well . . . I don't know. Actually I didn't want it but as it was a gift . . .

Pause.

FOREIGN WOMAN: Can I ask you another question?

HE: Yes.

FOREIGN WOMAN: No. I don't dare.

HE: What . . . what is it . . . ?

Pause.

FOREIGN WOMAN: Why do you dress up like a woman?

HE: What . . . ?

FOREIGN WOMAN: The other day you left the bathroom door half open and I almost went in. (*Pause.*) You don't have to answer. Besides, I've already asked you two questions.

HE: You see, when I used to work at the Liceu, I sometimes disguised myself in the opera costumes, and now that I'm not there any longer I occasionally do it it again, I disguise myself.

FOREIGN WOMAN: As a woman?

HE: At the Liceu I could dress up as all sorts of things, but now it's not so easy. When you put on a costume, it's as if you were another person, it's as if the costume made you something you aren't. I don't know if you understand.

FOREIGN WOMAN: Yes, I put on a costume for a carnival once.

HE: No, I do it here, at home, just for me.

Pause.

FOREIGN WOMAN: The dress wasn't very pretty.

HE: Yes. I know that.

FOREIGN WOMAN: If you want I can help you look for another one.

HE: No thanks. You don't need to.

FOREIGN WOMAN: Did you buy that one?

HE: Yes.

FOREIGN WOMAN: And didn't they ask who it was for in the shop?

HE: No.

FOREIGN WOMAN: I would have asked you. You see, that's why I'm all alone.

HE: Will you tell anyone?

FOREIGN WOMAN: About what?

HE: About the dress . . .

FOREIGN WOMAN: Does your wife know?

HE: Yes.

FOREIGN WOMAN: So what did she say to you?

HE: Nothing. She didn't say anything.

FOREIGN WOMAN: Wait . . . (SHE *gets up and searches in a make-up bag.*) Raise your head and look up.

HE: Why . . . ?

FOREIGN WOMAN: Just putting on a dress isn't enough.

HE: What do you mean . . . ?

FOREIGN WOMAN: You mustn't move now. (SHE *starts to put make-up on him.*)

HE: No . . . (HE *grabs her arm to stop her.*)

FOREIGN WOMAN: Did you ever try it?

HE: No.

FOREIGN WOMAN: You wash your face before you go to bed, right?

HE: Yes, but it's late.

FOREIGN WOMAN: It'll only take a moment. (SHE *begins to put make-up on him.*) You should have shaved first but it doesn't matter.

Lights down.

4

A large room in the same apartment. The same night. SHE *is standing while* SHE *dials the radio to get the station that broadcasts the opera. Then, when* SHE *turns around,* SHE *notices the presence of the* DOCTOR *who is seated in the shadows.*

DOCTOR: Did I frighten you?

SHE: No. (*Sits down.*) Who let you in?

DOCTOR: I slipped in when someone else was leaving.

SHE: I must give you a key.

DOCTOR: You don't need to.

Pause.

SHE: It's *La Bohème*. Do you remember it?

DOCTOR: Bits and pieces . . .

SHE: It's the third act, when Mimi goes to see Marcello, the friend of her lover Rodolfo, to tell him something, and Rodolfo intercepts him and she has to hide, and then while she's hidden she hears Rodolfo tell Marcello how very sick she is and that she's going to die. (*An overhead chandelier sways and some objects shakes.*) What can they be doing in the apartment upstairs this late at night?

DOCTOR: Wasn't it an earthquake?

SHE: There are no earthquakes in Barcelona. There's never been one. (*Pause.*) You look tired.

DOCTOR: No.

SHE: Have you eaten?

DOCTOR: At the hospital. In front of four anorexic girls I was teaching how to eat.

SHE: They don't know how?

DOCTOR: They've gotten out of the habit.

SHE: Why don't you ask them to transfer you to another area?

DOCTOR: I'm fed up with anorexia and fascinated at the same time.

SHE: Fascinated?

DOCTOR: Do you remember what you ate today?

SHE: Yes.

DOCTOR: And what you ate yesterday?

Pause.

SHE: Yes.

DOCTOR: And the day before yesterday? (*Pause.*) Well, those girls remember every crumb we make them swallow. One of them told me this afternoon that people in the street look at her as if she's a pig someone's fattening for the slaughter, and maybe she's right. All of them are right.

SHE: You agree with them?

DOCTOR: There's always a mirror that reminds them that what they are isn't enough, that in the long run what they appear to be is more important. That's how the majority of women, before they reach twenty, have been ruined forever.

SHE: What about men?

DOCTOR: They take a little more time, not much in any case.

SHE: Won't you ever do surgery again?

DOCTOR: Do you know why I became a surgeon? So that I could look for the soul, but I didn't find it anywhere, it wasn't there.

SHE: Did you think you'd find it by operating on someone?

DOCTOR: There are some extraordinary things in the human body; why shouldn't the soul be there too? Why shouldn't the soul be as tangible as kidneys, lungs, or intestines? Neither religion nor psychology have been able to show us a soul yet, even though they've had plenty of time, especially religion.

Pause.

SHE: This afternoon I went to the bullfights. Almost everyone there was a foreigner and by the second fight they were all on the side of the bull and against the toreros.

DOCTOR: What about you?

SHE: I left before it was all over and afterwards I took a walk down to the old railroad station [Estació de França]. Did you know that now there are no trains, no travellers, no nothing?

DOCTOR: There are no trains?

SHE: Maybe a few but they only go as far as Tarragona. Do you remember when I used to take you to that station to see the trains come and go from everywhere?

DOCTOR: Sure I remember.

SHE: When was the last time you took a train to go on a long trip?

DOCTOR: It's been a while.

SHE: And where did you go?

DOCTOR: To Venice.

SHE: To Venice?

DOCTOR: First to Milan and then to Venice.

SHE: Did you like Venice?

DOCTOR: It disappointed me at first.

SHE: Really?

DOCTOR: Until I came to the Arsenal district one afternoon. I saw colors there for the first time.

SHE: What colors?

DOCTOR: All of them.

SHE: What colors do you see now?

DOCTOR: Black and white.

SHE: Nothing else?

DOCTOR: The next time I saw them again was at the Olympic Games. I was volunteering at the Olympic Stadium. There was a great euphoria with the athletes parading and the crowd applauding. And suddenly, when I saw the colors of the flags, I felt it too.

SHE: What did you feel?

DOCTOR: That euphoria and the need to do something myself, and then I got the idea of dropping my pants.

SHE: Did you do that?

DOCTOR: Yes.

SHE: I never now whether you're telling the truth or not.

DOCTOR: I always tell the truth.

SHE: So what happened after you dropped your pants?

DOCTOR: Some security guards threw me out at once.

SHE: How did you come to volunteer?

DOCTOR: They needed doctors, and the psychiatrist I was seeing told me it would be a good way to get out of myself.

SHE: Do you still see the psychiatrist?

DOCTOR: Not anymore. Endogamy is an incurable ailment, sister dear. You only have to look at the good families of Barcelona that are left to realize that. (*Pause.*) Why did you call me?

SHE: I hadn't heard anything from you in some time. Do you remember when the last time was that we talked?

DOCTOR: No.

SHE: My husband is very ill. Did you know that?

DOCTOR: Yes, you told me.

Pause.

SHE: Do you know who's singing?

DOCTOR: No.

SHE: Callas. I never succeeded in getting you to like opera, or go with me even once to the Liceu.

DOCTOR: Do you still go to the Liceu?

SHE: No.

DOCTOR: Why?

SHE: It's very expensive and I'd be going by myself.

DOCTOR: If you want, I'll invite you one day and we'll go together.

SHE: You'd go to the Liceu with me?

DOCTOR: With one condition.

SHE: What?

DOCTOR: That afterwards the two of us would set it on fire.

SHE: The Liceu?

DOCTOR: They'd only build another one just like it as they did when the first one burned. No, we should set fire to something else.

SHE: What?

DOCTOR: The concert hall, the Palau de la Música, for example. And don't think we'd stop there.

SHE: Oh no?

DOCTOR: Then we could burn. . . the museum of contemporary art [the MACBA].

SHE: Why the museum?

DOCTOR: So that no one will think we have musical prejudices.

SHE: And then what could we burn?

DOCTOR: If we've gotten that far and no one's caught us, as I suspect, there are a few older skyscrapers and a few brand new ones we could do a great incendiary job on. Not forgetting the Barça soccer stadium, of course.

SHE: What about the Sagrada Familia?

DOCTOR: It's not finished but we could burn it too. And the Plaça de Catalunya naturally; in fact it ought to be set on fire every evening as a lure for the tourists who come up from the Ramblas.

SHE: I'd burn the Passeig de Gràcia also.

DOCTOR: Of course, and once it's burned I'd plant grape vines in tribute to the phylloxera that made it possible. (THEY *both smile.* HE *turns off the radio.*) Why did you call me?

SHE: I wanted to know how you were.

DOCTOR: And nothing more?

SHE: We've evicted all the lodgers, next week they'll all leave.

Pause.

DOCTOR: Is that what you wanted to tell me?

SHE: We thought it was better to be alone.

DOCTOR: Why alone?

SHE: He wants to die at home.

DOCTOR: Is he sure of it?

SHE: Yes.

DOCTOR: It'll be difficult for both of you.

SHE: Yes, we know that already.

DOCTOR: If you've already decided, then I won't try to change your minds.

SHE: If I call you, will you come sometime?

DOCTOR: Why?

SHE: He told me he wanted to consult you about something.

DOCTOR: Me?

SHE: Yes.

DOCTOR: Why doesn't he consult his own doctor?

SHE: He wants to discuss it with you.

DOCTOR: I'm not an oncologist.

SHE: It doesn't have anything to do with his illness.

DOCTOR: What is it?

SHE: He didn't want to tell me. It must be something to do with men.

DOCTOR: With men?

SHE: Something that's too embarrassing for him to tell me. Recently he only talks about the war, about the day the war ended. He says he remembers it very well, but until now he'd never talked about it.

DOCTOR: It'll be better for him to speak with his own doctor and consult with him.

SHE: Then you won't come?

DOCTOR: I don't know.

SHE: If you come I'll let you read my diary.

DOCTOR: Do you still keep one?

SHE: Yes.

DOCTOR: Every day?

SHE: Almost every day.

DOCTOR: And will you let me read it from the beginning?

SHE: Yes. (*Pause.*) Then you'll come?

DOCTOR: Show it to me now.

SHE: No. The next time you come.

DOCTOR: I want to read it now.

SHE: I'll let you have it now on condition you read it after you've left here.

DOCTOR: Can I take it with me?

SHE: Yes.

DOCTOR: Where is it?

SHE *takes a key from her pocket.*

SHE: It's in that drawer.

DOCTOR: (*Takes the key.*) People who lock things up with a key have always frightened me.

SHE: It's the only drawer in the entire house that you can lock with a key.

DOCTOR: Father kept everything locked up. Do you remember?

The DOCTOR *opens the drawer and looks inside.*

SHE: The green one is the oldest.

DOCTOR: (*Takes out a notebook with a green cover.*) This one?

SHE: Yes.

DOCTOR: Have you let anyone else read it?

SHE: No.

DOCTOR: What about your husband?

SHE: No.

DOCTOR: (*Opens it.*) What tiny handwriting.

SHE: I told you not to read it here.

The DOCTOR *puts the diary in his pocket.* HE *stands behind her and touches her hair.*

DOCTOR: Don't you go to the salon to have your hair done?

SHE: I seldom go out.

DOCTOR: Why?

SHE: I even have the groceries delivered.

DOCTOR: Do you have enough money?

SHE: Yes.

DOCTOR: And when he dies?

SHE: What?

DOCTOR: You'll only have half of his pension.

SHE: I'll get by.

DOCTOR: Will you rent out rooms again?

SHE: I don't know.

DOCTOR: If you need money, tell me.

SHE: But you're always broke.

DOCTOR: Would that we were as rich as we were before, right?

SHE: Yes.

Pause.

DOCTOR: Why don't you let me comb your hair the way I did when I was little.

SHE: You combed my hair?

DOCTOR: Don't you remember? You had hair down to here and I used to comb it for you.

SHE: I've thought about cutting it very short.

DOCTOR: No, don't cut it. I won't allow it. Where's your comb?

SHE: In the bathroom.

DOCTOR: Go get it.

SHE: No.

DOCTOR: Then I'll come another day and go with you.

SHE: Where?

DOCTOR: To the hair salon. We could go to the salon and afterwards to the Liceu. What do you think, sister dear? (*Pause.*) Are you all right? You're trembling.

SHE: I'm fine. (*Pause. The* DOCTOR *takes the diary from his pocket and gives it to her.*) Don't you want it?

DOCTOR: I'll take it with me another day.

Pause.

SHE: It's late. Sleep here if you wish.

DOCTOR: No. I have to go.

SHE: I'll bring you some sheets and you can sleep on the sofa.

DOCTOR: It's too hot here and, besides, someone's waiting for me.

SHE: Who?

DOCTOR: Someone, in the street.

SHE: Did you come with somebody?

DOCTOR: It's someone I don't know yet, who I must meet tonight, and who'll explain everything to me.

SHE: Everything?

DOCTOR: But no, it's impossible for me to meet him in this neighborhood, or even in all of Barcelona. I'd have to go much further.

SHE: So why don't you go?

DOCTOR: I always thought you would go first and that you would explain it to me.

SHE: I?

DOCTOR: If not, why did you take me to the train station? Just to see other people leave? Or maybe you were pretending to be a new Anna Karenina?

SHE: I was never that madly in love with anyone.

DOCTOR: Maybe that's the problem, that we've never felt that much love or hate for anyone.

SHE: You always liked Dostoevski more than Tolstoi.

DOCTOR: You're wrong. My hero has always been Count Vronski.

SHE: I haven't read Tolstoi for centuries. What about you?

DOCTOR: You know, the two of us should to to Russia, go to St. Petersburg, for example, take the Trans-Siberian railroad.

SHE: Would you go for both of us?

DOCTOR: All alone?

SHE: Aren't you seeing anyone now?

DOCTOR: No. But I thought I'd found someone tonight.

SHE: Who?

DOCTOR: A very handsome young man.

SHE: And what happened?

DOCTOR: I invited him home and while I was fixing a couple of drinks and making conversation so as not to go from the street straight to bed, he fell asleep.

SHE: So what did you do?

DOCTOR: Nothing.

SHE: You didn't wake him up?

DOCTOR: I left the house and came here.

SHE: You left him alone in your house?

DOCTOR: Yes.

SHE: What if he wakes up and you're not there?

DOCTOR: That's what I want, for him not to be there when I get back.

SHE: What if he is?

DOCTOR: Then I'll kill him, and tomorrow it'll be in all the papers, and they'll throw me in jail and you'll have to come see me there. You will come see me in prison? (*Pause.*) I can see you won't.

SHE: You have very beautiful hands, you should have been a pianist.

DOCTOR: Why do you always change the subject with my hands?

SHE: I'm sorry I've never seen you operate.

DOCTOR: I'm sorry you married someone with no imagination.

SHE: Then we're even.

DOCTOR: No. No we aren't. Come, come with me.

SHE: Where?

DOCTOR: Let's go far away tonight.

SHE: I can't go anywhere.

DOCTOR: Pack your suitcase and let's leave, come on.

SHE: And what about your job?

DOCTOR: Up their asses. Let's go.

SHE: I can't.

DOCTOR: Of course you can't.

SHE: And leave him here sick?

DOCTOR: Yes, it's true, now it's your turn to play the good samaritan with
    him.

SHE *slaps the* DOCTOR.

SHE: That's the second time I've slapped someone tonight.

DOCTOR: Yes, it's obvious you've had some experience.

Pause.

SHE: I'd never slapped you before, had I?

DOCTOR: No. It was the first time.

SHE: Did I hurt you?

The chandelier sways again; some objects shake a few seconds. After a pause, SHE *puts the diary in the* DOCTOR'*s pocket. Lights down.*

5

A brightly lighted room. The same night.

SHE: Did you put on make-up?

HE: Is it too much?

SHE: The eyes maybe.

HE: Then I'll take it off.

SHE: Don't.

HE: How does the dress look on me?

SHE: Stand up.

HE stands up. Pause.

HE: What . . .

SHE: It's not bad

HE: Truly?

SHE: What about the wig?

HE: I'll put it on another day. It's too hot now. (HE *sits down.* SHE *opens the wardrobe and takes from the pocket of a topcoat the pistol from Scene 2.*) What are you doing?

SHE: I'll show you how to load it.

HE: What for?

SHE: Don't you want to know how?

HE: Is it the security guard's pistol?

SHE: He let me have it tonight. It doesn't have any bullets but it doesn't matter. (*Opens and closes the pistol.*) You open it this way. You put the bullets in here, close it like this, and it it fires through here.

HE: Did the guard show you how?

SHE: My grandfather and my father showed me.

HE: Did they have a pistol?

SHE: They had one to protect what they ended up losing.

Pause.

HE: One day during the war I was playing on the beach and I found a pistol half-buried in the sand, but I wouldn't touch it; the older boys in our group snatched it up it right away.

SHE: (*Offers him the pistol.*) Come on, fire it.

HE: Huh . . . ?

SHE: I said shoot the pistol. (*Pause.* HE *takes the pistol and presses the trigger.*) Will you promise not to ask the security guard for the pistol again?

HE: Yes.

SHE: Fine.

HE *gives the pistol back to her and* SHE *puts it away in the wardrobe. Then* SHE *takes a man's suit from the wardrobe and begins to change clothes.*

HE: Are you going to cut your hair?

SHE: Yes.

HE: (*Weakly.*) I'm sorry.

SHE: What?

HE: I said I'm sorry you're cutting your hair.

SHE: I'm not. (*Pause.* HE *makes a gesture of touching her hair and then has second thoughts.*) What's wrong?

HE: Nothing. There was a smudge.

SHE: Where?

HE: You can't see it now.

Pause.

SHE: Tonight I spoke with my brother.

HE: And . . . ?

SHE: He'll come another day.

HE: Really?

SHE: Did I ever tell you that sometimes when I was little I wanted to be a boy? I wanted to be a boy and he wanted to be a girl.

HE: Your brother?

SHE: Does it surprise you?

HE: No.

SHE: Both of us wanted to be Russian.

HE: Russian?

SHE: At least to have Russian souls. Do you know what I mean?

HE: Not really.

SHE: Didn't you want to be something different you were a child?

HE: I don't know . . . I don't remember.

SHE: What was your ideal age?

HE: My what?

SHE: The best year you remember.

HE: When the war ended, the day the war ended, I suppose.

SHE: I didn't mean that.

HE: What did you mean?

SHE: It doesn't matter. (SHE *has finished dressing and pulls back her hair.*) What do you think?

HE: It's fine.

SHE: It's all right?

HE: You look younger.

SHE: Younger than who?

HE: Than before.

SHE: What do you mean?

Pause.

HE: The truth is we're not a bit alike. You and I have never been alike.

SHE *sits facing him. Pause.*

SHE: It's sufficient for me to disguise myself; you have no reason to.

HE: I know, but I want to go along with you. I don't want you to go alone.

SHE: It makes no difference to me at all.

HE: You should start practicing my signature.

SHE: I know that.

HE: But you don't do it.

SHE: There's time.

HE: Two months from now I have to go to the bank to sign for the pension.

SHE: By next month we'll have changed banks and I'll sign.

Pause.

HE: Have you explained that to your brother?

SHE: No.

HE: What have you told him then?

SHE: Nothing.

HE: Do you think he'll want to sign your death certificate instead of mine?

SHE: Of course he will.

HE: Your brother has never been very fond of me.

SHE: My brother's never been very fond of anyone, so don't worry about it.
    (SHE *begins to change.*)

HE: What are you doing?

SHE: I'm changing.

HE: Wait, don't change yet.

SHE: Why?

HE: I'm afraid to tell you.

SHE: Tell me what . . . ?

Pause.

HE: The foreign woman's baby is mine.

SHE: Yours?

HE: It was only once, the day they told me I had cancer. You weren't here that day, so I explained it all to her.

Pause.

SHE: How long have you known?

HE: She told me tonight.

SHE: And what did you say to her?

HE: Me? I didn't know what to say.

SHE: Did she ask you for money?

HE: She doesn't want money.

SHE: She didn't ask you for any?

HE: No.

SHE: Did she say she'd bring the child by sometime?

HE: No, I don't think so. (*Pause.*) Are you angry?

SHE: I also have something to tell you that I've never told because I was also afraid to.

HE: Afraid of me?

SHE: Yes.

HE: What is it?

SHE: My brother is not my brother, he's my son.

Pause.

HE: I don't understand.

SHE: I had him with my father.

HE: With your father?

SHE: He didn't force me or anything. I did it because I wanted to.

HE: But you were very young.

SHE: So what?

HE: I don't know . . .

SHE: He was the only person who loved me then.

Pause.

HE: Does he know? Your brother . . .

SHE: I suppose so. In any case I gave him my diary tonight.

HE: Is that why you haven't shown it to me?

SHE: The diary? You never asked me.

HE: Once you said you'd lend it to me and then you didn't.

SHE: Really?

HE: Don't you remember?

SHE: I'll let you read it now, if you wish.

Pause.

HE: I have something I want to give you too. (HE *takes something from the table drawer and gives it to her.*) It's a guidebook for Barcelona, a little old to be sure. One of the first jobs I had was to help put together this guidebook. A few like me went through the whole city marking all the streets there were at that time in Barcelona. It wasn't easy because there were a lot of shacks and you couldn't tell if some of the streets were really there or not, and the people threw rocks at us sometimes.

Pause.

SHE: Why is it all marked up?

HE: I marked it up later. One summer when it was very hot and I was working collecting light bills, I marked all the sidewalks where there was shade. The numbers at the top are the different hours of the day, because the shadows moved with the sun, they're never still.

SHE: But why did you do it?

HE: I thought that the following summer I'd go more rapidly with the guide and I wouldn't feel the heat so much, but it wasn't much use to me because that's when I started work at the Liceu.

Pause.

SHE: It's like a great map of shadows.

HE: Yes, you could say that. I've wanted to show it to you for a long tme, but I forgot about it. (*Pause.*) The Passeig de Gràcia isn't there.

SHE: Yes. I noticed.

HE: I tore out all the pages where I walked.

Long pause.

SHE: What's wrong?

HE: It suddenly seemed strange to see you dressed that way.

SHE: It didn't before?

HE: No.

SHE: The fact is I feel a bit hot in these clothes.

HE: My shoes are too tight. (HE *takes them off.*)

SHE: I'll take them to the shoe repair shop tomorrow.

HE: The shoe repair shop is closed.

SHE: Then I'll look for another one.

HE: Did you know that my grandfather repaired shoes?

SHE: Yes, you told me.

HE: Do you know how he died?

SHE: How?

HE: Burned to death.

SHE: Burned?

HE: One night when he was sleeping in the bed beside my grandmother he started to burn.

SHE: What do you mean?

HE: His body started to burn all by itself. It's called spontaneous combustion.

SHE: That's not possible. No one burns spontaneously.

HE: He was fatter than me and he also drank.

SHE: You haven't drunk in ages and you're not so fat. Besides, it's impossible. Nobody could suddenly start burning.

HE: Yes it is possible. I know how it's done.

SHE: How what's done?

HE: How to burn something without setting it on fire. I can burn things if I wish.

SHE: You?

HE: Yes.

SHE: How?

HE: By thinking it.

SHE: Thinking it?

HE: Do you see that facial tissue? (*There is a wadded tissue on the night table.*) For a while I've been thinking, thinking that it's getting so hot that at any moment it will burst into flames.

SHE: Are you serious?

HE: Yes. (SHE *looks at the tissue and starts to touch it.*) Don't touch it!

Pause.

SHE: It doesn't seem to be burning yet.

HE: It takes a while because it's damp and I'm out of practice. I haven't done it for a long time.

SHE: You've burned something that way?

HE: Yes.

SHE: What?

HE: At first I burned small things like the tissue until one day I tried it on something larger. Then I got scared and didn't do it anymore.

SHE: What did you burn?

HE: The Liceu.

SHE: What?

HE: I was the one who burned the Liceu.

Pause.

SHE: That's a joke, isn't it?

HE: No.

SHE: Do you really believe you burned the Liceu?

HE: Yes, it was me.

SHE: But you were at home that day.

HE: I did it from here.

Smoke begins to rise from the tissue. After a few seconds of surprise, SHE *puts out the tissue.*

SHE: It was already lighted, wasn't it?

HE: No.

SHE: How did it catch fire then?

HE: I've already told you. I did it.

SHE: With your thoughts?

HE: Yes.

SHE: And you burned the Liceu that way too?

HE: Yes, but it was harder because it was farther away.

SHE: But what reason did you have to burn the Liceu?

HE: Everyone was saying we needed a new Liceu, every day that passed I heard more people saying they wished it would burn so that there'd be a larger one. So finally I did it. I burned it.

Pause.

SHE: Have you told anyone all this?

HE: No. I was afraid to tell anyone.

SHE: To tell me, too?

HE: Especially you. (*Long pause.*) We forgot about the opera.

SHE: No.

HE: We can turn it on now.

SHE: What . . . ?

HE: We can turn on the opera now.

SHE: It must be almost over.

SHE *turns on a transistor radio that is on the night table and dials the opera.*

HE: You can't hear it very well here.

SHE: What you told me about Callas is true, isn't it?

HE: What was that . . . ?

SHE: What happened to you with Callas at the Liceu, it's really true . . .

HE: Yes, of course.

SHE: And what did she say to you when you returned her puppy?

HE: She thanked me. I've already told you that.

SHE: And that was all?

HE: She was in a hurry and only thanked me.

SHE: In Italian?

HE: Yes, in Italian. (*Pause.* HE *farts.*) I'm sorry.

SHE: Have you taken all your pills?

HE: Yes.

Pause.

SHE: Are you sleepy?

HE: Not yet. And you?

SHE: No.

HE: It's very hot tonight.

Pause.

SHE: Do you have to go to the bathroom?

HE: Yes. But you go first if you want to.

SHE: You're sure.

HE: Yes. I can wait.

SHE: I won't be long.

HE: You're going like that?

SHE: It's very late. Everyone's asleep.

SHE *leaves the room.* HE *lies down on the bed, remains for a few moments with his eyes open, listening to the end of* La Bohème. *Then* HE *closes his eyes, and mingled with the sound of the opera we hear the voice of General Juan Bautista Sánchez, in the speech he made the 26th of January, 1939, on the station Radiò Associació de Catalunya:* "I say first of all to the Barcelonans, to the Catalans, that I thank you with all my soul for the enthusiastic reception you have given our armed forces. I also say to the Spaniards that it was a great mistake to call Catalunya separatist, or anti-Spanish. I must say that they have given us the most enthusiastic reception I have seen, and remember that I have had the honor and the glory . . . of witnessing similar acts. Nowhere, I say to you, nowhere have we been received with the enthusiasm and the cordiality of Barcelona.

Lights down.

It's Raining in Barcelona

Pau Miró

Pau Miró

Photo: courtesy of the playwright

Pau Miró and *It's Raining in Barcelona*

Pau Miró (Barcelona, 1974) is an actor, director, and playwright who received his education at the Barcelona Theatre Institute, where he studied with Sergi Belbel, Carles Batlle, and José Sanchis Sinisterra, among others. After graduating in 1999, he founded his own company, Menudos, which was based at Barcelona's former Teatre Malic. As a stage actor, he has worked with Catalan directors including Lluís Pasqual, Oriol Broggi, Carlota Subirós, and Magda Puyo. In 2005, Miró staged at the Teatre Borràs (Barcelona) his own experimental adaptation of Anton Chekhov's *Uncle Vanya*, titled *Happy Hour*, which incorporated the music of contemporary composer/violinist/singer Kirsten Tinkler. That same year, he was invited to participate in the Teatre Lliure's publicly funded project to encourage text-based drama in Catalan. The result was a contemporary western titled *Bullets and Shadows* (*Bales i ombres*, 2004).

Miró's *Somriure de l'elefant* (*The Elephant's Smile*) premiered under his own direction, at the Barcelona Grec summer festival in 2006. The production, which theatre critic Marcos Ordóñez called "the black pearl of the Grec, the best 'local' premiere,"[1] was staged in a grassy medieval cloister of the Biblioteca de Catalunya, which masqueraded as the garden of a home for the aged. In *Somriure de l'elefant*, Miró infuses the everyday with a magical dimension, dreamlike and whimsical, offering us an homage to the theatre that is brought to light in a series of encounters between a retired theatre director and his former student. Additional projects include a modern-day version of Aeschylus's *The Persians*, which Miró co authored with director Calixto Bieito and presented at several venues and festivals throughout Spain in 2007 and 2008, and *The Singapore Trilogy* (*Trilogia de Singapur*, 2007), a play written and directed by Miró as part of the Teatre Nacional de Catalunya's "T-6" workshops for Catalan dramatists.

The blending of magical-lyrical elements with the everyday has become a common thread in Miró's work, and it also characterizes *It's Raining in Barcelona* (*Plou a Barcelona*). Perhaps his most well known play, *It's Raining in Barcelona* premiered at the Sitges International Theatre Festival under the direction of Toni Casares in 2004 and then moved on to the Sala Beckett, Barcelona's preeminent experimental theatre laboratory. The play was Miró's contribution to the award-winning series staged at the Beckett during the 2003-04 season titled "The Action Takes Place in Barcelona" ("L'acció té lloc a Barcelona"). Casares, in his role as Artistic Director of the Beckett, conceived the series at a time in which "Barcelona"— as concept, trope, image, or theme—had nearly vanished from the Catalan stage, and he encouraged both established and up-and-coming dramatists to create a theatrical imaginary grounded in visions of the city. The series earned him and the Sala Beckett a prestigious Generalitat de Catalunya prize (the Catalan national theatre award) in 2005. Barcelona spectators nominated *It's Raining in Barcelona* for five Butaca prizes, including "best text" and "best small-scale production," and the text has since been translated into several languages.

Miró situates the action of the play in the ever-changing Raval quarter of Barcelona. Throughout the past two decades, the Raval, infamously regarded as a haven for prostitutes, thieves, and drug dealers (with literary portrayals in the novels of Jean Genet and Manuel Vázquez Montalbán), has witnessed exponential growth in terms of the cultural diversity of its inhabitants, becoming a focal point for the city's new immigrant populations—especially those residents originally from Maghreb, Pakistan, and Latin America. At the same time, an overall renaissance in construction and design has characterized the post-Franco revitalization of this area of the city. As a consequence of several urban renewal projects of the 1990s, motivated in part by the Barcelona Olympic Games of 1992 and the municipal government's social democratic approach to urban development, the Raval has undergone numerous transformations. Dilapidated buildings in disrepair have been demolished to pave way for new apartment blocks. Several important cultural centers, such as the MACBA (Museu d'Art Contemporani de Barcelona), have taken up residence in the Raval district, and many of the old taverns and bordellos that for decades attracted sailors landing at the port of Barcelona have been replaced with fashionable cafés and galleries. In *It's Raining in Barcelona*, Miró captures the contemporary spirit of this area of the city, portraying it as a place of continual and striking change, as reflected in the eyes a prostitute (Lali), her client (David), and her pimp (Carlos). The linguistic register of Miró's dialogues contains a degree of spontaneity that is uncommon to the contemporary Catalan stage. The characters in *It's Raining in Barcelona* create with their words a kind of edginess and brutal realism that is refreshingly natural and sincere.

Born out of a workshop with Argentine playwright/director Javier Daulte—who is known for his original hybrid blends of science with the universals of love, life, and death—Miró's play operates in subtle ways to inject the prosaic harsh reality of his characters' world with an unexpected lyrical dimension. A series of candy wrappers containing poetic verses by the likes of Arthur Rimbaud, Giorgio Caprioni, Pere Gimferrer, and Charles Baudelaire become the pretext for unanticipated moments of existential reflection. The words of the poets role off the characters' tongues, bringing a new palette of color to their world and showing us, perhaps, that nothing is ever black and white. An ordinary seagull appears to have an almost mystical presence in their lives, as though she had the capacity to look into their souls. Robert Louis Stevenson's *Treasure Island* becomes a possible source of inspiration for Lali's desire to break with the present and aspire to a different sort of life. Miró knits together a series of ten brief, intimate scenes, most of them consisting of conversations between two characters. In the banal superficiality of their odd love triangle, and of their world of fast food, cheap rooms, and torn stockings, there are moments in which Lali, David, and Carlos reveal complex inner lives, a hidden magic that lies beneath the surface.

The Italian version of *Plou a Barcelona*, titled *Chiòve* (translated by Enrico Ianniello) and staged at the Piccolo Teatro di Milano in June 2008 by Francesco Saponaro, was awarded the Premio della Critica 2008 (from the Associazione Nazionale di Critici di Teatro). The play is scheduled to be staged in Paris (Bobigny) in January 2009.

SGF

NOTE

1. Marcos Ordóñez, "Gran Jefe Ojo de Halcón dice que os zurzan," *El País Babelia*, August 19, 2006. My translation.

Plou a Barcelona at the Sala Beckett in 2004.

Photo: courtesy of the Sala Beckett

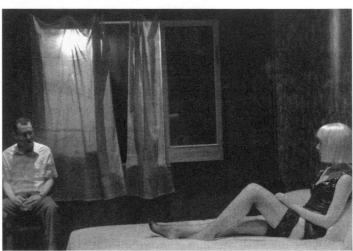

Plou a Barcelona at the Sala Beckett in 2004.

Photo: courtesy of the Sala Beckett

IT'S RAINING IN BARCELONA

by

Pau Miró

Translated by

Sharon G. Feldman

"The way I see it I'm not a failure, it's society that's failed. I've done everything possible . . . society has failed; it's not my fault. Society rejects us, it's catalogued us."

—Carol, a prostitute from the Raval quarter of Barcelona,
"The Whores Speak," by Regina de Paula Medeiros

AUTHOR'S NOTE: All grammatical and syntactical "errors" expressed by the characters are used as an expressive technique. They are unmarked so as not to complicate the reading.

CHARACTERS

CARLOS

LALI

DAVID

SPACE

A small apartment in the Raval quarter of Barcelona. An apartment that is, at most, 30 square meters in length.

Bedroom: There is a bed. The sheets of the bed drape down to the floor on both sides. Sheets with a printed design. Next to the bed there is a nightstand with two drawers. On top of the nightstand there is a radio-cassette player. There is a window with curtains. A light bulb without a shade hangs from the ceiling. On a wall there is a cracked mirror. Next to it, a clock whose face is an advertisement for Cinzano. Hanging on another wall is a 1980s-style telephone. There is a damaged chair. There is a small refrigerator with a rusted door and some old, brightly colored stickers.

There are two doors, one to the bathroom and the other marking the entrance.

Street noises. Summer. From time to time we hear a seagull.

1- THE SEAGULL

In the bedroom. Nighttime. There is a woman on the bed. Her name is LALI. SHE wears a blue velvet dress and is polishing her fingernails. SHE has a box of candy next to her. SHE is barefoot.

Sitting in the chair is CARLOS, wearing a t-shirt and grey pants. HE holds a candy wrapper in his hand and reads slowly:

CARLOS: "One evening, I took Beauty in my arms. And I thought her bitter."[1]

Pause.

LALI: That's nice.

CARLOS: Who is it?

LALI: It's . . . What's the name of the one from the other day?

Pause.

LALI: Dante?

CARLOS: No. Another.

Pause.

LALI: Shit, now I can't remember any of them.

CARLOS: Should I tell you?

Pause.

LALI: Yes.

CARLOS: Rimbaud.

LALI: Rimbaud?

CARLOS: A French poet (1854-1891).

LALI: That's OK. This one hadn't come up before, right?

CARLOS: I don't think so.

LALI: Read it again.

CARLOS: "One evening, I took Beauty in my arms. And I thought her bitter."

LALI: Of course, it means that . . .

Pause.

LALI: That beauty is sometimes bitter.

CARLOS: Right.

LALI: Do you understand it?

CARLOS: I guess.

LALI: "One evening, I took Beauty in my arms . . ." Of course, that means one night he was fucking a very good-looking woman and . . . I don't know . . . maybe when he was done . . . well he looked at her stretched out on the bed . . . and she didn't seem so good-looking anymore, and of course, her beauty became bitter.

CARLOS: You, you are good-looking.

LALI: And bitter?

CARLOS: No, well, sometimes, but not usually.

LALI: You want another?

CARLOS: Then you'll tell me I'm like a fat whale.

LALI: But you are getting to be like a fat whale.

CARLOS: In a little while, OK?

CARLOS *gets up and stands in front of the mirror.* HE *takes out a razor and begins shaving his beard.*

LALI: You're shaving again?

CARLOS: It's just that I still have some hairs over here. How did your morning go?

LALI: I went over to the university.

CARLOS: Which one?

LALI: Here, the one here at University Plaza.

CARLOS: And?

LALI: Two.

CARLOS: Two what?

LALI: Two, two.

CARLOS: That's all?

LALI: The semester is ending. There's not a lot going on.

CARLOS: Nude?

LALI: No. They were very nice.

Pause.

LALI: I crashed a class. At the university.

CARLOS: Why?

LALI: To see what it was like. I liked it.

CARLOS: Did they give you any dirty looks?

LALI: I don't know. I wasn't paying attention. I was really nervous. The money is in my purse.

Pause.

LALI: I really would have liked to go to the university.

CARLOS: Why?

LALI: I don't know. To know things and to be a little more normal.

CARLOS: You're better than normal.

CARLOS *places the razor in his pants pocket and moves toward the bed. HE grabs LALI's purse and takes out the money. Then HE gets on his knees in front of the bed and takes out a shoebox. HE opens it. The box is filled with money and candy wrappers.*

LALI: You should go deposit it in the bank. You haven't gone for days.

CARLOS: Right now there's not much. Lately, there's not much dinero, Lali.

LALI. Right.

CARLOS *places the money in the box first and then the candy wrapper that* HE *had placed in his pocket. Before putting in the wrapper,* HE *licks it a bit. Then* HE *puts the cover on the box and leaves it under the bed.*

We hear a seagull. CARLOS *gets up and goes over to the window.*

LALI: Is it here again?

CARLOS: Yes

LALI *goes over to the window.*

LALI: Is it the same one?

CARLOS: I guess so.

LALI: They're not so pretty up close.

CARLOS *turning toward the chair, passes by the refrigerator, opens it and takes a piece of candy out of the box. The* HE *closes the refrigerator and sits down in the chair.* HE *unwraps it and eats it.* HE *chews a bit and reads from the wrapper:*

CARLOS: "Without you a tree would no longer be what it is, nothing without you would be what it is."

LALI: I like that one better.

CARLOS: It's not bad. Who wrote it?

LALI: This one is definitely Dante.

CARLOS: No

LALI: The one who wrote the other one?

CARLOS: No, it's not that one, either.

Pause.

LALI: Go ahead, tell me.

CARLOS: G. Caprioni. Italian poet (1912-1990).

LALI: Without you a tree would no longer be what it is, nothing . . .

CARLOS: . . . without you would be what it is.

LALI: If she's not there, the trees are not there, either.

CARLOS: Right.

LALI: If she's not there then . . . everything would be different; things . . . things wouldn't be the way they are.

CARLOS: Right, of course.

And now the telephone rings. LALI *picks it up.*

LALI: Hello? . . . OK. I'm coming.

CARLOS: Already?

LALI: He's already here.

CARLOS: But it's only a quarter to eleven.

LALI: He always comes early.

CARLOS: Did he invite you to dinner today, too?

CARLOS *sitting in the chair, takes the razor out of his pocket and runs it over his beard.*

LALI: Yes, we're going to Mama's.

CARLOS: Bring me back a slice of pizza.

LALI: OK.

LALI *takes some stockings out of the drawer of the nightstand.*

CARLOS: You're putting on those stockings?

LALI: He likes them.

CARLOS: They have holes in them.

LALI: They only have two runs.

CARLOS: Don't you paint your toenails?

LALI: It's late.

CARLOS: You still have time, damn it.

LALI: I want to get there on time.

LALI *puts on the stockings.*

CARLOS: Why?

LALI: What?

CARLOS: Why?

CARLOS *cuts his chin and makes a faint sound of pain.*

LALI: What are you doing?

CARLOS: I cut myself.

Pause.

CARLOS: It's nothing, I hit a zit.

LALI *enters the bathroom. The sound of a faucet.* SHE *appears with a piece of wet paper with the intention of placing it on* CARLOS.

LALI: Here, put this on it.

CARLOS *shoves* LALI

CARLOS: It's nothing. Go ahead and paint your nails, you have time.

LALI: I'll do them tomorrow, it doesn't matter.

Pause.

LALI: Are you OK?

CARLOS *nods his head.* LALI *finishes putting on her stockings.*

CARLOS: You smell nice.

LALI: I bought a new deodorant at Dia, that supermarket. I have it in my bag if you want.

CARLOS: Yeah.

LALI *with her stockings half on, passes her bag to* CARLOS. CARLOS *goes through her bag.* HE *finds the deodorant.* HE *puts some on.*

LALI: It's nice, isn't it?

CARLOS: Yes.

LALI: It's on sale. It's Palmolive.

LALI *gets up from the bed and grabs a lipstick from the bag that* CARLOS *is holding.* SHE *paints her lips in front of the mirror.*

LALI: What do you think?

CARLOS: Of what?

LALI: The gloss. Wet look.

CARLOS: . . . ?

LALI: The lip gloss.

CARLOS: Oh, nice.

LALI: They look like they're wet, don't they? Go ahead, give me the wig.

CARLOS *takes a wig out of the bag. The wig is wrapped in a plastic bag.* LALI *takes it and goes about putting it on.*

LALI: Tomorrow I'm going to the CaixaForum museum. Do you want to come?

CARLOS: No, thanks. Some other time.

LALI: You don't go out much lately.

Silence.

LALI: Whatever you want. Where the hell are my shoes?

CARLOS: Under the bed.

LALI *kneels in front of the bed.*

LALI: I don't see them.

CARLOS: I saw them before.

LALI: Oh, right. Now I see them.

LALI *disappears under the bed and* CARLOS *takes a small packet of mustard out of the bag.*

CARLOS: You still have this packet of mustard.

LALI *under the bed.*

LALI: What?

CARLOS: I said . . .

LALI *under the bed.*

LALI: What did you say?

CARLOS: I said you still have the packet of mustard from McDonald's from the day we met.

LALI *comes out from under the bed holding the shoes.* SHE *sits on the bed and begins putting them on.*

LALI: There's a date on it.

CARLOS: The expiration date?

LALI: No, stupid. The day we met. Turn it over.

CARLOS: Oh, right. Now I see it. Do you remember what we ate?

LALI: What?

CARLOS: What we ordered. What we ordered that day.

Pause.

LALI: Crab salad for me.

CARLOS: Two portions of fries for me.

LALI: Onion rings for me.

CARLOS: And two "Mac-chickens" for me.

LALI: And we ordered the same dessert, two chocolate sundaes.

CARLOS: No, mine was caramel and yours was chocolate.

LALI: Oh, that's right.

CARLOS: And there was just one table.

LALI: And you sat down next to me and we finished off everything.

CARLOS: Yes, even the piece of cheeseburger that that girl left. You're not putting on blush?

LALI: I ran out. I'll buy more tomorrow.

LALI *takes the bag and goes into the bathroom.*

CARLOS: You look good anyway.

LALI *from the bathroom.*

LALI: There's a lot of shit under the bed.

CARLOS: I know.

LALI *from the bathroom.*

LALI: I'm telling you for your sake. I could care less.

CARLOS: Right. I know. I'll clean it tomorrow. Did you get any gold dust?

LALI *from the bathroom.*

LALI: I haven't had time.

Sound of sniffing from the bathroom. Then LALI *appears.*

LALI: I had a little left over from yesterday. I'm leaving, it's late.

CARLOS: You'll get there with plenty of time. Did you finish it off?

LALI: Yes. Later I'll go get some off of Vicente.

CARLOS: OK.

LALI: How's the ..

CARLOS: It's nothing.

LALI: Put a Band-Aid on it.

CARLOS: I'll put one on now.

LALI: See you in a little while.

LALI *gives* CARLOS *a kiss on the lips. Then* SHE *exits through the door.* CARLOS *gets up and goes to the window. Not half a minute goes by and* HE *waves from the window. Then* HE *goes in front of the mirror and looks at his wound. We hear the seagull.*

Darkness.

2- THE CANDY

The same bedroom. DAVID *is sitting in the chair.* LALI *is standing in front of the small refrigerator.* SHE *is wearing the wig and the blue velvet dress. There is a pair of glasses on top of the refrigerator. A romantic and very insipid ballad plays on the radio-cassette player.*

LALI: You haven't had much to eat.

DAVID: I'm not very hungry. You're not wearing any blush today, are you?

LALI: I ran out. The pizza was really good.

Pause.

LALI: How was it at the bookstore today?

DAVID: A lot of work. I don't know what's going on; lately people are buying a lot of books.

LALI: Ballantine's with Coke?

DAVID: Yes. It's really hot in this apartment.

LALI: It's summer.

LALI *goes toward the refrigerator.*

LALI: It's a generic brand, but it tastes just like Coke and it's half the price.

DAVID: Will you let me taste it?

LALI *pours the cola into a glass and brings it over to him.* DAVID *drinks some of it.*

LALI: Well?

DAVID *makes a gesture of disgust.* LALI *takes the glass and finishes preparing the drink.*

LALI: With the Ballantine's in it you won't notice.

DAVID: Don't make it too strong.

LALI: Oh, I don't have ice.

DAVID: Don't worry.

LALI *prepares the drink.*

LALI: Do you like this music? It's new. I bought it from one of the Pakistanis, three euros.

DAVID *makes a small gesture of approval. Pause.*

LALI: How's your wife?

DAVID: Dead.

LALI: Dead?

DAVID: More or less.

LALI: Poor thing.

LALI *gives* DAVID *the drink.* DAVID *takes a long sip.*

DAVID: Sit down on the bed.

LALI: All right.

LALI *sits on the bed.*

DAVID: Take off your shoes.

LALI *takes her shoes off with her feet.*

DAVID: Take off your stockings.

LALI *takes off her stockings.*

DAVID: You didn't paint your toenails?

LALI: I didn't have time. I didn't want to be late.

DAVID: That's OK. Do you have any nail polish?

LALI: Yes.

DAVID: Blue?

LALI: Yes.

DAVID: Then paint your toes.

LALI *gets up quickly, goes into the bathroom and comes out with a nail polish bottle in her hand.* SHE *sits down on the bed again and begins painting her nails.*

DAVID: Don't rush.

LALI: I won't.

Silence.

LALI: Will you recite some verses for me today?

DAVID: Today I didn't look for any for you. I'm not feeling very inspired.

LALI: Oh.

Pause.

LALI: Do you remember the one from the other day? It was really nice.

DAVID: I don't have any poetry today, Lali, I'm sorry, I didn't have time. I haven't had a very good day. I just want to look at you for a while. May I?

LALI: Of course.

Long pause.

DAVID: "As the sea has a mechanical movement, so has love its symbols."[2]

LALI: That's the one from the other day, right?

DAVID: Yes.

LALI: It's nice. It was Dante, right?

DAVID: Dante? No, it's Pere Gimferrer, a Catalan poet.

LALI: The one who you said always walks around with the overcoat and beret?

DAVID: Yes.

LALI: "As the sea has a mechanical movement, so has love its symbols." What does it mean?

DAVID: What does it mean to you?

LALI: What?

DAVID: What does it mean to you? How does it speak to you?

Pause.

LALI: I don't know, that . . .

DAVID: Your nails.

LALI: Right.

DAVID: Tell me, what does it evoke for you?

LALI: He compares the sea to love.

DAVID: And?

LALI: Love has symbols and the sea has its own inner workings.

LALI *begins blowing on her toenails.*

DAVID: Have you ever stared at the sea for a long time?

LALI: I don't know. I guess.

DAVID: It's always working, a mechanical movement, as though there were a meshing of gears that make it run constantly. The ebb and flow. And love, also seemingly mechanically, it's like it always happens in the same places. Hope and despair.

LALI: Oh.

DAVID *takes a long sip of the drink.*

DAVID: You're not drinking?

LALI: I'll have a sip of yours.

DAVID: Do you understand it a little better?

LALI: I think so.

DAVID: Stare at the sea and you'll understand.

LALI *moves near the bed and takes a sip of the drink. And* SHE *finishes it off.*

DAVID: Is there any candy left?

LALI: A little.

DAVID: Tomorrow I'll bring you some.

LALI: You'll be back tomorrow?

DAVID: Yes.

LALI: You've been coming around a lot lately.

DAVID: Do you mind?

LALI: Of course not.

DAVID: At eleven?

LALI: Yes. Will you bring me the book?

DAVID: The book?

LALI: Yes, you told me you would bring a book.

DAVID: Oh, yeah. With all the shit going on I haven't had a minute to think about it.

We hear a metallic sound.

DAVID: What was that noise?

LALI: What noise?

DAVID: Didn't you hear it?

LALI: What?

Pause.

LALI: It must be coming from another room.

DAVID: It seemed like it was here.

LALI: You said you would choose a book for me, one that would suit me.

DAVID: I'll think about it. You really didn't hear anything?

LALI: Nothing. There are fifteen minutes left; then I have to be someplace else.

DAVID: It's gone by so quickly.

LALI: That's because you're comfortable.

We hear the seagull.

DAVID: You did hear that.

LALI: Yes, I heard it.

DAVID: It seems like . . . a seagull.

LALI: It is a seagull. Look out the window and you'll see it.

DAVID *gets up from the bed and goes over to the window.*

DAVID: It's a seagull.

LALI: It's been here for the past two nights.

DAVID: What's a seagull doing on such a narrow street?

LALI: She comes here to sleep.

DAVID: It seems like it's looking at us.

LALI: She must like sleeping here.

DAVID: Should we throw it something?

LALI: Leave her alone, poor thing. She's not doing anything.

DAVID: It was a joke.

Pause. THEY *stare into each other's eyes.*

LALI: You're sure you don't want me to do anything for you?

DAVID: I just want to look at you.

LALI: Whatever you want.

DAVID *sits in the chair.*

DAVID: Take off your panties.

LALI *takes off her panties. Pause.*

DAVID: Close your eyes.

Darkness.

3- UNDER THE BED (BRIEF SCENE)

In the same bedroom. The light of day. CARLOS *is alone;* HE *wears a bandage on his chin.* HE *is cleaning under the bed.* HE *finds a candy wrapper and leaves it in the shoebox where* HE *keeps all the candy wrappers and the money.* HE *continues cleaning.* HE *finishes.* HE *gets up and goes over to the window.* HE *gazes out the window.*

4- I'LL TELL HER YOU CALLED.

In the same bedroom. Later. On the bed there is a cardboard bag from McDonald's. CARLOS *is sitting in the chair.* HE *wears the bandage on his chin and has a plastic cup from McDonald's at his feet.* LALI, *in front of the window, is putting drops in her eyes.* SHE *is not wearing a wig, or lipstick.* SHE *is scantily dressed.* CARLOS *holds a candy wrapper and reads with his mouth full:*

CARLOS: "And find frenzy in the everyday"

LALI: Find what?

CARLOS: Frenzy.

LALI: Frenzy.

CARLOS: Do you know whose it is?

LALI: Has it come up before?

CARLOS: I think so.

LALI: Rimbaud.

CARLOS: No

LALI: Dante

CARLOS: Not him, either.

LALI: Shakespeare

CARLOS: Last chance.

LALI: Oh, Bau . . . Bau . . . Baudelaire?

CARLOS: Very good. C. Baudelaire. French poet (1821-1867).

LALI: Finding the daily frenzy. What does it mean to you?

CARLOS: What what?

LALI: What does it say to you?

Silence.

LALI: To find a daily frenzy means: finding something each day that you like a lot, that. . . is very special to you.

CARLOS: When you bring me a double cheeseburger?

LALI: Yes. Or when Vicente brings us that really good shit.

CARLOS: Or you come back and nothing has happened to you and you tell me so with your eyes.

LALI: Or when I know who the author of the sentence on the candy wrapper is. Wow, it's late.

CARLOS: And are you going to the CaixaForum now?

LALI: I could do two or three; it's a good time.

CARLOS: Let's see.

CARLOS *grabs the cup from McDonald's that* HE *has at his feet and sips from the straw.* HE *makes a slurping sound.* LALI *takes a skirt out of the nightstand drawer.*

CARLOS: You've gotten very little sleep.

LALI: I'll sleep later.

LALI *puts the skirt on.*

LALI: Besides, David told me that there are some paintings there that I would like a lot.

CARLOS: When?

LALI: What?

CARLOS: He didn't tell that to you yesterday.

LALI: The day before yesterday.

CARLOS: The day before yesterday, when?

LALI: Was the MacChicken good?

CARLOS: Yes.

LALI: Is your cut healing?

CARLOS: Yes.

CARLOS *makes a slurping sound with the straw.* LALI *grabs the bag and goes into the bathroom.* SHE *sniffs.* CARLOS *makes the sound with the straw.* LALI *comes out of the bathroom.*

LALI: Do you want to come with me to the CaixaForum?

CARLOS: It's very hot.

LALI: There's air conditioning.

CARLOS: Another day.

LALI: Why don't you ever come with me anymore?

CARLOS: I don't like museums or those places where you go now.

CARLOS *makes the sound with the straw.* LALI *moves toward* CARLOS *and nuzzles his chest with her face.*

LALI: Are you wearing deodorant?

CARLOS: No.

LALI: Did it last from yesterday?

CARLOS: Yes.

LALI *caresses* CARLOS *and then stands up, takes off the t-shirt that* SHE *is wearing and puts on a tighter one.*

LALI: That Palmolive stuff is good. There's also Palmolive shower gel. When the one we have gets used up, I'll buy some.

CARLOS: The one we have is Heno de Pravia, right?

LALI: Yes.

CARLOS: I like it.

LALI: You'll like the Palmolive one more.

LALI *stands in front of the mirror and shakes her hair with her hands.*

LALI: Do I look normal?

CARLOS: Yes.

LALI: Really?

CARLOS: Of course you do.

LALI: My shoes?

CARLOS: Next to the bidet.

LALI *enters the bathroom.* CARLOS *leaves the cup on the floor.* LALI *enters and sits on the bed.* SHE *puts on her shoes. They are not the same ones that* SHE *had on last night.*

LALI: Will they let me in the museum?

CARLOS: Why not?

LALI: I'm a little nervous. They've changed security guards.

CARLOS: You just pretend you're looking at the paintings.

The telephone rings and the two of them look at each other. LALI *picks up the receiver.*

LALI: Hello? Hey, it got cut off.

LALI *hangs up the telephone.*

CARLOS: What, was it him?

LALI: Who?

CARLOS: David.

LALI: David?

CARLOS: What does he want now?

LALI: Maybe it wasn't him.

CARLOS: He's the only one who calls you on the landline. Why the hell does he have to call outside regular hours?

LALI: Oh, maybe it was him, I don't know, maybe something happened to him.

CARLOS: One of these days I'll take his phone.

LALI: You can't take his phone, Carlos. You know it.

CARLOS: I know it. I said it for the hell of it, damn. I said just to say it.

LALI: I'll wait and see if he calls again.

LALI *picks up the cup from the floor and puts it in the paper bag from McDonald's. Pause.*

LALI: Do you want me to bring you something?

CARLOS: A chocolate doughnut.

Pause.

LALI: It must have been the wrong number.

CARLOS: Right.

Pause.

LALI: I'm off.

CARLOS: All right.

LALI: Carlos.

CARLOS: What?

LALI: No, nothing. See you in a little while.

LALI *gives him a kiss and then leaves.* CARLOS *goes over to the window.* HE *waits.* HE *waves goodbye with his hand.* HE *leaves the candy wrapper in the shoebox under the bed. The telephone rings again.* HE *picks it up.*

CARLOS: Hello? . . . Hello. It's here . . . No . . . Huh? . . . I'm a friend of Lali's . . . A good friend, yes . . . Why are you calling? . . . Yes, I'll tell her. Yes.

CARLOS *hangs up the telephone.*

CARLOS: Son of a bitch.

CARLOS *sits on the bed and takes* LALI'*s wig and a comb out of the nightstand and begins combing it.*

Darkness.

5- THE SEA

It is nighttime once again in the same bedroom. We hear the seagull. In the bedroom are LALI *and* CARLOS. LALI *is wearing the blue velvet dress again.* SHE *wears her stockings up to her knees.* SHE *is finishing painting her lips. When* SHE *has finished* SHE *grabs the wig that is on the bed and begins putting it on in front of the mirror.* CARLOS *is eating a chocolate doughnut.*

LALI: There were some . . . ugly and . . . very sad paintings, but I don't know why I liked them a lot and I don't know . . . I began to look at the paintings and something very strange happened to me. I began to look at a painting and . . . I had never looked so carefully at a painting, I mean . . . for such a long time, and it was so sad, you know that emptiness that comes when you're down?

CARLOS: Yes.

LALI: Well that painting had it, it was like emptiness but it was . . . It was very . . . I don't know . . . it was very powerful, very sad and I don't know what came over me but I began to cry.

CARLOS: You've been crying?

LALI: I swear, I began to cry there in the middle of the CaixaForum.

CARLOS: But . . . Did they do something to you?

LALI: Who? No. They didn't do anything to me.

CARLOS: You cried because of the painting?

LALI: Yes. People began looking at me, they weren't looking at the fucking paintings, no, they were looking at me. I suppose in a museum it's not normal to begin crying and I couldn't take it anymore and I ran out.

CARLOS: Did you do anyone?

LALI: Are you kidding, nothing.

CARLOS: Lately there's not much dough coming in, Lali.

LALI: I know but it's just that every day it takes more out of me.

CARLOS: What?

LALI: That.

CARLOS: Right, but . . .

LALI: But what?

CARLOS: Nothing. How long were you at the . . . ? It's very late.

LALI: No it's that afterward I went down to the Barceloneta. I stared at the sea. For a long time.

CARLOS: The sea?

LALI: Yes.

CARLOS: Why?

LALI: I don't know, but it felt good.

CARLOS: And how are you feeling now?

LALI: Like I got my period.

CARLOS: But you didn't get it.

LALI: No.

CARLOS: But are you supposed to get it or not?

LALI: No, not now. I got it last week.

Pause.

CARLOS: I've never seen you cry.

LALI: I cried like an idiot. Shit, I didn't buy blush. Where are the shoes?

CARLOS: Next to the nightstand.

LALI *takes the shoes, sits on the bed and puts them on, while* CARLOS *takes the razor out of his pocket and begins passing it over his beard.*

CARLOS: And you haven't eaten anything?

LALI: What, are you kidding? With everything that happened I didn't have time.

CARLOS: Do you want a piece of doughnut?

LALI: No.

LALI *stands up.*

LALI: I'll have something to eat with David.

CARLOS: You could get more money out of him.

LALI: I'll bring you a piece of pizza. With a doughnut you can make it 'til later, right?

CARLOS: Yes.

LALI: We'll see if he brings candy. Carlos!

CARLOS: What?

LALI: Put down the razor, OK?

CARLOS: Why?

LALI *takes the razor from him and without meaning to throws it under the bed. Then* SHE *pulls up her stockings.*

CARLOS: What's going on, Lali? I wasn't—

LALI: You weren't, what?

CARLOS: I wasn't going to do anything.

Pause

CARLOS: You got a call again, before.

LALI: When?

CARLOS: Before, damn it, when you went out.

LALI: And?

CARLOS: I picked it up.

LALI: You picked it up?

CARLOS: Yes. It was him.

LALI: Why did you pick it up?

CARLOS: Why does he need to call you outside regular hours?

LALI: Did you speak to him?

CARLOS: Yes. Nothing happened. I asked him if he had something for you and he said that it wasn't important and he hung up.

LALI: And now what do I tell him?

CARLOS: About what?

LALI: About what? About you. If he asks me about you.

CARLOS: Well, the truth, nothing will happen. He's just another client, right?

The telephone rings. THEY *look at each other.* LALI *picks it up.*

LALI: Hello? . . . Yes, yes. I'm on my way.

LALI *hangs up the telephone.*

LALI: I'm leaving, it's late.

CARLOS: Aren't you going to give me a kiss?

THEY *remain still. Looking at each other. Pause.*

Darkness.

6- I WANT TO ASK YOU SOMETHING.

In the same bedroom. DAVID *sitting in the chair, with a Ballantine's and Coke in his hand.* LALI *sitting on the bed. Barefoot. With the dress, the wig, the lipstick and the stockings.*

DAVID: I didn't find any candy.

LALI: That's OK.

DAVID: Now that it's summer they stop making it.

DAVID *takes a sip.*

DAVID: I don't know where you put all that candy.

LALI: I burn a lot of calories.

Pause.

DAVID: I wasn't able to bring any verses today, either.

LALI: A lot of work?

DAVID *stares at* LALI.

DAVID: I like you better with makeup.

LALI: I didn't have time to go and buy the blush.

Pause.

LALI: Do you want me to do anything?

DAVID: No. I don't want you to do anything. I'll look at you. It's enough for me. Does it make you uncomfortable?

LALI: Of course not.

DAVID *takes a long sip from the drink. Pause.*

DAVID: I was at the hospital.

LALI: . . . ?

DAVID: She's almost dead.

LALI: Almost?

DAVID: One more day, at most.

LALI: Poor thing. And how are you doing?

DAVID: It will be a weight lifted from me. It sounds awful but it's true.

DAVID *takes a long sip and finishes the drink.*

DAVID: Will you make me another?

LALI: Of course.

LALI *goes toward the refrigerator and prepares the drink.*

DAVID: I've been coming here for two years already.

LALI: Two?

DAVID: Yes, today I counted while I was at the hospital.

LALI: They've flown by.

DAVID: Yes. I've told you a lot about her, haven't I?

LALI: A little bit.

Pause.

DAVID: I want to ask you to do something for me.

LALI: Whatever you like.

DAVID: I would like you to come to my wife's burial.

LALI: Me?

DAVID: Yes, you.

LALI: Why?

DAVID: I'd like you to be there.

LALI: I don't know if—

DAVID: I'll pay you.

LALI: No, I don't want money.

DAVID: Sorry.

Pause.

LALI: Do you really mean it?

DAVID: Yes. And I would like you to read something. An excerpt from whatever. A quote from the candy, or if you remember some verse that I've read to you. Whatever you like.

Pause.

DAVID: There won't be a lot of people there, my mother, a young guy who works at the bookstore and a couple of neighbors. And you, if you want. Do you want to do it?

LALI: I'm really flattered that you would suggest it.

Pause.

DAVID: Will you come?

Pause.

LALI: Yes.

DAVID: Thank you.

Pause.

LALI: But . . . is it really true? You want me to come? I don't embarrass you?

DAVID: It's important to me for you to be there.

LALI: Are you making fun of me?

DAVID: No. Not me. And you?

LALI: Me?

THEY *look at each other. Pause. Then* LALI *gives him the drink.* HE *grabs the glass and takes a sip.* THEY *stare at each other. Pause.*

DAVID: I called you this morning.

Silence.

DAVID: You weren't here.

Silence.

DAVID: A man answered.

LALI: Yes.

Pause.

LALI: Carlos

Pause.

LALI: The owner of the apartment. The apartment is his. I pay him the rent. Sometime he comes by to see how everything is going.

DAVID: He told me you were friends.

LALI: We get along.

DAVID: Good friends, he said.

LALI: And?

DAVID: Are you together?

LALI shakes her head no.

DAVID: Are you sure?

LALI nods her head.

Silence.

DAVID: You can tell me about it, it's OK. I'm just a client.

Pause.

LALI: There's nothing to tell.

DAVID: It's better that way.

Pause. Then we hear the seagull.

LALI: Look, she's already here.

DAVID: It's the seagull?

LALI: Yes.

LALI *goes by the window.*

LALI: She's so calm.

DAVID: I'm a little bit afraid of seagulls.

LALI: Why?

DAVID: Once a seagull bit me on the head.

LALI: On the head?

DAVID: I saw a seagull that was on the ground. It had crashed into . . . into I don't know what and it was on the ground and I went close up to see what was wrong with it, and suddenly another seagull came from behind and bit me on the head. I still have the scar. Look, touch it.

LALI *moves near* DAVID *and touches his head.*

DAVID: Can you tell?

LALI: Ah, yes. Maybe it was a mother defending her little one.

DAVID: Or maybe seagulls just watch out for each other.

DAVID, *sitting in the chair, takes a long sip.* LALI *with her back to the window.* THEY *stare at each other.*

Silence.

DAVID: Do you like this work?

LALI: Normally no.

DAVID: You must come across all kinds.

LALI: Yes, there are all kinds.

Silence.

DAVID: And wouldn't you like to leave it all?

Silence.

DAVID: Excuse me, it's none of my business.

LALI: It's OK. Yes, I would like to leave it but it's not so easy.

Pause.

LALI: Today I went down to look at the sea.

DAVID: Oh?

LALI: Yes. I stared at the sea for a long time.

DAVID: And how was it?

LALI: I was thinking about it.

DAVID: About what?

LALI: Leaving this job.

DAVID: And why don't you do it?

LALI: It's not so easy.

DAVID: I would feel disappointed as far as I'm concerned, but you should do it. Well, you could make an exception in my case. No, don't listen to me. You're very special, Lali, you could do a lot of things if you left this.

LALI: What things?

Pause.

DAVID: Sit down on the bed.

Pause.

LALI: OK.

LALI *sits on the bed.*

DAVID: Close your eyes.

LALI *closes her eyes.* DAVID *removes a book from the pocket of the sports jacket that is resting on the chair.* HE *gets up and places it between* LALI's *legs. Then he sits back down in the chair.*

DAVID: Open your eyes.

LALI *opens them.*

LALI: The book.

DAVID: *Treasure Island.*

LALI: Yes.

DAVID: Robert Louis Stevenson.

LALI *flips through the pages of the book.*

DAVID: It's a good start.

LALI: Does this book make you think of me?

DAVID: A little.

LALI: Why?

DAVID: I don't know, it talks about people who take risks, about people who
. . . discover new roads . . . and who aren't afraid of discovering them, I
don't know . . . look, I don't want to influence you with my opinion. When
you finish it we'll talk about it, we'll see what you make of it.

In a lower tone.

LALI: You're my favorite client.

THEY *stare at each other.*

DAVID: Put the book down.

LALI: OK.

LALI *leaves it on the nightstand.*

DAVID: Take off your dress.

LALI: OK.

LALI *takes the dress off, underwear, sky blue in color.*

DAVID: Close your eyes.

LALI *closes her eyes.* DAVID *stands up and when he is in front of* LALI *he gets on his
knees.* DAVID *looks between* LALI's *legs. Suddenly we hear the seagull,* DAVID *turns
to look toward the window and when* HE *turns his head back in the direction of* LALI's
legs HE *remains staring at the floor for a while.* HE *touches something on the floor with
his finger, then* HE *looks at his finger.*

DAVID: Is this blood?

LALI *opens her eyes.*

LALI: What?

DAVID: There's blood. Blood is coming out of you?

LALI: From where?

DAVID: Do you have your period?

DAVID *looks at* LALI*'s feet.*

LALI: I got it last week—.

DAVID: You don't have any cuts on your feet?

LALI: I don't know. Oh, yes! . . . It must be a nail that I broke this morning.

DAVID *stares at the floor once again.*

DAVID: There are like some little drops of blood. There's like a stream that stops under the bed. Do you see it?

LALI: Leave it. It's late.

DAVID: It's like it's coming from under the bed.

DAVID *follows the stream and lifts up the sheets that go down to the floor.*

LALI: No. There's nothing under the bed. Don't look under the bed.

DAVID *looks under the bed and lets out a scream. Then* HE *stands up.* HE *looks at* LALI. LALI *remains paralyzed. Silence. Long pause.* DAVID *goes out the door. Silence. Some seconds go by and* HE *reenters.* HE *grabs the sports jacket that is resting on the chair and without looking at* LALI *goes out the door. The door shuts. A bit of time passes. Then* CARLOS *appears under the bed with his left hand grabbing his right wrist.* CARLOS *looks at* LALI *and* LALI *returns his look. Silence.*

LALI: What did you do?

CARLOS: I'm sorry. It was an accident.

LALI: You're bleeding a lot.

Darkness.

7- TRILOGY AROUND A MINOR DETAIL (BRIEF SCENE)

CARLOS. *Alone in the bedroom. Sitting in the chair.* HE *is putting a bandage on his right wrist.* HE *finishes putting it on and goes over to the window.* HE *remains staring out the window.*

Darkness.

LALI. *Daylight. Alone.* SHE *is not wearing a wig but* SHE *is wearing the blue velvet dress. A bit less made up as a result of the passing hours.* SHE *is sitting on a bench in the J. Mª. Folch i Torres Plaza in the Raval quarter of Barcelona. With a bag from Pans & Company at her side.³ And reading* Treasure Island.

Darkness.

DAVID. *Alone. In the waiting room at the Hospital del Mar.⁴ We hear the peep peep peep of those machines that mark the heartbeats in a hospital.* DAVID *stares at the emptiness. Suddenly he scratches his knee. And he happens to look at it. There he finds a hair from* LALI's *wig.* HE *blows on it, as though* HE *were making a wish and then we hear a longer peeeeep that announces that whoever's heart was beating is no longer beating.*

Darkness.

8- A SENTENCE

In the same bedroom. Afternoon. LALI *sitting on the bed, reading* Treasure Island, SHE *is scantily dressed.* CARLOS *sitting in the chair, with the bandage on his right wrist, staring at* LALI. *Pause.*

CARLOS: Lali.

Silence.

CARLOS: I left you some of the Bacon and Cheese. It's really good.

Silence.

CARLOS: Aren't you going to eat anything?

Silence, then CARLOS *makes the sound with his straw. Pause.*

CARLOS: Do you mind if I finish it?

Silence.

CARLOS *grabs the sandwich from the bag from Pans & Company and begins eating. With his mouth full:*

CARLOS: Are you going out?

LALI: No. Would you let me read?

CARLOS: OK, sorry.

Pause. Then CARLOS *makes the sound again with the straw.*

LALI: Would you stop making that noise?

CARLOS: Sorry.

CARLOS *swallows the sandwich, trying not to make too much noise. Pause. Then* CARLOS *with his mouth full:*

CARLOS: Are you mad?

Silence

CARLOS: I'm sorry about what I . . .

LALI *stops reading the book and stares at* CARLOS. *Silence.*

CARLOS: It wasn't on purpose. I moved a little because my back was hurting and I don't know how I cut myself, but it wasn't on purpose.

THEY *continue to stare at each other. Pause.* CARLOS *swallows the sandwich that had become rolled up.* HE *doesn't move. Pause.*

CARLOS: Maybe he'll call you

LALI: Why? To find out how you're doing?

Silence.

LALI: He was the only client that was worthwhile.

CARLOS: You used to spend a lot of time with him but it's not like he paid you so much.

LALI: But I learned things.

CARLOS: What things?

LALI: Things you can't understand.

CARLOS *continues chewing.*

CARLOS: He was just another client, right?

LALI: No.

CARLOS: No?

LALI: He made me feel like . . . like I could be something else in this life.

CARLOS: And me?

LALI: What about you?

CARLOS: How do I make you feel?

LALI: You want me to tell me how you're making me feel right now?

Silence. CARLOS *finishes the piece of sandwich that* HE *was eating as discreetly as possible and leaves the wrapper in the bag.*

CARLOS: Today you're feeing a little that way, but tomorrow you feel better.

Silence.

CARLOS: Do you want to go out?

Silence.

CARLOS: We can go to McDonald's.

LALI: Today you want to go out?

CARLOS: We can go to the Barceloneta. To look at the sea. And then we can get something to eat at McDonald's. Or if not at that chicken place.

LALI: I want to leave this job.

Pause.

CARLOS: You're having a bad day. Everything seems grim. It's normal.

LALI: I really mean it.

CARLOS: If you want, tomorrow I'll go with you to the museums and to those places you go to.

LALI: Why?

CARLOS: So you have company.

LALI: When I'm working I don't see green anymore, I just see sad men.

CARLOS: What do you mean?

LALI: You don't understand anything, Carlos.

CARLOS: It's like you were reading one of those sentences that come with the candy. Can't you talk like a normal person?

LALI: Normal?

CARLOS: Yeah, when you did the ones in construction, or in the offices, or the ones who unload the trucks at the docks, you used to speak like a normal person and . . . and you were also happier. Now you spend the day like you're sad, always thinking about things that are useless.

LALI: I used to spend the day working.

CARLOS: I've tried to follow your thing with the goddamned pieces of candy. Fuck the damned candy, Lali. The stuff they put on those wrappers is useless. It's got nothing to do with real life.

Pause.

LALI: I'm sick of sucking rotten dicks. Does that make any sense to you?

Pause.

CARLOS: You want to leave?

LALI: Yes.

CARLOS: OK. Leave.

LALI: I'm leaving.

CARLOS: Leave.

LALI: I want to do other things, I can do other things.

CARLOS: What things? Work the cash register in a supermarket and not make even as much working double the amount of hours?

LALI: It's a possibility.

CARLOS: OK. Do it.

LALI: I will do it.

CARLOS: And me?

LALI: You?

CARLOS: Yeah. Me. What about me? What do we do? What will we do?

The telephone rings.

CARLOS: Don't pick it up no, fuck!

LALI *gets up quickly from the bed and grabs the telephone.* SHE *speaks in between many silences.*

LALI: Yes? . . . Yes . . . Yes . . . Yes? . . . Yes . . . Not yet . . . Yes, yes . . . Yes.

LALI *hangs up the telephone. Pause.*

LALI: His wife died.

Pause.

LALI: He wants me to go to the burial tomorrow.

CARLOS: He still wants you to go?

LALI: Yes, yes. He said he wants me to go.

Pause.

LALI: Nine o'clock at the Mortuary at Les Corts.

CARLOS: Are you going?

LALI: Of course.

Pause.

LALI: How do I get there?

CARLOS: It's up near the Camp Nou, where the transvestites are.[5] I think you have to grab the number 3 line until Maria Cristina or the University, and it leaves you pretty close.

Pause.

CARLOS: He wasn't mad?

LALI: He was weird.

CARLOS: But not angry?

LALI: I don't know.

Pause.

CARLOS: And did he say anything about what happened yesterday?

LALI: No.

CARLOS: He didn't say anything else?

LALI: He wanted to know if I'd found the passage.

CARLOS: What passage?

LALI: He wants me to read something tomorrow at the burial.

CARLOS: Oh, right, the passage.

LALI *stretches out on the bed, grabs the volume of* Treasure Island *and begins reading. Long pause. We hear the seagull.* CARLOS *gets up and goes over to the window. Pause.*

CARLOS: It's going to rain tomorrow.

Pause.

LALI: It doesn't matter, I have an umbrella.

Silence.

CARLOS: Lali.

LALI *stares at* CARLOS.

LALI: What is it?

CARLOS: And what about me . . . ?

LALI: Again?

CARLOS: No, I mean what do I do now, if I can help you?

Pause.

LALI: If you want, look in the box with the wrappers, and see if you can find a sentence for me to recite at the burial, something nice or something about the sea or . . . I don't know, see if you find anything.

Pause. Then CARLOS *goes over to the bed and crouches down.* HE *picks up the box and sits down in the chair.* HE *takes off the cover and begins reading the wrappers.*

LALI: How's your wrist?

CARLOS: Fine, fine. It's nothing.

Both of them continue reading. Long silence.

Darkness.

9- SILVER

In the same bedroom. Morning, a grey day. It's raining outside incessantly. CARLOS is sitting in the middle of the bed. Both his legs are hanging down. With his feet touching the ground. HE's chewing on a piece of candy. HE holds the razor in this left hand resting on his head. A distracted look. Outside the rain intensifies. We hear some bells in the background. We hear, at the same time that CARLOS is eating the candy, the voice of LALI who is slowing reading:

LALI: "Of Silver we have heard no more. That formidable seafaring man with one leg has at last gone clean out of my life; but I dare say he met his old negress, and perhaps still lives in comfort with her and Captain Flint. It is to be hoped so, I suppose, for his chances for comfort in another world are very small." Robert Louis Stevenson (1850-1894).[6]

Darkness among the sound of the bells.

10- DOES SHE KNOW?

In the same bedroom. A grey afternoon. Outside the rain is coming down. Some lightening. Some thunder. CARLOS is seated in the chair. DAVID is in front of the window with his back to CARLOS. DAVID gazes out the window. CARLOS looks at the floor. A long pause before speaking.

DAVID: Do you own it?

CARLOS: The apartment?

DAVID: Yes.

CARLOS: Rental.

Pause.

DAVID: The building is a mess.

CARLOS: They want to sell the building and they're letting it go to hell to see if we'll leave.

THEY *stare at each other. Pause.*

DAVID: She's taking a while, isn't she?

CARLOS: Yes.

THEY *continue staring at each other. Pause.*

DAVID: Did she go very far?

CARLOS: Close by. Here on Sant Pau Street.

THEY *continue staring at each other. Pause.*

CARLOS: How did the burial go?

DAVID: OK.

THEY *stare at each other. Pause.*

DAVID: She read very well.

Staring. Pause.

DAVID: Would you pour me some Ballantaine's?

Staring. Pause.

CARLOS: Of course

THEY *stop staring at each other.* CARLOS *gets up from the chair and goes over to the refrigerator to prepare the drink.*

CARLOS: With Coke?

DAVID: Yes. Don't make it too strong.

CARLOS *prepares the drink. Silence.*

CARLOS: There's no ice.

DAVID: It doesn't matter. Don't worry.

CARLOS *prepares the drink and gives it to him.*

DAVID: Thank you.

DAVID *takes a large sip.*

Pause.

DAVID: Did she take the umbrella?

CARLOS: I don't know.

Pause.

DAVID: It's good that it's raining.

CARLOS: Yes.

DAVID: Because of the fires.

DAVID *takes another long sip.*

DAVID: Here. Finish it.

CARLOS: No, but . . .

DAVID: I'm getting queasy. I have an empty stomach.

CARLOS *takes the drink from him.*

DAVID: I didn't eat anything yesterday.

Pause.

DAVID: Today either.

Pause.

DAVID: Don't you all have anything to eat?

CARLOS: I don't think so.

CARLOS *takes a long sip and opens the small refrigerator. HE opens the box of candy.*

CARLOS: There's a piece of candy left. They're good.

Pause.

DAVID: Have you tasted them?

CARLOS *gives him a piece of candy.*

CARLOS: Some.

DAVID *unwraps the piece of candy and eats it quickly.* HE *remains with the wrapper in his hand.*

DAVID: Where . . . . . ?

CARLOS *makes a gesture with his hand and* DAVID *gives him the wrapper.* CARLOS *reads it to himself.*

DAVID: What does it say?

CARLOS: What?

DAVID: What does it say?

THEY *stare at each other. Pause. Then* CARLOS *reads slowly.*

CARLOS: "If the band is not to break, bite it first."

DAVID: If the . . . what?

CARLOS: "If the band is not to break, bite it first."[7]

Pause.

DAVID: Who's it by?

CARLOS: Do you know?

DAVID: By . . . it seems like a short saying, it must be by some philosopher, right?

CARLOS: Should I tell you?

Pause.

DAVID: Yes.

CARLOS: F. Nietzsche.

DAVID: Nietzsche.

CARLOS. German philosopher (1844-1900).

CARLOS *crounches in front of the bed and lifts the sheets.* HE *searches. Then* HE *disappears somewhere under the bed.*

DAVID: What are you doing?

CARLOS *from underneath the bed.*

CARLOS: It's just that she keeps all the candy wrappers in a box.

CARLOS *continues searching under the bed.*

Silence.

DAVID: Were you always under the bed?

CARLOS *sticks his head out from under the bed.*

CARLOS: Yes.

CARLOS *goes under the bed again. Pause.*

DAVID: You must have heard everything.

Silence.

DAVID: A lot of shit, I suppose.

CARLOS *from underneath the bed.*

CARLOS: Pretty much.

Silence. Then CARLOS *comes out from under the bed with the wrapper in his hand and a box in the other.* HE *sits in the chair, removes the top of the box and places the wrapper inside.* DAVID *sits on the bed and stares at him.*

DAVID: And that business of hiding under the bed was your idea or hers?

Pause.

CARLOS: Both.

Pause

DAVID: Why?

CARLOS: I kept her company.

DAVID: Company?

CARLOS *nods his head. Pause.*

DAVID: In reality, I came here for the same thing, for the company, I suppose, like everyone, we come for the company, and of course, someone had to keep her company.

CARLOS *moves toward the bed, kneels and leaves the box on top of the sheets. From under the bed* HE *takes out a red umbrella from McDonald's.* CARLOS *holds the umbrella.* THEY *stand one in front of the other. Close.*

CARLOS: The umbrella was left here.

DAVID: How long have you been together?

CARLOS: Seven years.

Pause.

DAVID: I've asked her to come work at the bookstore.

Pause.

DAVID: She said yes.

Pause.

DAVID: She's very happy.

Pause.

CARLOS: Will she go and live with you?

Pause.

DAVID: No. The whole thing would lose its appeal. Besides, now that my wife is no longer around, I don't want anyone.

Pause.

DAVID: She wants to continue here, with you.

Pause.

DAVID: She wants us to behave, you and me.

CARLOS: How much will you pay her?

DAVID: 900 euros a month.

Pause.

DAVID: Gross.

Pause.

DAVID: Services included.

CARLOS: What services?

DAVID: What do you think?

Pause.

CARLOS: Does she know?

DAVID: About the services?

CARLOS: Yeah.

DAVID: For the time being, no.

Long pause.

CARLOS: 1200 net.

DAVID: Net? No. It's too much.

CARLOS: The bookstore's going real well.

DAVID: Not so well.

CARLOS: 1100 net.

DAVID: 1000 gross.

CARLOS: 1000 net.

DAVID: 1000 net.

THEY *stare at each other. Pause. A vague smile.*

LALI *enters through the door with a pair of plastic bags.* HER *hair is wet. The umbrella that* CARLOS *is holding falls to the ground.*

LALI: Sorry. There were a lot of people.

LALI *leaves the bags on the bed and goes into the bathroom.* LALI *from the bathroom drying her hair.*

LALI: I found the seagull.

LALI *comes out of the bathroom.*

LALI: Here, downstairs, in the doorway.

LALI *takes three sandwiches wrapped in foil out of the plastic bag.*

LALI: She was so calm, wet but calm. I got wet too, I didn't bring the umbrella.

LALI *leaves the sandwiches on the bed.*

LALI: It seemed like she was looking right at me, the seagull.

SHE *takes a bottle out of the other bag.*

LALI Ballantaine's. The other one's almost finished, right?

CARLOS: It is finished.

LALI *takes a bottle of Pepsi Light out of the plastic bag.*

LALI: I gave her some of the hotdog.

DAVID: To the seagull?

LALI: Yeah. She ate it.

CARLOS: Hotdogs?

LALI: Yeah. The roast chickens were all gone. I got three hotdogs.

LALI *gives a hotdog to* DAVID, *who is now sitting in the chair, and then* SHE *gives another to* CARLOS, *who is now sitting on the bed. Then* SHE *gives them each a plastic cup and serves them the Pepsi Light.* LALI *sits down on the bed, next to* CARLOS. THEY *begin unwrapping the sandwiches.*

LALI: Oh, here, Carlos, I forgot, mustard.

LALI *takes an envelope with mustard out of one of the plastic bags and gives it to* CARLOS. CARLOS *puts some of it on his hotdog.* THEY *begin eating.* CARLOS *with his mouth full.*

CARLOS: Lali?

LALI: Yes.

CARLOS *finishes chewing and swallows the piece of hotdog. Pause.*

LALI: What?

CARLOS: No, nothing.

Pause.

LALI: What?

CARLOS: No, no, nothing. It was stupid.

Pause. Then THEY *continue eating.*

LALI: Should I put some music on?

DAVID *nods yes,* CARLOS *too.* LALI *goes over to the radio-cassette player and puts on a lively song. Then* SHE *sits and begins to eat, the* THREE *eat and sip the Pepsi Light. Slowly the scene is enveloped in darkness.*

Final darkness.

NOTES

1. "Un soir, j'ai assis la Beauté sur mes genoux.—Et je l'ai trouvée amère." Arthur Rimbaud, *Un saison en enfer*, trans. Paul Schmidt (New York: Harper and Row, 1976).

2. "Tiene el mar su mecánica como el amor sus símbolos." Pere Gimferrer, "Oda a Venecia ante el mar de los teatros," *Arde el mar* (Madrid: Cátedra, 1994). TRANSLATOR'S NOTE: My thanks to Enric Bou for his assistance in translating this verse.

3. TRANSLATOR'S NOTE: Pans & Company is a popular Catalan fast-food sandwich chain.

4. TRANSLATOR'S NOTE: Hospital del Mar is a well-known Barcelona hospital, situated on the oceanfront.

5. TRANSLATOR'S NOTE: The Camp Nou is the stadium that is home to FC Barcelona (the Barcelona football team).

6. Robert Louis Stevenson, *Treasure Island* (Edinburgh: Edinburgh University Press, 1998).

7. Friedrich Nietzsche, *Beyond Good and Evil*, trans. Helen Zimmern (New York: The Macmillan Company, 1907).

The Institut Ramon Llull has a mission to promote Catalan language and culture internationally, in all of its variations and methods of expression. In order to accomplish this task, it carries out the following activities:

a) Foster Catalan language classes in universities and other centers of higher learning, placing special emphasis on the study and research of Catalan language and culture beyond its linguistic domain.

b) Promote the teaching of Catalan to the general public beyond the linguistic domain.

c) Broaden the familiarization with Catalan literature on an international level by encouraging and supporting translations into other languages and corresponding promotional activities for such works when deemed appropriate.

d) Contribute to the international dissemination of works of philosophy, nonfiction, and research by providing encouragement and support for translations into other languages, organizing meetings, seminars and exchange programs, and other activities towards the advancement of the Catalan academic, intellectual, and scientific community abroad.

e) Promote and provide support to international Catalan societies in their initiatives, projects, and activities.

f) Further the international impact of Catalan visual arts through the use of appropriate promotional strategies and activities, encourage the internationalization of outstanding artistic work, provide aid towards the exposure of artists and artwork abroad, and broaden the international awareness of Catalonia's artistic patrimony.

g) Promote collaborations, projects, and joint initiatives with institutions and organizations dedicated to the diffusion of Catalan culture, whether within the boundaries of the linguistic domain or without; placing a special emphasis on the homologous institutions of other counties or cultures.

The Institut Ramon Llull carries out its activities in the areas of Language, Artistic Creation, and Humanities and Science.

Please check: http://www.llull.cat/_eng/_home/

The Martin E. Segal Theatre Center (MESTC), is a non-profit center for theatre, dance and film affiliated with CUNY's Ph.D. Program in Theatre. The Center's mission is to bridge the gap between academia and the professional performing arts communities both within the United States and internationally. By providing an open environment for the development of educational, community-driven, and professional projects in the performing arts, MESTC is a home to theatre scholars, students, playwrights, actors, dancers, directors, dramaturges, and performing arts managers from the local and international theatre communities. Through diverse programming—staged readings, theatre events, panel discussions, lectures, conferences, film screenings, dance—and a number of publications, MESTC enables artists, academics, visiting scholars and performing arts professionals to participate actively in the advancement and appreciation of the entire range of theatrical experience. The Center presents staged readings to further the development of new and classic plays, lecture series, televised seminars featuring professional and academic luminaries, and arts in education programs, and maintains its long-standing visiting scholars-from-abroad program. In addition, the Center publishes a series of highly-regarded academic journals, as well as books, including plays in translation, written, translated and edited by leading scholars. For more information, please visit http://web.gc.cuny.edu/mestc

The Graduate Center, CUNY, of which the Martin E. Segal Theatre Center is an integral part, is the doctorate-granting institution of The City University of New York (CUNY). An internationally recognized center for advanced studies and a national model for public doctoral education, the school offers more than thirty doctoral programs, as well as a number of master's programs. Many of its faculty members are among the world's leading scholars in their respective fields, and its alumni hold major positions in industry and government, as well as in academia. The Graduate Center is also home to twenty-eight interdisciplinary research centers and institutes focused on areas of compelling social, civic, cultural, and scientific concerns. Located in a landmark Fifth Avenue building, The Graduate Center has become a vital part of New York City's intellectual and cultural life with its extensive array of public lectures, exhibitions, concerts, and theatrical events.
To find out more, please visit: http://www.gc.cuny.edu

Ph.D. Program in Theatre, The Graduate Center, CUNY, is one of the leading doctoral theatre programs in the United States. Faculty includes distinguished professors, holders of endowed chairs, and internationally recognized scholars. The program trains future scholars and teachers in all the disciplines of theatre research. Faculty members edit MESTC publications, working closely with the doctoral students in theatre who perform a variety of editorial functions and learn the skills involved in the creation of books and journals.
For more information on the program, please visit: http://web.gc.cuny.edu/theatre

The MESTC Publication Wing produces both journals and individual volumes. Journals include *Slavic and Eastern European Performance* (SEEP), *The Journal of American Drama and Theatre* (JADT), and *Western European Stages* (WES). Books include *Four Melodramas by Pixérécourt* (edited by Daniel Gerould and Marvin Carlson—both Distinguished Professors of Theatre at the CUNY Graduate Center), *Contemporary Theatre in Egypt* (which includes the translation of three plays by Alfred Farag, Gamal Maqsoud, and Lenin El-Ramley, edited by Marvin Carlson), *The Heirs of Molière* (edited and translated by Marvin Carlson), *Seven Plays by Stanisław Ignacy Witkiewicz* (edited and translated by Daniel Gerould), *The Arab Oedipus: Four Plays* (edited by Marvin Carlson), *Theatre Research Resources in New York City* (edited by Jessica Brater, Senior Editor Marvin Carlson), and *Comedy: A Bibliography of Critical Studies in English on the Theory and Practice of Comedy in Drama, Theatre and Performance* (edited by Meghan Duffy, Senior Editor Daniel Gerould). New publications include: *BAiT-Buenos Aires in Translation: Four Plays* (edited and translated by Jean Graham-Jones), *roMANIA AFTER 2000: Five New Romanian Plays* (edited by Saviana Stanescu and Daniel Gerould), *Four Plays from North Africa* (edited by Marvin Carlson), and *Benet i Jornet: Two Plays: Fleeting and Stages* (edited and translated by Marion Peter Holt).
To find out more, please visit: http://web.gc.cuny.edu/mestc/subscribe.htm